QUALITATIVE INQUIRY IN NEOLIBERAL TIMES

D0139957

Qualitative Inquiry in Neoliberal Times is written from the perspective that the scholarly lives of academics are changing, constantly in flux, and increasingly bound to the demands of the market – a context in which the university has increasingly morphed into a business enterprise, one that treats students as consumers to be marketed to, education as something to be purchased, and research as something to be capitalized on for financial gain. The effects of this market-orientation of scholarly life, especially on those in the social sciences and humanities, are ones that demand serious examination. At the same time, qualitative inquiry itself is changing and evolving within and against the rhythms of this 'new normal'.

This volume engages with these emerging debates in qualitative research over new materialism, 'data', public policy, research ethics, public scholarship, and the corporate university in the neoliberal age. World-renowned contributors from the United States, United Kingdom, Spain, Norway, Australia, and New Zealand present a global perspective on these issues, framed within a landscape of higher education marked if not marred by efficiency metrics, accountability, external funding, and university rankings.

Qualitative Inquiry in Neoliberal Times is a must-read for faculty and students alike interested in the changing dynamics of their profession, whether theoretically, methodologically, or structurally and materially.

This title is sponsored by the International Association of Qualitative Inquiry, a major new international organization that sponsors an annual congress.

Norman K. Denzin (PhD, University of Iowa) is Distinguished Emeritus Professor of Communications, College of Communications Scholar, and Research Professor of Communications, Sociology, and the Humanities at the University of Illinois, Urbana-Champaign.

Michael D. Giardina (PhD, University of Illinois) is an Associate Professor of Media, Politics, and Culture at Florida State University.

QUALITATIVE INQUIRY IN NEOLIBERAL TIMES

Edited by
Norman K. Denzin and Michael D. Giardina

Routledge
Taylor & Francis Group

NEW YORK AND LONDON

First published 2017
by Routledge
711 Third Avenue, New York, NY 10017

and by Routledge
2 Park Square, Milton Park, Abingdon, Oxon OX14 4RN

Routledge is an imprint of the Taylor & Francis Group, an informa business

© 2017 selection and editorial matter, Norman K. Denzin & Michael D. Giardina; individual chapters, the contributors

The right of Norman K. Denzin and Michael D. Giardina to be identified as the authors of the editorial material, and of the authors for their individual chapters, has been asserted in accordance with sections 77 and 78 of the Copyright, Designs and Patents Act 1988.

All rights reserved. No part of this book may be reprinted or reproduced or utilised in any form or by any electronic, mechanical, or other means, now known or hereafter invented, including photocopying and recording, or in any information storage or retrieval system, without permission in writing from the publishers.

Trademark notice: Product or corporate names may be trademarks or registered trademarks, and are used only for identification and explanation without intent to infringe.

Library of Congress Cataloging-in-Publication Data
A catalog record for this book has been requested.

ISBN: 978-1-138-22643-2 (hbk)
ISBN: 978-1-138-22644-9 (pbk)
ISBN: 978-1-315-39778-8 (ebk)

Typeset in Bembo
by diacriTech, Chennai

Printed and bound in the United States of America by Sheridan

CONTENTS

ACKNOWLEDGMENTS

We thank Hannah Shakespeare, Dylan Ford, and Matt Bickerton at Routledge for their support of this volume and the larger ICQI project. Thanks also to Christina Nyren and her team for production design, and to Neal Ternes for assistance in compiling the index. Many of the chapters in this book were presented as plenary or keynote addresses at the Twelfth International Congress of Qualitative Inquiry, held at the University of Illinois, Urbana–Champaign, in May 2016. We thank the Institute of Communications Research, the College of Media, and the International Institute for Qualitative Inquiry for continued support of the Congress as well as those campus units that contributed time, fund, and/or volunteers to the effort.

The Congress, and by extension this book, would not have materialized without the tireless efforts of Mary Blair, Katia Curbelo, Bryce Henson, Robin Price, Nathalie Tiberghien, and James Salvo (the glue who continues to hold the whole thing together).

For information on future Congresses, please visit http://www.icqi.org

Norman K. Denzin
Michael D. Giardina
October 2016

INTRODUCTION

Qualitative inquiry in neoliberal times

Norman K. Denzin and Michael D. Giardina

> In this moment we, as academics, are depersonalized, quantified, and constrained in our scholarship via a suffocating array of metrics and technologies of governance.
>
> — Marc Spooner, in press, p. 2

Annual evaluations. Efficiency metrics. Merit indices. Bibliometrics. Impact Factors. Accountability. Transparency. Effectiveness. University rankings. Strategic planning. Benchmarking. Managerialism. New Public Management. All are buzzwords of a contemporary audit culture in which the market logics of life in the neoliberal university – of life in the new normal – are structured and perpetuated.

Consider the following:

In 2013, Florida State University (FSU) was designated as one of two "preeminent" universities in the state of Florida (the other being the University of Florida), which made it eligible to receive additional state funding of $15 million per year for five years in order to "hire faculty members and escalate research" as part of a strategic plan to increase its university ranking among public universities from 43rd (at the time) into the top 25.[1] Also that year, as well as the year following (i.e., 2014). FSU was named by *U.S. News & World Report* as the nation's "most efficient high quality university," meaning it had been deemed the leading institution in the country in terms of being able to "deliver a best-quality higher educational experience while maximizing efficiencies and effectiveness" (FSU Press Office, 2014, para. 2). Two years later still (in 2016), the university proudly announced it had leapt ahead five spots (from 43rd to 38th) in the national rankings put forth annually by *U.S. News & World Report*, based on metrics used by that publication to determine such rankings (Elish, 2016).[2]

As a faculty member at this particular institution, these pronouncements have a very real effect on the orientation of my scholarly life.[3] In terms of performance metrics used to calculate preeminence status and national rankings, the health of my university is understood to be strong and growing stronger. Moreover, the outcomes of the increased funding allocation and push to be a Top 25 public university are beginning to be visibly realized. By way of examples, many faculty members at the university have recently received market equity raises to bring their salaries in line with competitive national averages; money for merit bonuses has been readily available in the last few years; new tenure-track professors are being hired at a healthy pace; professional development money and on-campus grant opportunities seem to be holding steady; new construction and renovation projects can be found all over campus (including ones for a new Institute for Global Entrepreneurship; a new Earth, Ocean, and Atmospheric Sciences building; improvements to Doak Campbell Stadium; and several new student dormitories, among others); and, anecdotally at least, morale among faculty is on the rise.

On the face of it, the above developments are assuredly positive, and suggest a new period of prosperity for the university community. After all, who wouldn't want to be a faculty member at an institution whose national and world rankings are on the rise, where opportunities for professional development are plentiful, and which is making major capital investments in student life? Indeed, it is safe to say that FSU is doing everything 'right' to compete in a new context of neoliberal higher education, and it has concrete 'metrics' to document its improved and improving status over the last five years. Yet here and elsewhere, the guiding light of such success stories (or failures, depending on the particular college or university) is one that is frequently related to how well the university performs under the conditions of contemporary audit culture within an era of neoliberalism (or market fundamentalism).

We have written at length about our current neoliberal condition (see, e.g., Denzin & Giardina, 2014, 2015, 2016; Giardina & Denzin, 2011, 2012, 2013), and will not rehash those arguments here. Suffice to say, as a (political) economic governing formation,

> proponents of neoliberalism throughout the 1980s (and into today) advocated for unbridled entrepreneurial freedom, free markets, free trade, a radically reduced state, and vigorously promoted consumerism. Deregulation, privatization, market forces, and consumer choice became the watchwords of neoliberal states as they extolled the virtues of economic globalization and sought to provide the appropriate institutional setting within which economic growth could be maintained and corporations could significantly increase rates of profit by generating increasing consumption of goods and services. (Smart, 2010, p. 19)

With respect to its impact on the context of higher education, the principle mechanisms of this neoliberal rationality have resulted in a structural reorienting of the university's role in society (i.e., public debates over the role of academia; political struggles over state and federal funding; the commodification and commercialization of the university in terms of branding campaigns, corporate research parks, student housing options, etc.) and the conduct of its research mandates in terms of the commodification of knowledge and the marketization of science (Denzin & Giardina, 2015, pp. 10–12; see also Bok, 2003; Canaan & Shumar, 2008; Giroux, 2007; Tuchman, 2009). Olof Hallonsten (2016) puts the outcomes of these changing conditions more bluntly: "As academic capitalism spreads, universities abandon traditional meritocratic and collegial governance to hunt money, prestige, and a stronger brand" (para. 2).

Within this climate, audit culture has emerged as a key strategy for producing efficient and productive subjects, whether in the manufacturing or technology industries, healthcare and hospital settings, or for our purposes here, in higher education. Cris Shore (2008), drawing from Michael Power (1994), explains that audit culture "refers to the contexts in which the techniques and values of accountancy have become a central organizing principle in the governance and management of human conduct – and the new kinds of relationships, habits and practices that this is creating" (p. 279). As a consequence of its ready acceptance throughout other forms of corporate life, it is unsurprising to find "the language of metrics ... has been transported into the language of research" (Cheek, Garnham, & Quan, 2006, p. 424). This imperative has become firmly ensconced within contemporary higher education – both in the United States and elsewhere – where the emphasis on metrics and deliverables has never been more prevalent, in large measure due to the "hard realities that college success and survival rests on retention and achievement rates," and where, because of these realities, "many college staff ... believe that these things are important and that there is no other way things can be done" (Hodkinson, 2008, p. 314).[4]

As part of this new normal, Yvonna Lincoln (2011) argues, faculty are increasingly having to make an accounting of oneself – an accounting of their scholarly and professional existence and productivity – through the codes and parameters of sometimes arbitrary metrics, which are then used to make decisions about the relative worth of the individual and his or her research insofar as annual evaluations or promotion and tenure processes. We do not suggest, of course, that promoting quality research outputs among one's faculty is inherently 'bad.' In fact, as Julianne Cheek, Bridget Garnham, and James Quan (2006) remind us,

> The pursuit of quality, in terms of producing research that is useful, has impact, and makes a difference is not in itself problematic. However, what

is, and might well increasingly become, problematic is the way in which quality is being reduced to particular measures. (p. 424)

Thus, the issue would seem to be that our research output – or, rather, *our productivity* – is now quantified in measures that do not really account for anything other than for being (ac)counted. It is for this reason that Chris Holligan (2010) identifies the functions of audit culture as "a ritual of verification" in which "originality and truth are replaced by the application of the technoscience of citation metrics and impact indicators" (p. 292).

Additionally, Marc Spooner (in press) suggests one result of this "suffocating array of metrics and technologies of governance" is that "in this moment we, as academics, are depersonalized, quantified, and constrained in our scholarship" (p. 2). Subject to and regulated by market interests, "research becomes not an integral part of one's being as an academic – the manifestation of a desire to know – but a matter of survival" by which, in "constantly producing for others, we simultaneous reconstitute ourselves" (Roberts, 2013, p. 40). In Trent Hamman's (2009) telling of it, scholars are increasingly becoming "compelled to assume market-based values in all of their judgments and practices," such that they effectively reconstitute themselves as "entrepreneurs of themselves" (p. 38) – what Michel Foucault (2004) and others have termed *homo oeconomicus*, or the economic subject who is defined by rational action meant to maximize his or her own value toward the purposes of consuming itself. In this way, argues Wendy Brown (2015), the project of neoliberalism

does not merely privatize – turn over to the market for individual production and consumption – what was formerly publicly supported and valued. Rather, it formulates everything, everywhere, in terms of capital investments and appreciation, including and especially humans themselves. (p. 176)

In other words, it is the imperative of the neoliberal state to assert itself in the marketplace, as the market is not a natural phenomenon but rather a series of logics that must be maintained and ordered. Thus the state, which is subject and subservient to market logics, *must also serve to create and maintain both the market and its conditions in order for them to exist* (Foucault, 2004; Brown, 2015). In this context, governmentality is marketed as economized under the logics of *homo oeconomicus*, pulling the act of governing itself into a position where public and private interests are fused. Moreover, the seemingly corrupt fusion of politicians and private business, which form the backbone of the corporate welfare state, is normalized into a politically rationalized choice reflective of power-knowledge relationships inherent to the neoliberal state (Foucault, 2004; Brown, 2006, 2015). The effect, Brown (2011) maintains, is that although democracy is fundamentally defined through rule by the people, such rule also requires a people who are educated, thoughtful, and democratic in sensibility. This means a people modestly knowing about these constellations and powers; a people with capacities of discernment and judgment in relation to what it reads, watches, or hears about a range of developments in its world; and a people oriented toward common concerns and governing itself. Such knowledge, discernment, and orientation is what a university liberal arts education has long promised and what is now being sacrificed on the pyre of neoliberal rationality, metrics, and imperatives in every sphere. (p. 36)

Or, more briefly stated, contemporary audit culture under neoliberalism serves as a technique of governance, transforming faculty (or, rather, free human agents) into "calculating, responsible, self-managing subjects" (Shore & Wright, 2015, p. 421) – a transformation which hollows out if not erases the promise of higher education.[5]

In sum, what faculty bring to balance sheets, contribute to graduate and undergraduate credit hours, or otherwise directly impact large-scale university quality metrics (such as high-impact research or doctoral students graduated per year) now matter more than ever, and have replaced – or at least significantly decreased the emphasis on – public intellectualism, quality over quantity of outputs, community engagement, and the free exchange of controversial ideas in the classroom.[6]

* * *

One of the great paradoxes of audit culture within higher education is how seemingly easily we give ourselves over to these new metrics and accounts of the self even though they might be radically altering the conduct of our research, teaching, and service (though, granted, many would argue we have no choice). But it should not be terribly shocking. Julianne Cheek (2016; see also Cheek, this volume) reminds us, in stark terms, that all qualitative inquirers and their various forms of inquiry are inextricably embedded within the contemporary research marketplace. The problem, she notes,

> is not how to get out of the research marketplace, *because the reality is that one cannot.* Rather, the problem qualitative researchers face is, in fact, itself, made up of a series of problems related to how we are adapting, or might adapt, for qualitative inquiry to conform to the brands in demand in the research marketplace + how far we are prepared to go in terms of such adaptation + our individual research undertakings + qualitative inquiry more generally. (p. 3, emphasis ours)

To that end, we should ask ourselves what the stakes are for those in the qualitative tradition who have to operate under such conditions.

Writing on the logics of being a qualitative researcher in the neoliberal university, Andrew Hermann (2012) reminds us that, broadly speaking, our very existence as qualitative scholars who wish to have impact on the world "calls us to move *beyond* the ivory halls of higher education, *beyond* our own fruitful story-telling, *beyond* academic journals and boutique presses" (p. 143, emphasis original). But the context and support for doing so is not one that is currently in favor within most universities. To wit, the methodological struggles of the 1970s and 1980s – fights over the very existence of qualitative research – although part of a distant past, remain very much alive in the current moment. They are present in the tenure battles that are waged every year for junior faculty when their qualitative research is criticized for being "not scientific." They are alive in the offices of grant agencies, when only mixed-methods studies or those drawn from the post-positivist paradigm are funded. And they are alive in the slavish adherence to Impact Factors and other metrics that do not accurately reflect any meaningful idea about the real-world ramification of a given piece of scholarship. In fact, as Handel Kashope Wright (2006) makes clear, the changing conditions of the corporate university necessarily promote a climate in which "every overtly social justice-oriented approach to research … is threatened with de-legitimization by the government-sanctioned, exclusivist assertion of positivism … as the 'gold standard' of educational research" (Wright, 2006, pp. 799–800).

Yet we would be remiss if we didn't point out that the landscape *has* changed some over the last decade-plus (and continues to do so). Which is to say, as Hermann (2012) somewhat radically posits, qualitative researchers may no longer need 'protection *in* the academy' so much as 'protection *from* the academy' (pp. 143–144, emphasis original). For perhaps we have become *too* successful at playing the game of the neoliberal scholar. After all, we increasingly have more and more journals with high ISI Impact Factors[7] in which to publish our research (e.g., *Qualitative Inquiry* [1.934 IF], *Qualitative Research* [1.671] IF, *Qualitative Health Research* [2.181 IF]), large-scale international conferences dedicated to the pursuit of excellence in qualitative inquiry (e.g., International Congress of Qualitative Inquiry, European Congress of Qualitative Inquiry, Ethnographic & Qualitative Research Conference, The Qualitative Report Conference, etc.), and growing opportunities for external funded research (if still relatively limited in comparison to our [post-]positivist colleagues). Long-standing arguments over Institutional Review Boards vis-à-vis qualitative research may also soon become moot or radically altered if suggested changes to the Office of Human Research Protections "Common Rule" go into effect (see NPRM Summary, U.S. Department of Health and Human Services, 2015). These developments, enacted through advocacy and constant pushback against evidence-based research mandates and 'gold standard' discourses, do suggest a change in the offering.

We are cautious, however, of celebrating these changes *too* earnestly: whilst better positioning qualitative researchers to attain success and advance *within the neoliberal university*, the above developments say little to the kind of research being conducted or the extent to which it impacts various communities: it says only that we can play their game with more tools at our disposable to be successful in a system – a neoliberal academy – that many critical scholars would take issue with in the first place. It is to this end that Morten Levin and Davydd Greenwood (2011) have called for a reinvention of the social sciences in the corporate spaces of the neoliberal university. To wit, they argue that action researchers – which we would extend here to include all qualitative researchers (*nee, all public intellectuals*) – have a responsibility to do work that is socially meaningful and socially responsible. But to do so, the relationship between researchers, universities, and society must change.

Importantly, we must recognize that the fields of qualitative inquiry and qualitative research are *themselves* transition, always in flux; there is no one singular unifying theory or method, no singular community to speak of (Torrance, 2017; Dimitriadis, 2016). Post-interpretive paradigms are on the horizon (Kuntz, 2015). Older paradigms are being reconfigured. Hybrid paradigms are emerging alongside new geographies of knowledge and new decolonizing epistemologies. Radical feminists are using biostatistics and pursuing biosocial studies. Poststructuralists and post-humanists are interrogating the underlying assumptions and practices that operate in the era of big data, digital technologies, the data sciences, software analytics and the diverse practices of numeracy (de Freitas, Dixon-Roman, & Lather, 2016). Alternative ontologies of numbers and subversive uses of statistics question the kinds of computational practices that saturate everyday life (de Freitas, Dixon-Roman, & Lather, 2016). New global communities of interpretive practice span the globe, stretching from North to South, East to West (see Coburn, 2015; Steinmetz, 2005; Walter & Anderson, 2013; Wyly, 2009). A blurring of discourses and borders are upon us.

Because of these changes and the work of those pushing for such change, the social science tent *has* gotten bigger. For example, there are now many different versions of what is science. Margaret Eisenhart (2006), for one, proposes a model of qualitative science that is interpretive (Geertz, 1973) and practical. After Bent Flyvberg (2001), she wants a science that matters, a science based on common sense, focused on values and power, relevant to the needs of ordinary citizens and policy makers. There are related calls for local science, for new ontologies and epistemologies (critical realism), indigenous science, interpretive science, post-human, post-materialist science, de-colonizing sciences, science as a socially situated practice, science based on feminist standpoint methodologies (Harding, 2005). Michael Burawoy (2005) likewise calls for a policy-oriented, non-elitist, organic public social science – a social science wherein the scholar collaborates with local communities of practice, neighborhood associations, labor and social justice movements (pp. 511–512). These alternatives to traditional positivist science improve the status of qualitative inquiry in the current political environment. They offer strategic forms of resistance to the narrow, hegemonic SBR framework. It is no longer possible to talk about a monolithic model of science. The mantel of authority has been tarnished. *It is, likewise, no longer possible to speak of a monolithic model of qualitative inquiry.*

The chapters

Qualitative Inquiry in Neoliberal Times is situated within the debates outlined above. The authors in this volume take up debates over issues of post-qualitative research, new materialism, 'data,' public policy, research ethics, public scholarship, and the corporate university in the neoliberal age. Collectively, they engage with the key debates concerning our existence as faculty members within and against the imperatives of neoliberalism – within and against the changing nature of our profession and our field(s) of inquiry.

The volume is comprised of eleven chapters and a Coda spread between two sections: *Theory, 'data,' and entanglements* and *Ethics, politics, and resistance.* Julianne Cheek ("Qualitative inquiry, research marketplaces, and neoliberalism") begins our volume by addressing the problems qualitative researchers face in what she terms the 'research marketplace,' or the place where "research-related products are bought and sold." It is within this marketplace that products such as publications and external grants, and throughputs such as students who complete degree programs on schedule provide researchers with 'currency' to "buy" goods such as "promotion, tenure, and jobs." Cheek argues that all researchers are inextricably wedded to the research marketplace, and negotiate the demands of the market in order to survive if not flourish. One of the challenges, she argues, is not that qualitative research is suspect within this marketplace, but that certain forms of qualitative research are becoming normalized and market-friendly, to the detriment of other forms of (non-normalized) research outputs. She concludes by offering a way forward for qualitative researchers in the historical present to engage with the actual problems of higher education and in turn actively (re)claim a space for the kind of qualitative inquiry we seek.

In Chapter 2 ("Post qualitative inquiry"), Elizabeth Adams St. Pierre reflects on past generations of qualitative inquiry to look ahead to the generation to come, asking in part "How do we dislodge the taken-for-granted to make room for something different, something 'new'?" Writing against conventional humanist qualitative inquiry, St. Pierre engages with questions of post-qualitative inquiry, ontological turn(s), and 'methodology free' inquiry ("how inquiry might begin and proceed without a pre-existing, methods-driven methodology that determines what to do next and then next"). She also makes an impassioned argument for the importance of studying philosophy, history, and the philosophy of social science, and the promise so doing holds for rethinking qualitative inquiry.

Continuing this line of thinking, in Chapter 3 ("Qualitative methodology and the new materialisms"), Maggie MacLure explores the potency of new materialist thought and its implications for qualitative, or 'post-qualitative' methodology.

At the same time, however, she also wonders how far methodology has really put itself at risk. Taking her cue from a remark by Deleuze, she asks: In trying to free thought from the hierarchies of representation, and restore ontologies of difference, are we merely trying to revivify conventional method with a safe dose of impure Dionysian blood? Are we just acting the drunkard and whistling a Dionysian tune? To this end, she argues that the turn to materiality has powerful, but also powerfully dangerous, implications for qualitative research – and that these implications are not always fully recognized by those of who have embraced, and been embraced by, the new materialisms.

In Chapter 4 ("The importance of small form"), Mirka Koro-Ljungberg, Anna Montana Cirell, Byoung-gyu Gong, and Marek Tesar engage in conversation over the relationship between data and neoliberalism, including ways to resist the privileging of 'BIG data' for "the less and little." Writing against audit culture metrics and the fetish of data, they consider not what data are or how they profit, "but how they function beyond production and financial profit, how they resist, deconstruct, counter, transgress, transform, multiply, what they enable and disable, and how they meet the other, the unknown, the strange and yet becoming." To that end, they propose a focus on the mundane, the minor, 'the small details and smaller nuances and smallest differences' through which to rethink take-for-granted practices and assumptions. The look, therefore, to a data beyond neoliberalism, and the promise so doing offers.

Connecting the ideas contained in the previous chapters to policy research, Harry Torrance in Chapter 5 ("Be careful what you wish for") addresses data entanglements in qualitative research, policy, and neoliberal governance. To do this, he engages with conversations over 'data' in the natural and social sciences, especially as it relates to assumptions over what are and what can be done with and to data. He then connects these conversations to policy imperatives in education, as well as to arguments over data within the post-qualitative tradition. He concludes by addressing the ways in which data is implicated in neoliberal governance and the 'unintended consequences' (and solutions) that may arise from engaging with such entanglements.

Bronwyn Davies, Margaret Somerville, and Lise Claiborne open Section II with Chapter 6 ("Feminist poststructuralisms and the neoliberal university"), which presents a conversation with each other about what new modes of thought and being have emerged from feminist poststructuralist thought and how these modes of thought and being are positioned within the neoliberal university. Their discussion is oriented around these three primary questions: (1) how might we understand the neoliberal university?; (2) what is the position of poststructuralism in a neoliberal university?; and (3) how can they work together and/or apart? Drawing from their own experiences as situated actors within various neoliberal universities, Davies, Somerville, and Claiborne illustrate the potential for feminist poststructuralism to make contributions to university governance (broadly conceived).

Michelle Fine in the chapter ("Leaky privates") on the political imperatives of public scholarship – of being public scholars. She begins by presenting a narrative accounting of her educational activism in a local school district and the resultant legal and political fallout and opposition by corporate education reformers. She then connects this discussion to the changing face of the public university in neoliberal times, examining several key dynamics "through which the construct 'public' is undergoing dramatic reconstruction within higher education": state budgetary support of public universities, increasing admissions requirements and cutting financial aid, the gowing influx of corporate dollars and a concomitant corporate assault on higher education, the increasing militarization of university campuses, and a correlative increase in provocative public scholarship and the building of activist coalitions by academics. Fine concludes her chapter with a call to arms for public intellectualism and activism to retake the public in public university and forge a new way forward.

In Chapter 8 ("Assembling a we in critical qualitative inquiry"), Stacy Holman Jones continues the theme of building alliances and assembling against assaults on higher education – of how qualitative researchers exist in such a space. Drawing from and engaging with the work of Judith Butler, Holman Jones presents a manifesto for "assembling a 'we'" in qualitative inquiry, an assembly that views qualitative inquiry performatively "as action and speech that creates a space between participants. To this end, she explains how our work in critical qualitative inquiry might be thought of "as a relation of the freedom to speak" that enables us to act ethically, equitably, supportively, persistently, and resistently with and toward one another. She concludes by reminding us that those who have "the power and privilege of speaking" in the academy "assume the responsibility of supporting and acting ethically and justly toward those of us who do have such privileges."

Taking up the impacts of neoliberalism on Indigenous research and methodologies in Chapter 9 ("Trickster as resistance"), Roe Bubar and Doreen E. Martinez turn our attention to resisting neoliberalism in research processes and ethics, especially as it relates to Native Nations and Peoples. More specifically, they reimagine notions/practices of Native sovereignty as a way to consider ethics in academic research and in Indigenous knowledge making with Indigenous Peoples. They begin by discussing the unique relationship Native nations have with the United States and the 'trust responsibility' that flows from that relationship. They then consider how academic research – and specifically research ethics, bound within a Western paradigm and couched within neoliberal academic contexts – aggravates (if not aggrieves) Indigenous knowledges systems that arise from Native belief systems and are intimately tied to tribal sovereignty and daily lifeways. They conclude by suggesting "a re-centering of tribal sovereignty and respect of Indigenous knowledges as mile markers to cover the distance that must be overcome in the academy in order to embrace Native nations as political entities rather than simply as human subjects."

Broadening debates over the use of qualitative software, Kristi Jackson in Chapter 10 ("Turning against each other in neoliberal times") examines the narrative strategies used by qualitative researchers to discuss the role of Qualitative Data Analysis Software (QDAS) – narrative strategies that often act in the service of boundary-work, or "the collective activities of a profession to demarcate acceptable from unacceptable scholarship and knowledge, regardless of the veracity of the claims being scrutinized." Rather than a thorough, systematic, and well-reasoned boundary week, Jackson argues, many of the narratives surrounding QDAS have been oversimplified or carelessly deployed. At issue is not the technical usage of such software packages in the production of qualitative research, but rather the polarizing nature of QDAS itself and what can be done to better understand its place within the field.

Section II concludes with Aitor Gómez's chapter on communicative methodology and social impact. He begins by summarizing the primary postulates of the communicative perspective – universality of language and action; individuals as transformational social agents; communicative rationality; common sense; the lack of interpretive and epistemological hierarchies; and dialogic knowledge – and then outlines how this translates into and through, communicative action, organization, data collection, and data analysis. He then examines the social impact of such research, turning to the example of two projects (INCLUDE-ED and WORKALO) to illustrate how a communicative perspective can contribute to social change.

The volume is brought to a close by Johnny Saldaña, who in his Coda ("All I really need to know about qualitative research I learned in high school") borrows from Robert Fulgham's classic essay, "All I Really Need to Know I Learned in Kindergarten," to draw humorous parallels between high school culture and the world of qualitative inquiry. Such cultural components of adolescent education include cliques, bullies, popularity, learning new subjects, and first-time experiences. In this Coda, he thus examines how qualitative researchers replicate in hybrid forms typical aspects of high school life through their methodologies, epistemologies, publications, leaders, and interpersonal relationships. The satiric comparison of two cultural worlds suggests the field of qualitative inquiry is still in adolescent development with much more growth yet a promising future ahead.

By way of a conclusion

Our scholarly lives are changing, constantly in flux, and increasingly bound to the demands of the market. The university has fully morphed into a business enterprise, one that treats students as consumers to be marketed to and education as something to be purchase; privileges the science, technology, engineering, and math (STEM) fields due to perceived economic and employment benefit to the state; monetizing faculty research; engages in research partnership with global corporations; marginalizing non-revenue-generating disciplines, especially those in the humanities; restocks the faculty ranks with adjuncts and non-tenure earning 'teaching professional' lines instead of tenure-track lines; and focuses on efficiency and other audit culture metrics. These changes have not happened overnight, of course; they are the outcome of neoliberalism's decades-long impact (some would say attack) on public universities that can largely be traced to political economic shifts in the 1970s and 1980s, "when policy-makers started to see higher education more as a private (rather than public) good" (Bagakis, 2016, para. 8). Thus, the struggle for faculty is one that reaches far beyond the walls of their profession. As Henry Giroux (2016) maintains,

> The struggle is not over specific institutions such as higher education or so-called democratic procedures such as elections but over what it means to get to the root of the problems facing the United States and to draw more people into subversive actions modeled after both historical struggles from the days of the underground railroad and contemporary movements for economic, social and environmental justice. (para. 2)

Such efforts cannot be measured in Impact Factors, or be realized in the balance sheets of a university. And they certainly can't be witnessed simply through our advancement up the faculty ranks or through the accolades we receive for publishing in this journal or that journal. Rather, it is the kind of research we choose to engage in, the publics we choose to speak with and to, and the ends toward which our research endeavors that determines our worth as scholars. Working within the system so as not to get worked over by it (as Cheek once said) is crucially and practically important, yes. But at the same time, we should be doing everything we can to push back, resist, and change for the better the conditions under which our scholarship is governed.

Giroux (2016) writes that a progressive Left

> needs a language of critique that enables people to ask questions that appear unspeakable within the existing vocabularies of oppression. We also need a language of hope that is firmly aware of the ideological and structural obstacles that are undermining democracy. [And] [w]e need a language that reframes our activist politics as a creative act that responds to the promises and possibilities of a radical democracy. (para. 16).

As teachers, researchers, and public servants, qualitative researchers of all traditions are uniquely equipped to take up this charge, to reach beyond the walls of the profession, to engage with disparate and competing publics, to conduct research that materially effects if not changes the course of the historical present. That is the charge of this volume. *We have a job to do; let's get to it.*

Notes

1   The Florida preeminence bill outlines 12 metrics by which universities are evaluated, including retention rates, graduation rates, research expenditures, endowments, and the like. A university must meet 11 of the metrics in order to receive or hold onto its 'preeminent' status. A change in the bill created a category for a university to be considered an 'emerging preeminent' university by achieving 6 of the 12 metrics. Since its receipt of preeminence status, the yearly funding rate has been increased from $15 million per year to $35 million per year beginning in 2016. For an in-depth look at these categories, see Bakeman (2016).

2   The seven categories *U.S. News & World Report* uses to determine university rankings are: graduation and retention rates (22.5 percent); assessment of excellence, i.e., peer and high school counselor assessment (22.5 percent); faculty resources, (20 percent); student selectivity (12.5 percent); financial resources (10 percent); graduation rate performance, that is, the difference between actual and predicted graduation rate (7.5 percent); and alumni giving (5 percent) (see Elish, 2016). The 5 ranking spot leap for FSU was noted as the most dramatic move up the list of all public universities in 2016; when considering both public and private universities, FSU's rank was 92nd out of 310 schools, tied with North Carolina State University, University of Colorado–Boulder, and the University of Vermont. In the 2016–2017 *Times Higher Education World University Rankings* league table of 980 universities in the world, FSU was ranked in the 201–250 bracket (a bracket which included schools such as Boston College, George Washington University, University of Iowa, University of Otago [New Zealand], Queen's University [Canada], and University of Barcelona [Spain]).

3   Giardina is speaking here.

4   The belief smacks of the "There Is No Alternative" slogan used by former British Prime Minister Margaret Thatcher in reference to neoliberalism (i.e., there is no alternative to neoliberalism).

5   Shore (2008) defines the larger terms of the debate in this manner:

> [A]udit changes the way people perceive themselves: it encourages them to measure themselves and their personal qualities against the external 'benchmarks,' 'performance indicators' and 'ratings' used by the auditing process. An audit society is one where people are interpolated as auditees, where accountability is conflated with elaborate policing mechanisms for subjecting individual performance to the gaze of external experts, and where every aspect of work must be ranked and assessed against bureaucratic benchmarks and economic targets. (p. 281)

6   This transformation is witnessed in other national contexts as well, where quality assessment schemes such as the Research Excellence Framework (REF) in the United Kingdom rely heavily on the notion that research outputs can (and should) be both measurable and used as one of the primary benchmarks for allocating funding to a university. In terms of the REF, units (departments) are ranked across four panels: overall quality profile; outputs ('originality, significance' and 'rigour'); impact ('reach and significance'); and environment (the 'vitality and sustainability' of the academic unit). Each panel is awarded a four-star, three-star, two-star, one-star, and 'unclassified' designation, with four-star being 'quality that is world-leading in terms of originality, significance, and rigour,' three-star being "internationally excellent," two-star being

"recongised internationally," one-star being "recognised nationally," and unclassified being "falls below the standard of nationally recognized work." For more see the official *Assessment framework and guidance on submissions* document, available at www.ref.ac.uk/media/ref/content/pub/assessmentframeworkandguidanceonsubmissions/GOS%20 including%20addendum.pdf

7   In simple terms, the ISI Impact Factor of a journal is essentially the number of times published articles are cited, divided by the number of articles that could theoretically be cited, for a given journal in a given period of time.

References

Bagakis, G. (2016, October 15). Neoliberalism's decades-long attack on public universities. *Truthout*. Retrieved from www.truth-out.org/news/item/37988-neoliberalism-s-decades-long-attack-on-public-universities

Bakeman, J. (2016, October 3). A new dilemma for public universities: Performance or preeminence? *Politico*. Retrieved from www.politico.com/states/florida/story/2016/09/a-new-dilemma-for-public-universities-performance-or-preeminence-106000

Bok, D. (2003). *Universities in the marketplace: The commercialization of higher education*. Princeton, NJ: Princeton University Press.

Brown, W. (2006). Sacrificial citizenship: Neoliberalism, human capital, and austerity politics. *Constellations, 23*(1), 3–14.

Brown, W. (2011). The end of educated democracy. *Representations, 116*(1), 19–41.

Brown, W. (2015). *Undoing the demos: Neoliberalism's stealth revolution*. Boston: MIT Press.

Burawoy, M. (2005). Provincializing the social sciences." In G. Steinmetz (Ed.), *The politics of method in the social sciences: Positivism and its epistemological other* (pp. 508–526). Durham: Duke University Press.

Canaan, J. E. & Shumar, W. (2008). Higher education in the era of globalization and neoliberalism. In J. E. Canaan and W. Shumar (Eds.), *Structure and agency in the neoliberal university* (pp. 1–32). London: Routledge.

Cheek, J. (2016). Qualitative inquiry and the research marketplace: Putting some + s (pluses) in our thinking, and why this matters. *Cultural Studies ↔ Critical Methodologies 1532708616669528*, first published online ahead of print September 26, 2016 doi:10.1177/1532708616669528

Cheek, J., Garnham, B., & Quan, J. (2006). What's in a number? Issues in providing evidence of impact and quality of research(ers). *Qualitative Health Research, 16*(3), 423–435.

Coburn, E. (2015). A review of *Indigenous Statistics: A Quantitative Methodology. Decolonization: Indigeneity, Education, & Society, 4*(2), 123–133.

de Freitas, E., Dixon-Roman, E., & Lather, P. (2016). Alternative ontologies of number: Rethinking the qualitative in computational culture. *Culture Studies Critical Methodologies, 16*(6), 431–434.

Denzin, N. K., & Giardina, M. D. (Eds.) (2014). *Qualitative inquiry outside the academy*. Walnut Creek, CA: Left Coast Press.

Denzin, N. K., & Giardina, M. D. (Eds.) (2015). Qualitative inquiry and the politics of research. Walnut Creek, CA: Left Coast Press.

Denzin, N. K., & Giardina, M. D. (Eds.) (2016). *Qualitative inquiry through a critical lens*. Walnut Creek, CA: Left Coast Press.

Dimitriadis, G. (2016). Reading qualitative inquiry through critical pedagogy: Some reflections. *International Review of Qualitative Research, 9*(1), 140–146.

Eisenhart, M. (2006). Qualitative science in experimental times. *International Journal of Qualitative Studies in Education, 19*(6), 3–13.

Elish, J. (2016, September 13). FSU leaps ahead in national rankings. *Florida State University.* Retrieved from https://news.fsu.edu/news/university-news/2016/09/13/fsu-leaps-ahead-national-rankings/

Flyvbjerg. B. (2001). *Making social science matter.* London: Cambridge University Press.

Foucault, M. (2004). *The birth of biopolitics: Lectures at the College de France 1978–1979* (G. Burchell, Trans.). New York, Picador.

FSU Press Office (2014, February 11). For second year, Florida State named 'most efficient' by *US News & World Report. Florida State University.* Retrieved from http://news.fsu.edu/news/university-news/2014/02/11/second-year-florida-state-named-efficient-u-s-news-world-report/

Geertz, C. (1973). *Interpreting cultures.* New York: Basic Books.

Giardina, M. D., & Denzin, N. K. (2011). Acts of activism⇔politics of possibility: Toward a new performative cultural politics. *Cultural Studies⇔Critical Methodologies, 11*(4), 319–327.

Giardina, M. D., & Denzin, N. K. (2012). Policing the "Penn State crisis": Violence, power, and the neoliberal university. *Cultural Studies⇔Critical Methodologies, 12*(4), 259–266.

Giardina, M. D., & Denzin, N. K. (2013). Confronting neoliberalism: Toward a militant pedagogy of empowered citizenship. *Cultural Studies⇔Critical Methodologies, 13*(6), 443–451.

Giroux, H. A. (2007). *University in chains: Confronting the military-industrial-academic complex.* London: Routledge.

Giroux, H. A. (2016, April 10). Radical politics in the age of American authoritarianism: Connecting the dots. *Truthout.* Retrieved from www.truth-out.org/news/item/35573-radical-politics-in-the-age-of-american-authoritarianism-connecting-the-dots

Hallonsten, O. (2016, October 3). Corporate culture has no place in academia. *Nature.* Retrieved from www.nature.com/news/corporate-culture-has-no-place-in-academia-1.20724

Hamman, T. (2009). Neoliberalism, governmentality, and ethics. *Foucault Studies, 6*(1), 37–59).

Harding, S. (2005). Negotiating with the positivist legacy: New social justice movements and a standpoint politics of method. In G. Steinmetz (Ed.), *The politics of method in the social sciences: Positivism and its epistemological others* (pp. 346–365). Durham: Duke University Press.

Hermann, A. F. (2012). "Criteria against ourselves?" Embracing the opportunities of qualitative inquiry. *International Review for Qualitative Research, 5*(2), 135–152.

Hodkinson, P. (2008). Scientific research, educational policy, and educational practice in the United Kingdom: The impact of the audit culture on further education. *Cultural Studies Critical Methodologies, 8*(3), 302–324.

Holligan, C. (2010). Building one-dimensional places: Death by the power of audit. *Power and Education, 2*(3), 288–299.

Kuntz, A. M. (2015). *The responsible methodologist: Inquiry, truth-telling, and social justice.* Walnut Creek, CA: Left Coast Press.

Levin, M., & Greenwood, D. (2011). Revitalizing universities by reinventing the social sciences: Bildung and action research. In N. K. Denzin and Y. S. Lincoln (Eds.), *The SAGE handbook of qualitative research* (4/e). Thousand Oaks, CA: Sage.

Lincoln, Y. S. (2011). "A well-regulated *faculty…*" The coerciveness of accountability and other measures that abridge faculties' right to teach and research. *Cultural Studies⇔Critical Methodologies, 11*(4), 369–372.

Power, M. (1994). *The audit explosion.* London: Demos.

Roberts, P. (2013). Academic dystopia: Knowledge, performativity, and tertiary education. *Review of Education, Pedagogy, & Cultural Studies, 35,* 27–43.

Shore, C. (2008). Audit culture and illiberal governance: Universities and the politics of accountability. *Anthropological Theory, 8*(3), 278–298.

Shore, C., & Wright, S. (2015). Governing by the numbers: Audit culture, rankings, and the new world order. *Social Anthropology, 23*(1), 22–28.

Smart, B. (2010). *Consumer society: Critical issues and environmental consequences.* Thousand Oaks, CA: Sage.

Spooner, M. (in press). Audit culture. In N. K. Denzin and Y. S. Lincoln (Eds.), *The SAGE handbook of qualitative research* (5/e). Thousand Oaks, CA: Sage.

Steinmetz, G. (Ed.). (2005). *The politics of method in the human sciences: Positivism and its epistemological others.* Durham, NC: Duke University Press.

Torrance, H. (2017). Experimenting with qualitative inquiry. *Qualitative Inquiry , 23(1), 69–76.* doi: 10.1177/1077800416649201

Tuchman, G. (2009). *Wannabe U: Inside the corporate university.* Chicago: University of Chicago Press.

U.S. Department of Health & Human Services. (2015). NPRM 2015 – Summary. Retrieved October 29, 2016 from www.hhs.gov/ohrp/regulations-and-policy/regulations/nprm-2015-summary/index.html.

Walter, M., & Anderson, C. (2013). *Indigenous statistics: A quantitative methodology.* Walnut Creek: Left Coast Press.

Wright, H. K. (2006). Are we (t)here yet? Qualitative research in education's profuse and contested present. *International Journal of Qualitative Studies in Education, 19*(6), 793–802.

Wyly, E. (2009). Strategic positivism. *The Professional Geographer, 61*(3), 310–322.

SECTION I

Theory, 'data,' and entanglements

1

QUALITATIVE INQUIRY, RESEARCH MARKETPLACES, AND NEOLIBERALISM

Adding some +s (pluses) to our thinking about the mess in which we find ourselves

Julianne Cheek

What this chapter is about and why I wanted to write it

My motivation for writing this chapter stems from a long interest in trying to better understand the social mess that we, as qualitative researchers in neoliberal times, find ourselves in − a social mess that no part of our qualitative research endeavors remains untouched by, or can stand apart from. This is because "the qualitative researcher is not an objective, politically neutral observer who stands outside and above the study of the social world. Rather, the researcher is historically and locally situated within the very processes being studied" (Denzin, 2010, p. 23).

Ackoff (1974) defined a problem that is a mess in this way: "No problem ever exists in complete isolation. Every problem interacts with other problems and is therefore part of a set of interrelated problems, a system of problems ... I choose to call such a system *a mess*" (p. 21, emphasis in original). Put another way, a "Social Mess is a set of interrelated problems **and other messes**" (Horn & Weber, 2007, p. 6, emphasis in original) that connect to make up the problem that we face. A concept that is sometimes used interchangeably with, and that is very closely related to, the idea of social messes is that of "wicked problems" (Rittel & Webber, 1973). Wicked problems are those that actually are not problems at all, "in the sense of having well defined and stable *problem statements*. They are too messy for this, which is why they have also been called *social messes and unstructured reality*" (Ritchey, 2013, p. 1, emphasis in original).

As part of trying to better understand the social mess that qualitative inquirers are situated in in neoliberal times, in the discussion to follow I want to make us less certain about what the problems facing us are. In other words, I want to introduce some complexity and/or uncertainty into the way that we think about the *problems themselves* that qualitative researchers and their qualitative inquiries face. As a system of thought or "a peculiar form of reason" (Brown, 2015, p. 17), neoliberalism permeates and connects to all aspects of social, political, economic, and research life. This peculiar form of reason "consists of making select problems recognizable even as it posits select responses to problems as commonsensical" (Kuntz, 2015, p. 35). In so doing, neoliberalism works to also make select problems *not* visible and select responses to problems *not* commonsensical.

For example, we all recognize the neoliberal-derived series of problems that are very visible in the daily lives of researchers related to researchers having to be accountable and "auditable" (Tuchman, 2009, p. 61) for their research-related performance, both to governments and to the institutions in which they work. Furthermore, we all recognize the seemingly commonsensical, ordinary, and routinized neoliberal-derived solutions to this problem of us having to be accountable for our research-related performance; solutions such as the development, use, and proliferation of a series of metric-based measures to judge our research performance. These are solutions that are viewed as commonsensical even if the metrics used, such as impact factor, measure things they were never intended to (see Seglen, 1997; Garfield 1999), or are known to be flawed: "(i)mpact factor is not a perfect tool to measure the quality of articles but there is nothing better and it has the advantage of already being in existence and is, therefore, a good technique for scientific evaluation" (Hoeffel, 1998, p. 1225).

Conversely, a situation in which such auditability is *not* required, or one in which metrics of some form are *not* used to measure research related performance, increasingly is one that we do not recognize. In fact, such a situation seems quite extraordinary given the mainframe afforded to neoliberalism in contemporary research contexts. This mainframe results in other ways of thinking about things or other possible responses to problems that appear to be *not commonsensical* and even *nonsensical* – solutions such as entertaining the idea of not using metrics at all to demonstrate research achievements.

As Cannella and Lincoln (2015) reminded us, neoliberalism is "a total emersion within competition and enterprise formation throughout daily life, politics, government and action … . The infiltration is so complete that the condition is made invisible" (Cannella & Lincoln, 2015, p. 60). Such invisibility sustains the seeming "ordinariness" and common sense of this way of thinking and acting, both about what the problems facing us actually are and what solutions to these problems might be (Cheek, in press). In order to make visible the infiltration of neoliberalism in, and effects of that infiltration on, our research and our daily lives as researchers, I argue in the discussion to follow that we need to put some pluses (+s) in our thinking (Cheek, 2016, in press) about the problems we face as qualitative inquirers in neoliberal times.

Without adding these +s to our thinking in order to see the problems for what they really are, we are never going to be able to move beyond dealing with the symptoms, or parts, of the underlying mess that actually *is* the problem.

Put another way, putting some +s in our thinking will help us move our focus off of parts of the problem, such as an individual metric, to focus instead on the connections (+s) or interrelated problems that *are* the mess – such as those between metrics + publication + promotion + tenure + research funding + rankings + methods + a research marketplace + neoliberalism + all the other +s that form constellations around each of the +s in this example.

From the outset, however, a word of caution is needed about trying to do this. When trying to put the +s in our thinking, the discussion to follow will get very messy at times, as the argument being made may splinter and go in multiple directions all at once. This is because each + is *itself* a point around which many dynamic connections cluster, with each of those clusters having many other "dynamic connections (or +s) intersecting with them and from which they have emerged … [resulting in a] … complex matrix and web of connections made up of hundreds of such interwoven threads that impact on the everyday decision making and research life of individual researchers" (Cheek, in press). Nevertheless, as I argue in the discussion to follow, such messiness is to be embraced rather than "cleaned up" or hidden. Embracing and actively seeking such messiness is a way to resist "boxed-in thinking" (Alvesson & Spicer, 2016, p. 135) that results in a situation where "few people have a comprehensive understanding of the situation [we can substitute "mess" here for our purposes]. They do not make connections" (Alvesson & Spicer, 2016, p. 135). In other words, they do not put the +s into their thinking.

In the next section I build on the ideas introduced here by taking a closer look at, and thereby adding some +s in our thinking about, the research marketplace – a place where many +s meet and intersect with qualitative inquiry in a neoliberal context. A place that is all about the "right" connections (+s). A place that is both an example *and* a symptom of complex, connected issues and problems. A place that is *itself* "a form of social mess, a system of interrelated problems that connects to other systems of interconnected problems at a number of points" (Cheek, in press). And a place, that like it or not, we as researchers in neoliberal times are connected to.

The research marketplace: It's all about the connections (+s)

In a nutshell, the research marketplace is a place where research-related products are bought and sold. This buying and selling is symptomatic of the pervasiveness and reach of the logic of the competitive market into all aspects of contemporary life – including research (Baumann, 1988; Cannella & Lincoln, 2015; Cheek 2011, 2016, in press; Denzin & Giardina 2016; Kvale, 2008; Lincoln, 2012). The centrality of the market, and the competition that underpins the buying and selling that goes on in it, are fundamental tenets of neoliberalism, which "adopts the self-regulating free market as *the* model for proper government" (Steger & Roy, 2010, p. 12, emphasis in original), and the "solution to all problems" (Lucal, 2015, p. 5).

Products highly valued in this research marketplace include outputs such as publications (especially refereed journal articles in high-impact-factor journals), inputs such as monies that are gained externally for research, and throughputs such as the number of students who complete higher education degrees "on time" – that is, within the time allocated by administrators of these degrees (Cheek 2011, 2016, in press). These products provide researchers with currency in the research marketplace – currency that can be used to "buy" goods such as promotion, tenure, and jobs. In this marketplace, what matters most is the relative position of, or the relative amount of currency held by, a researcher, compared to other researchers who are their market competitors.

Buyers in the research marketplace include funders of research who provide monetary or in-kind support to buy both our research ideas and our research expertise to conduct that research. Other buyers in this marketplace are publishers and editors of scientific journals. They want us to submit our research papers to their journals so they can publish our research, but also so they can increase their submission rates to show strong market presence, raise the journal's impact factor to improve the journal's relative market position, and sell more subscriptions to the journal to increase the market share of, and therefore the profit made from, their journal. Publishers of research-related books also buy our written accounts of our research to sell to others in the research marketplace. Often they work out what are in-demand "brands" of books such as text books or step-by-step, how-to-do manuals about research, and commission researchers (or put another way, buy a researcher's knowledge of and expertise with methods and research) to write a brand of book that meets this market-driven demand.

Sellers in the research marketplace include universities that compete with each other to sell their courses to prospective students. Students invest in degrees offered by higher-education institutions in the form of paying fees. Thus, prospective students, especially full-fee-paying overseas students, are a source of income for many universities (Ball, 2012). This is income that is badly needed by the universities given that governments no longer fully fund core activities of universities in many countries (Ball, 2015; Clawson & Page, 2011; Lucal, 2015). Students look to invest their fees wisely in terms of maximizing return on that investment, and shop for "top" universities at which to study. To help them shop and invest wisely, companies design, produce, and/or sell what are, in effect, student investment guides to the higher-education and research marketplace; for example, *The Good Universities Guide* (Hobsons, 2015), *The International Student Barometer* (i-graduate International Insight, 2015), and any number of variants on this theme.

Also selling in the research marketplace are "private sector firms (such as Elsevier, producer of Scopus; Thomson Reuters, producers of the ISI Web of Knowledge; and Google, producer of Google Scholar), and their inter-firm relations," who are able to "generate a profit from gathering and selling information" (Robertson, 2012, pp. 237, 242) that research-related metrics are based on and that can be used to rank institutions, individuals, and even countries in terms of their research performance (Cheek, 2016). Ranking has become big business in the research marketplace; institutions are increasingly becoming dependent on it as a marketing device or an "economy of persuasion, circulating around promotion, desire and expectations" (Alvesson, 2013, p. 218). For example, in the quest to be as attractive as possible to potential students-as-investors, universities display their relative rankings on a number of metrics such as amount of research income received or number of high-impact journal articles (Cheek, 2016), in what Lincoln termed a "rankings rodeo," which reflects and signifies "the capitalist-corporatist-marketing nexus in higher education" (Lincoln, 2012, p. 1456). Such displays of rankings are part of persuading students that a particular university is a good choice, or preferred brand, or place at which to study, and of course that it offers good returns on the fees paid for that privilege.

More than a decade ago, Johnson observed that "(h)igher-education institutions are no longer virtually guaranteed an existence through governmental funding streams. As funding now follows students higher-education institutions must literally be *attractive*, hence the importance of marketing" (Johnson, 2003, p. 142, emphasis in original). What Johnson asserted then remains just as relevant today, if not even more so, given that since she wrote this we have seen the continued chronic underfunding of higher education in many countries (Clawson & Page, 2011; Lucal, 2015). What has changed, however, is that there are many more +s that we can put into her observation, as it is no longer only students that the funding follows. Discretionary performance-based funding from governments also follows certain research metrics, such as external funding for research, and publications in high-impact journals. In other words, the amount of external funding for research and the number of high-impact journal articles can be cashed in for extra funding from governments and top up university budgets.

Qualitative inquirers: We, too, are selling in a research marketplace

Individual qualitative researchers embedded in a research marketplace (Cary, 2006) are also selling and buying in that place. For example, when we submit our research manuscript to a journal, or our book manuscript to a publishing house, we are in effect transacting in the research marketplace; we are seeking to "sell" our manuscript, and the time and ideas that went into it, to that journal or publishing house. It might not always be money that changes hands in such transactions, although for some authors, publishing in-demand products such as how-to research-type manuals can be big business. Rather, what is gained from the transaction or sale is currency, and therefore exchange value and relative ranking, in a research marketplace driven by supply and demand. Thus, individuals and their research products that meet the criteria or demands or expectations of buyers sell well, are highly sought after, and consequently become quite entrenched in the marketplace. Those individuals and products that do not meet the requirements of the marketplace are positioned as peripheral in it, and either disappear completely or adapt themselves and their research in order to better compete by meeting the needs or requirements of the buyers/customers in that marketplace.

In such a competitive place, the researcher-as-seller must provide evidence of the high standard of what she or he is "selling," in keeping with what potential buyers perceive a "high standard" to be. Consequently, as qualitative inquirers, we find ourselves in a paradoxical situation in this research marketplace: free to act, but constrained in how free we can be if we want to be able to sell our research products in this place. As a result, "at one level we are completely independent, but we all march to the same tune without even thinking about it" (Alvesson & Spicer, 2016, p. 193). In so marching, we regulate ourselves and our actions by, for example, thinking about "needing" to publish in high-impact-factor journals, or "needing" to obtain external research funding from highly prized brands of funders, such as National Institutes of Health (NIH) funding in the United States, or Horizon 2020 funding in the European Union (see Cheek, 2016). Thus, far from being free to decide what tune to march to, or even whether to march at all, it is more a matter of marching or risking being left behind and becoming increasingly irrelevant in the research marketplace.

To reduce this risk, researchers push themselves to produce more than their competitors, and seek to be associated with high-value brands in the research marketplace, such as publications in high-impact-factor journals, and external funding from high-brand funders. In acting in this way, the thinking and actions of researchers are "more influenced by losses than gains" (Alvesson & Spicer, 2016, p. 55). In a zero-sum research marketplace, one cannot afford to lose ground because, by definition, that means someone else has gained ground and therefore the competitive edge. Since we are ranked and positioned in relation to each other, one researcher's/research method's/research or higher institution's gain is another's loss or disadvantage (see Alvesson, 2013, p. 117). This is because it is where one ranks – how much market-derived currency one has in relation to the currency that others have – that matters in this marketplace. Put simply, we can only gain market position if another loses it.

The increasing scarcity of jobs, and especially tenure, in higher education in most countries makes it difficult for researchers to ignore the connections between the accumulation of research market currency and individual-researcher viability in a highly competitive employment marketplace (Lucal, 2015). These are connections such as publications + funding + tenure + promotion + jobs + amount of marketplace currency + high-impact-factor journals + the huge number of other possible +s we can put into our thinking here. We are increasingly required to market ourselves and our research. Put another way, we have to "tell" (Ball, 2015) about our success using "skills of presentation and of inflation, making the most of ourselves, making a spectacle of ourselves" (Ball, 2012, p. 19). This is all part of what Ball (2012, p. 17) called making ourselves "calculable rather than memorable," and Tuchman (2009, p. 61) referred to as making ourselves "auditable."

One way we make ourselves calculable, and therefore auditable, is by displaying evidence of the amount of our market currency in our research track record. In a zero-sum research marketplace, with its emphasis on relative marketplace position, far from being a neutral or objective résumé of research-related achievements, the track record of the researcher is a selling device. Research track records are produced by, and in turn are productive of, economies of persuasion (Alvesson, 2013) in a contemporary context "permeated by a powerful consumption orientation" (Alvesson, 2013, p. 35). They are designed to display, and persuade others about, the individual researcher's "attractiveness" in terms of the relative amount of research marketplace currency that that individual researcher has. Such persuasion is imperative to gain market advantage in a zero-sum research marketplace, where a researcher's research-related products and credentials "are increasingly viewed by both universities and their clients as tradable goods, just like any other commodity" (Sidhu, 2006, p. 144).

For example, employers of researchers use this display of market-related products to calculate the relative worth of researchers when deciding who to offer jobs and/or tenure to, or who to promote over others. Likewise, funding bodies use market-derived metrics, such as the number of peer-reviewed articles in high-impact-factor journals in a track record, to calculate the relative worth of the researchers comprising a research team when deciding the most competitive research application to award funding to. This focus on measuring researchers' comparative research output has resulted in the development and use of more and more metrics to calculate, rank, and make visible the market position or ranking of the individual researcher and/or individual higher-education/research institution. What is important in this ranking exercise is not so much what the performance level actually is, but rather how that performance "measures up" compared to the performance of competitors.

The irony in all this is, that despite the centrality of the free market in neoliberal-derived thinking, a thinking *"in which the individual is (in theory), free to pursue his or her own ends with minimal state intervention"* (Denzin & Giardina, 2015, p. 13, emphasis in original), never before have we had more government interference in what actually is a research quasi-market (Le Grand & Bartlett, 1993), in which the government increasingly interferes and "provides significant guidance and influence on how the market operates" (Foskett, 2011, p. 30). Such interference includes determining what research will "count" and be rewarded, what types of publications will gain more funding for an institution, or what types of research grants and methods used in those grants will be more highly prized and gain more performance-related discretionary funding from the government, as well as other forms of currency in the research marketplace for that institution (Cheek, 2011, in press).

Thus, supposed freedom, either of markets or of individuals, is not actually the case in neoliberal-derived contexts. Constraints on researchers emanate from the research marketplace in which they find themselves because of the way that their research products and goods are bought, sold, and thought of in terms of brand, value, and currency in that place. While in theory as individuals in a research marketplace we are free to pursue our own ends with minimal state intervention, what in fact we are "free" to do is to produce as many, and as much, of certain high-value research brands and products as we choose to, and to work as hard as we want to in order to make ourselves competitive, "calculable" (Ball, 2012, p. 17), and therefore marketable in this place. All of this is exacerbated by the fact that while the idea of the market being involved in some way in universities/higher education/research, or the exposure of universities/higher education/research to markets and the idea of "commercialization, is not new (Bok, 2003; Brown, 2011; Furedi, 2011), what is new is a process of enhanced marketisation, with markets driving the world of universities [and we can add research here for the purposes of our discussion] in a way unprecedented in their history" (Foskett, 2011, p. 26).

In the next part of the discussion I want to develop further the idea of putting some pluses (+s) or connections in our thinking about being attractive or calculable in the research marketplace. However, when doing so, I will overtly shift the focus of the discussion to the individual qualitative researcher trying to survive and thrive in the social mess that is the research marketplace. In so doing, I will focus on exploring "how the private troubles of individuals which occur within the immediate world of experience, are connected to public issues and public responses to these troubles" (Denzin, 2010, p. 9). As my point of departure I use a specific, seemingly "normal" or "ordinary" event in the course of a research/academic career: namely the rejection of a manuscript sent to a journal to be considered for publication.

A fairly ordinary event that, when the +s are added, is actually quite extraordinary

One of the problems I faced when preparing the presentation for the 12th International Congress of Qualitative Inquiry on which this chapter is based, was where to begin. If the presentation was to be about adding +s to our thinking about the problems facing qualitative inquiry in neoliberal-saturated times, then which +, or part of the problem, should I begin with? As luck would have it, a rather ordinary event – but one that was also actually quite extraordinary, as we shall see – occurred during this time. The research team of which I am a member received a review of a manuscript that we had submitted to a journal for publication. As part of the review, the reviewer had written, in bold, "I am not an expert at qualitative research, but the methods used in this manuscript do not appear to be rigorously based on any standard qualitative methodology." The reviewer also went on to say in another part of the review (this time not in bold), "You use the term 'constantly' (letters were constantly compared), consider [sic] using a different term such as 'iterative'/iteratively reviewed"[1] (review received May 2016).

In order to begin to come to terms with this review and to try to, or decide whether to, address the points raised in it, I needed to understand what the problem was that the review exemplified; however, this was extremely difficult. Questions kept arising, such as, What *really* was the problem with this review, and what was the *real* problem that the reviewer wanted us to address? – the word "constant," the appearance of a lack of rigor, not using standardized forms of qualitative inquiry, the reviewer's self-declared lack of expertise, or not writing our qualitative inquiry in "the" way the reviewer had come to expect? Trying to work out a specific, clearly defined problem to address was impossible, as every time I did so the seemingly "specific" problem fractured in many different directions, all of which led to other problems that also fractured into other series of problems – some of which took me back to where I had begun. Put another way, I found myself, and my thinking, enmeshed in a problem that was *itself* a web, or a multidimensional matrix, of problems; in other words, I found myself in a mess. It was this mess, with its web of connected problems, that was the underlying problem, of which the review was a symptom.

For example, consider the statement made by the reviewer: "I am not an expert in qualitative research." It is certainly part of the problem that the reviewer was setting him- or herself up as what I will call "an expert nonexpert" *and* justifying that action by recourse to notions of standard qualitative methodology, *and* did not need to state what that standard or normalized version of qualitative inquiry is because the word 'standard' suffices, *and* that this can lead to a normalized version of qualitative inquiry promulgated by nonexperts in the field, *and* that this may privilege some forms of qualitative inquiry and exclude others on the basis of not being 'standard," *and* that this connects to other series of +s or *ands* such as those connected to the development and use of guidelines and checklists for assessing qualitative inquiry,[2] *and* they are used by expert nonexperts to base their claims of expertise on.

The actions of the individual reviewer, however, their version of standard qualitative inquiry, and even their statement, "I am not an expert in qualitative research," are not all of the problem. Connecting to the use of such a reviewer, who is open about not being an expert in the area they are reviewing, is a series of problems related to the journal's editorial process and the peer-review process itself. For example, what was it that enabled the reviewer to be in a position to review this article, to be able to say what he or she said; *and* who had selected this reviewer and on what basis; *and* why was a review from a self-proclaimed nonexpert accepted and acted on; *and* how does one become a reviewer for that journal; *and* what quality controls or assurances (or whatever other sort of term we want to use) are applied to the peer reviews; *and* what series of problems does this raise about the use (or abuse) of the peer-review process, which is the fundamental plank in academic publishing *and* determines whether research is *published* and publications in peer-reviewed journals provide researchers with much currency in the research marketplace, *and* the number and type of publications that a researcher has are used to make decisions about the quality and impact of both the research *and* the researcher, *and* this is able to be used and traded for promotion, tenure, and other commodities in the academic and research marketplace (Cheek, 2016, in press). The connections (*ands*) just went on and on in my thinking.

Therefore, simply removing this particular reviewer and replacing him or her with another from the database of that particular journal might solve one part of the problem, but it will not solve other parts of the problem, such as that this reviewer will continue to, *and* is able to, review papers about qualitative inquiry, *and* will do so according to notions of a standard or normalized qualitative inquiry, *and* since these will be the papers published *and* the view of qualitative inquiry that the readership is presented with, these views of qualitative inquiry will become the norm; therefore, the actions of the nonexpert reviewer, in effect, work to produce certain views of qualitative inquiry *and* repress others, *and* other nonexperts in qualitative inquiry will gain their understandings from these views, *and* they too will review papers about qualitative inquiry according to such views.

The problem here is not that qualitative inquiry is not being published by this journal, or any other, for that matter; the problem is far more complex than that. The problem is also that certain normalized market-/reviewer-friendly forms of qualitative inquiry are becoming the type of qualitative inquiry that is being published by default in this journal, *and* becoming normative versions of what our qualitative inquiry is measured against by nonexpert reviewers. Then guidelines can be produced for nonexpert reviewers based on these normative versions of qualitative inquiry, *and so*, if a piece of qualitative inquiry doesn't measure up or conform to what is in the guidelines, then it can't be the "real" form or the desired brand of qualitative inquiry, *and* this results in market-friendly brands of qualitative inquiry being developed, *and* in the rise of market-based connoisseurs of, and experts about, qualitative inquiry, who may not necessarily have much experience, if any at all, of qualitative inquiry itself. This is what enables the reviewer to be able to write, "I am not an expert at qualitative research, but … ."

Thus, how I might think about, or act in relation to, such a review was complicated, because each *and* (or +) in the examples above is *itself* a point around which many dynamic connections emanate and/or converge. The review is a symptom of a series of connected problems that together make up a social mess. This series of connections goes well beyond the specific review we received, the content of our paper, or the findings of our research. Thinking about this reflexively, I came to realize that the rejection, or even the review itself, was not the problem but only part of it. What *was* the problem was the series of connections that enabled that reviewer to write that review, *and* the series of connections that enabled the editor of that journal to act on that review, *and* the series of connections that meant that this reviewer and review could affect both my own and qualitative inquiry's currency in the research marketplace. Dealing with only one part of this series of *ands* (+s) that comprise the mess that is the problem, will not "solve" that mess.

Consequently, I found myself thinking about what I could, might, or should do about this review, and most importantly, why I was thinking this. Far from worrying about whether to change the word "constant" to "iterative/iteratively reviewed," I found I was asking questions of myself about what method could I, should I, must I use, and why? + What journal could I, should I, must I publish in, and why? + Why is it important to ask those questions? + Crucially, how important to me are the answers to those questions? It was this last + that I really struggled with: "How important to me are the answers to those questions?"This was because thinking about how important the answers to those questions were to me forced me to confront how far I was willing to adapt my qualitative inquiry to the nonexpert's standardized or normalized view of qualitative inquiry in order to get the paper published.

The research marketplace: Qualitative inquirers as victims, complicit, or both?

When thinking about how I have adapted, or might adapt, both myself as a qualitative inquirer and the qualitative research I do to the research marketplace and all the +s it is connected to (including the nonexpert "expert" review), I was reminded of a question posed some 20 years ago by Edward Said (1996). He asked "whether there is or can be anything like an independent, autonomously functioning intellectual" [or for our purposes here, qualitative inquirer], "one who is not beholden to, and therefore constrained by, his or her affiliations with universities that pay salaries, political parties that demand loyalty to a party line, think tanks that while they offer freedom to do research perhaps more subtly compromise judgment and restrain the critical voice" (pp. 67–68). I was struck by how relevant, and even more important to consider this question is in contemporary times when neoliberalism continues its relentless march, unchecked and seemingly unstoppable.

The question posed by Said (1996) is one that qualitative inquirers need to ask about their affiliations with a research marketplace that is itself derived from affiliations with universities, political parties, and think tanks – a research marketplace that gives the illusion of freedom for individuals to do research in that place, yet compromises researchers' judgments by market-driven insistence on certain types of research outputs and emphasis on certain types of currency in that marketplace. Even more confronting is the thought of a research marketplace in which we ourselves, of our own volition, may act to restrain our own critical voice by choosing to play all or some of the "games" of the research marketplace in order to gain more currency and therefore get "ahead" of others in that place. Looked at in this way, this might be a place in which we "are not simply victims," but also a place where we are "complicit, indeed we are sometimes beneficiaries. At times … we participate in all of this, not reluctantly, but 'imaginatively, aggressively, and competitively'" (Ball, 2015, p. 259).

Chubb and Watermeyer's (2016) study of the way academics write their research-grant applications provides us with a good example of such imaginative, aggressive, and competitive participation. The study focused on how researchers write the section of the funding application that requires researchers to identify the "impact" of the proposed research. In this section of the proposal, researchers are required to demonstrate "how they will ensure economic and/or societal returns from their research" (p. 3). Chubb and Watermeyer were interested in the way researchers in the United Kingdom and Australia wrote this particular section of the grant, what they wrote, as well as why they wrote what they did. In other words, they were interested in the thinking behind the writing. They interviewed academics who had recently been involved in writing grant applications and probed the thinking behind the writing about the impact of their research. The following excerpts from the interviews (Chubb & Watermeyer, 2016) provide insights into that thinking:

- "They're telling a good story as to how this might fit into the bigger picture. That's what I'm talking about. It might require a bit of imagination, it's not telling lies. It's just maybe being imaginative." (p. 8)
- "If I want to do basic science I have to tell you lies." (p. 5)
- "It's virtually impossible to write one of these grants and be fully frank and honest in what it is you're writing about." (p. 5)
- "I don't think we can be too worried about it. It's survival … . People write fiction all the time, it's just a bit worse." (p. 6)
- "People might, well not lie but I think they'd push the boundaries a bit and maybe exaggerate!" (p. 9)

Putting some +s in our thinking about these excerpts exposes the connections between the writing of the impact statement and the research marketplace. Pluses (+s) such as market-derived forms of how to write about impact in a grant (the winning formula); + it is hard (even impossible) to get research funded that is not in line with those understandings of what impact is; + therefore, researchers must play the game of writing about the impact of their research in reviewer-preferred ways, even if it means that they act in ways they are not really comfortable with or even would critique in other settings; + the goal is to get external funding; + external funding gives researchers much currency in the research marketplace; + external funding is highly prized by institutions that researchers work in or to which they apply for jobs, promotion, or tenure; + the ends justify the means.

Here the problem is not having to write about the impact of the research that funding is being sought for. Requiring researchers applying for funding to demonstrate some societal and/or economic benefit or return from their research is in itself not necessarily a bad thing; rather, the problem is what Alvesson and Spicer (2016) referred to as "self-stupidifying" (p. 91), exhibited in the descriptions given by those interviewed of the way that the impact statement was written and why. Self-stupidifying "starts to happen when we censor our own internal conversation" and "try to give some sense to our often chaotic experiences" (p. 91). Thus, in the interview excerpts cited previously, we see academics justifying what is in effect lying in the writing of the impact statement, in terms of such lying being imaginative or creative or necessary or just part of what one has to do to get a grant. Analysis of these interviews led Chubb and Watermeyer (2016) to suggest that many academics "are complicit with the system they protest and upon which focus their criticism" (p. 9) when they write the impact statement section in their grant applications. A consequence of this, they suggested, is that "the hyper-competitiveness of the higher education market is resulting in impact sensationalism and the corruption of academics as custodians of truth" (p. 1).

Such a suggestion acts as a reality check for us as qualitative inquirers in market-driven competitive times. It puts the focus squarely back on us as individuals and the way that we ourselves position our qualitative inquiry and ourselves in the many connections that make up the contexts in which we research daily. It again reminds us that in the research marketplace, we "are not simply victims" (Ball, 2015, p. 259). Therefore, it is not sufficient for us to blame others or to take the high moral ground by claiming that we are not part of the problem or mess in which we are embedded, but rather the mess is "making" us have to act in certain ways that we do not want to act, or that it is just common sense to go along with it all and just get on with our research. Rather, we must think deeply about choices we make and actions we take in relation to those choices – actions such as choosing to write our qualitative research to fit the requirements of funders (such as impact statements; on the surface a seemingly commonsensical or ordinary position to adopt if winning the funding is the goal); or actions such as choosing **not** to write our qualitative inquiry to fit the requirements of funders (on the surface a seemingly nonsensical or extraordinary position to take in a competitive research marketplace, given the loss of currency in that place that will result).

End thoughts: The power and possibility of the pluses (+s)

Mainelli and Harris (2011) reminded us that "the real world is messy, circular and aggressive. Wheels within wheels [or for our purposes here, +s within +s] … lead to bigger messes and unintended consequences" (p. 2). It is important for us as qualitative inquirers to recognize the mess that we are in, and see it for what it is: a series of connected problems that connect and reconnect with each other in many different permutations. Like it or not, we are part of the mess, and the question for us then becomes how we will position ourselves as researchers, and the qualitative inquiry we do, in this mess.

Exposing and better understanding the +s that comprise social messes such as the research marketplace in which both we and our qualitative inquiry are embedded, enables us to actively choose which of those +s we will choose to ignore, which we will choose to engage with, and which we will choose to negate. In this way, putting the +s in our thinking opens up the possibility for us to "have the space in which to stand and talk back to authority, since unquestioning subservience to authority in today's world is one of the greatest threats to an active, and moral, intellectual life" (Said, 1996, p. 121). In so doing, it will be possible to remind ourselves that we are the ones "who can choose between actively representing the truth to the best of your ability and passively allowing a patron or an authority to direct you" (Said, 1996, p. 121). Furthermore, it will open up the possibility for us to have a space in which to stand and talk back to *ourselves*, thereby stopping the self-censoring in the conversations we have with ourselves about the choices we can, must, or should make in a neoliberal-derived research marketplace.

Refusing to be passively positioned by the research marketplace and the neoliberalism that it is both derived from and acts to sustain, allows for the possibility that we can escape forms of neoliberal-derived "boxed-in thinking" (Alvesson & Spicer, 2016, p. 135) about how we can, even must, enact our qualitative inquiry. Speaking back to ourselves in the spaces that adding the +s to our thinking creates is a way of trying to avoid the feeling of losing, and actually losing, control both of ourselves as researchers and of our qualitative inquiry. In this way, putting some +s in our thinking is a way of pushing back at what Ball described as the feeling of being "a neo-liberal academic working for a global HE[3] brand, ranked in international performance sites for performance-related pay" (Ball, 2015, p. 258), and an academic (or for our purposes here, a qualitative researcher) being what Butler described as "other to myself precisely at the place where I expect to be myself" (Butler, 2004, p. 15).

In all of this we must be realistic. We are qualitative inquirers conducting qualitative inquiry that is embedded in neoliberal-saturated times. Putting the +s in our thinking might decrease the volume of the neoliberal tune we are all, to varying degrees, marching to, and/or slow the pace of that marching. Nevertheless, it won't stop either the *tune itself* or the marching to that tune; indeed, in the relentless competition of the research marketplace, putting the +s in our thinking may even leave us feeling left behind in that march, and reduce our value in the eyes of those orchestrating the tune, for as Alvesson and Spicer (2016) pointed out, "If you persist in asking tough questions, you are likely to cause problems for yourself. You will most likely upset the smooth workings of a group, threaten relationships with key people, and disturb existing power structures. Play dumb, and the status quo survives; team relationships can continue unthreatened. All this allows you to focus on 'delivering the goods'" (p. 75).

What putting the +s into our thinking *will* enable us to do, however, is to connect the fragmented symptoms of the neoliberalism that we engage with daily – symptoms such as the imperative to publish, or the development of metrics such as the h-index and impact factor, or the transformation of students into customers. Focusing on what actually *is* the problem, not the solutions to symptoms of it, may offer the possibility that despite the fact that we might not be able to get out of the mess we are in, we can better understand it, and therefore manage it, navigate it, and even escape parts of it.

Part of this is seeing these symptoms for what they are: fragments that are part of the mess that we are in, but not all of it. Recognizing the symptoms for what they are can work to prevent us from focusing only on "treating" those individual symptoms rather than addressing the mess that is the underlying problem itself. Treatments such as adapting the way we write our research to fit with a funding body's understanding of research impact, as exemplified by the tradeoffs made by the researchers in Chubb and Watermeyer's (2016) study. Treatments that take our focus away from the fact that we are dealing with symptoms of the problem and not the problem itself. The *real* problem, namely the underlying series of connected problems that these symptoms and treatments arise from, marches on relentlessly.

Hence, putting some +s in our thinking is about developing "the capacity to question assumptions and to think differently … [thereby avoiding] the problem of people who only have a hammer in their toolbox, and as a result are inclined to treat everything as a nail" (Alvesson & Spicer, 2016, p. 135). It is about breaking open any boxed-in thinking we might have about what our problem is, thereby opening up a politics of possibility (Madison, 2003) in which we can "turn away from neoliberalism and towards ourselves, to begin the difficult – but also joyous – work of managing our affairs for ourselves" (Purcell, 2016, p. 620) rather than passively allowing a journal reviewer or a market-based metric or a zero-sum, quasi-research marketplace direct us and our research. Joyous in that we will no longer have to self-censor our thinking about how to do or write our qualitative inquiry. Joyous that we do not inevitably have to outsource our thinking (Alvesson & Spicer, 2016) about our research to the research marketplace and customers in that place, such as the nonexpert reviewer, or granting panels wanting to know about the impact of our research in a certain way. And, most of all, joyous as a result of a renewed optimism that maybe, just maybe, we might be able to avoid becoming other to ourselves in the very place where we hoped and expected to be ourselves – in our qualitative inquiry.

Notes

1 We had talked about constant comparison of data, theories, and ideas as part of the analytical process.
2 For example, see Hammersley's (2008) probing discussion in his critical essay on "the issue of quality in qualitative research."
3 "HE" refers to higher education, but for the purposes of this discussion we can substitute "research" for HE.

References

Ackoff, R. L. (1974). *Redefining the future: A systems approach to societal problems.* London: Wiley.

Alvesson, M. (2013). *The triumph of emptiness. Consumption, higher education, & work organization.* Oxford, United Kingdom: Oxford University Press.

Alvesson, M., & Spicer, A. (2016). *The stupidity paradox: The power and pitfalls of functional stupidity at work.* London, United Kingdom: Profile Books.

Ball, S. J. (2012). Performativity, commodification and commitment: An I-spy guide to the neoliberal university. *British Journal of Educational Studies, 60*(1), 17–28.

Ball, S. J. (2015). Living in the neo-liberal university. *European Journal of Education, 50*(3), 258–261.

Baumann, Z. (1988). Is there a postmodern sociology? *Theory, Culture and Society, 5,* 217–237.

Bok, D. (2003). *Universities in the marketplace: The commercialization of higher education.* Princeton, NJ: Princeton University Press.

Brown, R. (2011). The march of the market. In M. Molesworth, R. Scullion, & E. Nixon (Eds.), *The marketisation of higher education and the student as consumer* (pp. 11–24). Oxon, United Kingdom: Routledge.

Brown, W. (2015). *Undoing the demos: Neoliberalism's stealth revolution.* Boston: MIT Press.

Butler, J. (2004). *Undoing gender.* New York: Routledge.

Cannella, G. S., & Lincoln, Y. S. (2015). Critical qualitative research in global neoliberalism: Foucault, inquiry, and transformative possibilities. In N. K. Denzin & M. D. Giardina (Eds.), *Qualitative inquiry and the politics of research* (pp. 51–74). Walnut Creek, CA: Left Coast Press.

Cary, L. J. (2006). *Curriculum spaces: Discourses, postmodern theory and educational research.* New York: Peter Lang.

Cheek, J. (2011). The politics and practices of funding qualitative inquiry. In N. K. Denzin & Y. S. Lincoln (Eds.), *The Sage handbook of qualitative research* (4th ed., pp. 251–268). Thousand Oaks, CA: Sage.

Cheek, J (2016). Qualitative inquiry and the research marketplace: Putting some +s (pluses) in our thinking, and why this matters. *Cultural Studies ↔ Critical Methodologies 1532708616669528*, first published on September 26, 2016 doi:10.1177/ 1532708616669528

Cheek, J. (in press). The marketization of research: Implications for qualitative inquiry. In N. K. Denzin & Y. S. Lincoln (Eds.), *Sage handbook of qualitative research* (5th ed.). Thousand Oaks, CA: Sage.

Chubb, J., & Watermeyer, R. (2016). Artifice or integrity in the marketization of research impact? Investigating the moral economy of (pathways to) impact statements within research funding proposals in the UK and Australia. *Studies in Higher Education,* 1–13. doi:10.1080/03075079.2016.1144182

Clawson, D., & Page, M. (2011). *The future of higher education.* New York and London: Routledge.

Denzin, N. K. (2010). *The qualitative manifesto. A call to arms.* Walnut Creek, CA: Left Coast Press.

Denzin, N. K., & Giardina, M. D. (2015). Introduction. In N. K. Denzin & M. D. Giardina (Eds.), *Qualitative inquiry and the politics of research* (pp. 9–25). Walnut Creek, CA: Left Coast Press.

Denzin, N. K., & Giardina, M. D. (2016). Introduction. In N. K. Denzin & M. D. Giardina (Eds.), *Qualitative inquiry through a political lens* (pp. 1–16). New York: Routledge.

Foskett, N. (2011). Markets, government, funding and the marketisation of UK higher education. In M. Molesworth, R. Scullion, & E. Nixon (Eds.), *The marketisation of higher education and the student as consumer* (pp. 25–38). Oxon, United Kingdom: Routledge.

Furedi, F. (2011). Introduction to the marketisation of higher education and the student as consumer. In M. Molesworth, R. Scullion, & E. Nixon (Eds.), *The marketisation of higher education and the student as consumer* (pp. 1–7). Oxon, United Kingdom: Routledge.

Garfield, E. (1999). Journal impact factor: A brief review. *Canadian Medical Association Journal, 161*(8), 979–980.

Hammersley, M. (2008). *Questioning qualitative inquiry. Critical essays*. London: Sage.

Hobsons. (2015). *The good universities guide*. Retrieved from http://ebook.gooduniguide.com.au/#folio=FC

Hoeffel, C. (1998). Journal impact factors [Letter]. *Allergy, 53*, 1225.

Horn, R. E., & Weber, R. P. (2007). New tools for resolving wicked problems: Mess mapping and resolution mapping processes. Retrieved from www.strategykinetics.com/New_Tools_For_Resolving_Wicked_Problems.pdf

i-graduate International Insight. (2015). *International student barometer*. Retrieved from www.i-graduate.org/services/international-student-barometer/

Johnson, H. (2003). The marketing orientation in higher education: The perspectives of academics about its impact on their role. In G. Williams (Ed.), *The enterprising university* (pp. 142–153). Buckingham: SRHE & Open University Press.

Kuntz, A. M. (2015). *The responsible methodologist: Inquiry, truth-telling, and social justice*. Walnut Creek. CA: Left Coast Press.

Kvale, S. (2008). Qualitative inquiry between scientific evidentialism, ethical subjectivism and the free market. *International Review of Qualitative Research, 1*(1), 5–18.

Le Grand, J., & Bartlett, W. (1993). *Quasi-markets and social policy*. Basingstoke, United Kingdom: Macmillan.

Lincoln, Y. S. (2012). The political economy of publication: Marketing, commodification, and qualitative scholarly work. *Qualitative Health Research, 22*, 1451–1459.

Lucal, B. (2015). 2014 Hans O. Mauksch address: Neoliberalism and higher education: How a misguided philosophy undermines teaching sociology. *Teaching Sociology, 43*(1), 3–14. doi:0092055X14556684

Madison, D. S. (2003). Performance, personal narratives, and the politics of possibility. *Turning Points in Qualitative Research: Tying Knots in a Handkerchief, 3*, 469–486.

Mainelli, M., & Harris, I. (2011). *The price of fish: A new approach to wicked economics and better decisions*. London: Nicholas Brealey.

Purcell, M. (2016). Our new arms. In S. Springer, K. Birch, & J. MacLeavy (Eds.), *The handbook of neoliberalism* (pp. 613–622). New York: Routledge.

Ritchey, T. (2013). Wicked problems: Modelling social messes with morphological analysis. *Acta Morphologica Generalis, 2*(1), 1–8.

Rittel, H. W. J., & Webber, M. M. (1973). Dilemmas in a general theory of planning. *Policy Sciences Amsterdam, 4*, 155–169.

Robertson, S. L. (2012). World-class higher education (for whom?). *Prospects, 42*(3), 237–245.

Said, E. W. (1996). *Representations of the intellectual*. New York: First Vintage Books.

Seglen, P. O. (1997). Why the impact factor of journals should not be used for evaluating research. *BMJ, 314*(7079), 498–502.

Sidhu, R. K. (2006). *Universities and globalization: To market, to market.* Mahwah, NJ: Lawrence Erlbaum.

Steger, M. B., & Roy, R. K. (2010). *Neoliberalism: A very short introduction* (Vol. 222). Oxford: Oxford University Press.

Tuchman, G. (2009). *Wannabe U: Inside the corporate university.* Chicago: University of Chicago Press.

2

POST QUALITATIVE INQUIRY

The next generation

Elizabeth Adams St. Pierre

This chapter comes out of a conference session I organized for the 2016 International Congress of Qualitative Inquiry titled, "A History of Qualitative Research in Four Generations." Session participants kindly agreed to be slotted into the rather arbitrary four generations: Norman Denzin and Frederick Erickson in the first; Patti Lather in the second; I represented the third; and Alecia Jackson, the fourth. I believe that Denzin and Erickson helped invent the radical interpretive qualitative methodology of the 1970s and 1980, that Lather led its troubled engagement with the postmodern, that I continued Lather's critique by inventing post qualitative inquiry, and that Jackson (in press) is a leader in the "new" work, which she has recently called "thinking without method." There is a postmodern lineage of sorts for the last three generations, because I was Patti Lather's student, Alecia Jackson was mine, and we all employ the "posts" in our work. There are, of course, other histories of qualitative methodology.

The generation-to-come loomed large in my mind as I listened to our presentations. How will we make the next generation of inquirers? What projects will they take on? What historical events – like the social movements of the 1960s and 1970s that called for interpretive and critical qualitative methodologies – will inspire them to think, do, and live differently? Of course, the next generation has already begun its work that is spreading like a rhizome to upend what we thought was true and real about social science research methodology.

The conference session was well attended, and I believe it was a fruitful exercise for the participants as we thought back through the years about what qualitative inquiry had been – and been differently – when each of us came to it; about its early and continuing struggle to legitimate itself against positivist social science's recurring dismissals as being prescientific or even nonscientific; its elaboration, structuring, centering, and normalization through textbooks, university research courses, conferences, and journals as part of that legitimation process; its battering and rejection by positivist "scientifically based research" in the first decade of the 21st century; and then, for me and others now, its failure in the face of the "new" coming out of the ontological turn prompted decades ago by postmodernism and by the more recent new materialism, new empiricism, posthuman, and nonhuman, as well as by affect theory, thing theory, assemblage theory, actor network theory, complexity theory, and so on.

As for me, I began my "third generation" doctoral studies at Ohio State University in 1991, when some feminists (e.g., Braidotti, 1994; Butler, 1990, 1992; Haraway, 1991; Hekman, 1990; Lather, 1991; Weedon, 1987; Wolf, 1992) were taking up postmodernism. The proliferation of qualitative textbooks and handbooks had just begun. We surely didn't study the history of qualitative inquiry because it was still new, *still being invented*. But I would argue that studying the history of a discursive and material formation such as conventional humanist qualitative methodology today, several decades later, should be de rigueur in order to demystify its truth claims by calling into question the foundational assumptions it has laid down. Historicizing a taken-for-granted structure helps us understand the very fragile history of its present, a present that did not have to be, that, indeed, would *not* be, without a particular foundation that conditions its emergence. More importantly, there are, in fact, different presents with different histories that have enabled different approaches to social science inquiry that do not look like conventional humanist qualitative methodology. Some of those are now moving into the mainstream.

The conventional humanist qualitative methodology described in textbooks and handbooks and university research courses is, indeed, an invention, a fiction – we made it up. For that reason, we must understand that its taken-for-granted processes, procedures, and practices now embedded in powerful institutional forces are aligned with a Platonic, Cartesian, modernist, representational, transcendent trajectory, which Deleuze (1968/1994) would likely call a "dogmatic image of thought" (p. 148). Again, historicizing a discursive and material formation such as conventional humanist qualitative methodology enables us to understand that other formations, other methodologies, or *no methodology at all*, are possible when other images of thought are in play, such as the Liebnizian, Nietzchean, Deleuzian, postmodern, nonrepresentational, immanentist trajectory that post qualitative inquiry makes room for.

It should not be surprising that those incompatible images of thought produce incompatible empiricisms (see St. Pierre, 2016a), which then enable different empirical inquiry. It is this problem, the incompatibility of different onto–epistemological arrangements, that becomes more evident as history calls into question the necessity and, what Nietzsche might call, the *goodness* of dominant methodologies. In general, dominant forms of inquiry are recognizable; taken-for-granted; considered proven, reliable, valid, and good. What Mazzei (in press), following Deleuze and Guattari (1975/1986), recently called "minor inquiry" becomes suspect because it is not recognizable but different, unproven according to the standards of the dominant model, perhaps false, and, hence, not good.

How do we dislodge the taken-for-granted to make room for something different, something "new"? Derrida's deconstruction is helpful in that work because it is a critique of a structure one intimately inhabits but must say no to. Relieved at the beginning of my doctoral studies that I could work with words and not numbers in my research, I accepted without question the structure of conventional humanist qualitative methodology. After all, it was radical and new, exciting, and seemingly limitless. Conventional humanist qualitative methodology grounded in what people say and do, in their everyday lived experiences, quickly became my methodological home, as it does for many doctoral students like me who love language. This research begins and ends with the *cogito*, with participants who have knowledge the researcher wants to know too. Language, words from interviews and field notes, becomes data, brute data, which, it is assumed, can contain *meaning* that language, in turn, can *represent*. The assumption is that language not only *is* the truth (data, evidence) but can also *stand in* for the truth (be clear, transparent, objective) in mirroring reality.

At the same time, however, I fell in love with the poststructural understanding of language which is incommensurable with the description found in conventional, humanist qualitative methodology. In this understanding, meaning always escapes the capture, the closure, of language. This understanding also refuses the logic of representation which posits a hierarchy of knower–language – the real in favor of a flattened ontology with representations on the same plane as humans and the real. Humans, then, are not prior to language but exist on the same horizontal plane as everything else. For me, poststructural understandings of language, as well as the subject, produced the failure of conventional humanist qualitative methodology, a structure I happily inhabited early on that became increasingly restrictive and inadequate as I turned away from its dogmatic image of thought.

Given the incompatibility of the humanist and the "post" descriptions of language and being, especially human being, deconstruction was inevitable. Derrida (1990) wrote that "deconstruction is neither a theory nor a philosophy. It is neither a school nor a method. It is not even a discourse, nor an act, nor a practice. It is what happens" (p. 85). Indeed, as I read Derrida and Foucault and Butler and Spivak and Deleuze and Guattari, qualitative methodology deconstructed itself. I could neither think it nor do it.

This, then, is where my so-called *third*-generation engagement with conventional humanist qualitative methodology began – in its postmodern impossibility and a groping toward an inquiry that beckoned but remained largely unintelligible. It was only when I returned, years later, to Deleuze and Guattari, whom I had read early in my doctoral program – to their radical, experimental ontology and transcendental empiricism – that I began to fully understand that my inability to *do* conventional humanist qualitative inquiry emerged from my inability to *think* it. Here, *application*, or *the inability to apply*, marked the failure of a theory of methodology in the always imbricated theory-practice, theory-methodology relation. I could not resolve the incompatibility of the onto-epistemologies of conventional humanist qualitative methodology and those of the "posts" in some pragmatic "smoothie"[1] (see Erickson in Moss, Phillips, Erickson, Floden, Lather, & Schneider, 2009, p. 508) and proceed as usual. I agreed with Wyly (2009) who wrote that "many have warned of the dangers of a mix-and-match eclecticism; there are some features of alternative epistemologies and methodologies that simply cannot be reconciled" (p. 319). For me, "mixed" onto-epistemologies were as impossible as "mixed" methods.

In this regard, it might be helpful to think of the "turns" in the humanities (e.g., postmodern turn, ontological turn), much like Kuhn's paradigm shifts in the natural sciences, as creating what Harvey (1989) called "incommensurable spaces that are juxtaposed or superimposed upon each other ... Characters are forced to ask, 'Which world is this? What is to be done in it? Which of myselves is to do it?" (p. 48). Kuhn (1970), writing about the paradigm shifts of the natural sciences, explained that "what differentiated these various schools was not one or another failure of method – they were all 'scientific' – but what we shall come to call incommensurable ways of seeing the world and of practicing science in it" (p. 4). He added, "the two groups of scientists see different things when they look from the same point in the same direction;" thus, "they practice their trades *in different worlds*" (p. 150, emphasis added). Further, "within the new paradigm, old terms, concepts, and experiments fall into new relationships with the other" (p. 149), resulting in misunderstanding. For example, the concept *empirical* in transcendental empiricism does not mean the same as *empirical* in logical empiricism. I remember someone once telling me I didn't do empirical research. I replied that I did, but that I used a different kind of empiricism. The accuser was not convinced, but, understanding the incommensurability of our positions, I knew better than to try to convince him. I suspect the Deleuzian inquirer who thinks with transcendental empiricism is unlikely to do conventional ethnographic "fieldwork" focused chiefly on interviewing humans and observing humans even though she is, indeed, doing empirical research.

Perhaps this problem illustrates how the possibilities of one generation become the impossibilities of another as they invent and work in different worlds. The Nobel Prize–winning quantum physicist Max Planck (as cited in Kuhn, 1970) explained that "a new scientific truth does not triumph by convincing its opponents and making them see the light, but rather because its opponents eventually die, and a new generation grows up that is familiar with it" (p. 151). Indeed. I take that warning to heart and worry about the truths I and my generation espouse that shut down experimentation and the "new" for the next. These incommensurabilities are very real and cannot be resolved or disappeared by working harder to understand the previous or next generations. I have come to believe that the romance of using rational dialogue to "talk across differences" to reach understanding and consensus (e.g., Habermas, 1981/1984) is just that, a romance and a cheat. In fact, consensus — too often a power move in which those who disagree are silenced — can disappear difference, diversity. For that reason, Lyotard (1979/1984) wrote that dissensus — not consensus — is the motor of democracy.

But our generational positioning, our beginnings and subsequent training, will always get in our way:

> Who did we study with as doctoral students?
> What onto-epistemologies enabled our research questions and our methodologies?
> What methods and methodologies were privileged?
> What methodological textbooks did we study and believe?
> What were the objects of our knowledge at that historical moment?
> What counted as science?
> What couldn't we think and so do?
> What were we doing that could not be captured by our conceptual and theoretical categories?

What struck me as I listened to Denzin, Erickson, Lather, and Jackson in that conference session was how very radical their work was as each generation pushed through taken-for-granted limits established by prior generations. Of course, these four scholars and researchers are extraordinary in the breadth and depth of their reading and risk-taking. Their work is not typical, and they model the rich possibilities of the finest scholarship that embraces working in discomfort and being lost in rigorous confusion. When I really think about it, I realize that the space in which each generation thinks and works is always so very small, so limited, and so closed off that it may take the very radical work of many generations to explode the paradigm, to force the turn, to produce a different world. Whether we want to do that, of course, is another matter altogether. How comfortable do we need to be? Are we willing to think outside our training? What truths have we learned that we're unable to give up, and why do we cling to them? How devastating does a crisis in our historical moment (e.g., climate change, World War II) have to be to shatter the foundations on which we rely for authority so we can move toward *difference*.

During the last 20 years or so, I've tried to both teach conventional humanist qualitative methodology and disrupt it, to make it historical and contingent and so not necessary. But I've watched many students become trapped in its pre-given "process" and then produce what Kuhn (1970) called "normal science" (p. 10), perhaps aiming for more elaborate and precise methods and richer and thicker descriptions with alternative representations aimed at getting closer to the authentic real. For me, that work has become repetitive and predictable. Our dutiful doctoral students learn what we teach and then teach it themselves, thus passing down beliefs, for example, that data analysis is coding data and that systematicity is the marker of science. It doesn't take us long to latch onto something we can understand fairly quickly, to a process that is easily repeatable, to a prescriptive methodology that more or less resolves confusion.

Lately, I've begun to wonder what it would be like to work with students who are "methodology free" (St. Pierre, in press), who haven't already fallen into the groove of a pre-given methodology, who might be lost from the beginning and prefer to stay lost as they "inquire," whatever that involves. I've wondered whether transcendental empiricism, which could be categorized in the domain of philosophy, might be possible in social science inquiry. My chief concern is that philosophers are charged with reading deeply whereas social scientists must rush to application and produce data and evidence and findings, no matter how little they've read. For that reason, undertheorized social science research is not uncommon.

There is much to think about, much we've taken for granted in social science research methodology that must be de-naturalized if we are to open up space for the next generation to do its own radical work. The conference session I've focused on here with four generations of qualitative researchers emerged from being in academia long enough to have a history with qualitative methodology. I encourage those who are just beginning their careers in social science research not to take its current methodologies too seriously but to historicize them by studying how they came to be accepted as true and good, what methodologies had to be excluded for them to become dominant and privileged, how the current methodologies are maintained and perpetuated and normalized, who counts as a real researcher in a methodological formation, and so on. Clearly, these are questions of politics and power and not of truth or goodness.

In the past couple of years, I have written a brief personal history about my relation with conventional humanist qualitative methodology during my years in academia (St. Pierre, 2016b), a paper recommending some practices for a new researcher who might want to resist the old methodologies (St. Pierre, 2015), and I have co-edited several special issues of journals whose papers provide citational authority to support those who want to try something different (*International Journal of Qualitative Studies in Education*, 2013, 26(6) on post qualitative inquiry, St. Pierre & Lather, Eds.; *Qualitative Inquiry*, 2014, 20(6) on data analysis after coding, St. Pierre & Jackson, Eds.; *Cultural Studies⇔Critical Methodologies* 2016, 16(2) on the new empiricisms and new materialisms, St. Pierre, Jackson, & Mazzei, Eds.; *Qualitative Inquiry* (in process) on using concept as/instead of method, St. Pierre & Lenz Taguchi, Eds.). We editors encouraged the authors of the papers in those special issues to attend to what could not be contained in but escaped the normal procedures, processes, and practices of the methodologies they'd learned. For example, in the special issue on data analysis after coding, we asked authors to write about what they did, other than coding data, when they did something they thought was analysis. In the special issue on using a concept instead of a method or methodology to inquire, we asked authors to experiment, to imagine how inquiry might begin and proceed without a pre-existing, methods-driven methodology that determines what to do next and then next. For example, how might the Deleuzo-Guattarian concepts *refrain* or *heacceity* open up inquiry? The risky work authors in those special issues accomplished does not look like conventional qualitative methodology, and it is inspiring to see what researchers can do when not constrained by what they think have to do or should do to be methodologically correct. It is also inspiring when journal editors seek out and encourage scholarship that goes beyond the bounds of the norm.

As I worked with these authors, I realized, again, the importance of being well read and especially of studying philosophy, history, and the philosophy of social science. If we don't have anything much to think with, our work is not likely to be very interesting. I also realized, again, that some of the best writing is writing to think what could not have been thought except in writing. As I read those experimental papers, I could feel the surge, the risky energy collected in one sentence that led to the next spectacular sentence and the next. This is not writing to repeat, to represent, but writing to inquire (Richardson & St. Pierre, 2005). This editing work over several years confirmed my belief that two of the most important research practices are reading and writing even though neither counts as such in conventional qualitative methodology since reading is typically confined to the "literature review" which one does before one inquires, and writing is typically confined to "representation" which one does at the end, after one has inquired. Actually, I believe the authors of papers in these special issues used at least the practices I recommended for post qualitative inquiry in 2015: to refuse methodology; read, read, read; begin with theory and concepts; trust yourself and get to work, which, I think, involves writing. Of course, they used other practices as well.

I would like to be more specific about what one might read – and what we might teach – to prepare for this "new" work of the ontological and empirical turns and of post qualitative inquiry. As I thought about my own research training as a doctoral student while I wrote my paper for the conference session described in this paper, I realized that though doctoral students were then and are now expected to do empirical social science research, we seldom study the various empiricisms and their history and politics. Because of that, when the "new empiricism" appeared, we had no idea what the "old" empiricisms (e.g., logical empiricism, the empiricism of phenomenology) were, how they were different from each other, or how they were different from the new empiricism (e.g., transcendental empiricism).

Nor had we, even those of us who had studied postmodernism, which is shot through with ontological concerns, studied ontology. The identity politics that dominated much conventional humanist qualitative research for decades had insisted we study and use, for example, feminist epistemologies, Chicana epistemology, various race epistemologies, queer epistemologies, and so on. Epistemology seemed to have sidelined ontology as we focused on the marginalized knowledges of oppressed groups. Methodology adjusted somewhat to account for those standpoint epistemologies coming out of identity politics (e.g., Lather, 1991; Morrow, 1994; Moustakas, 1994; Reinharz, 1992; Sandoval, 2000; Scheurich, 1997; Smith, 1999; Stanfield & Routledge, 1993), but it remained within the closure of human exceptionalism. Even though some postmodernists had declared the death of the subject (e.g., Barthes, 1984/1986; Butler, 1992; Foucault, 1979; Haraway, 1988), the Cartesian *cogito* remained alive and well in the new standpoint epistemologies and the methodologies that accommodated them. In other words, we had not taken up the postmodern charge of rethinking ontology, the nature of being and, especially of *human* being.

But it is ontology – the nature of being – that drives much of the new empirical, new material work. I'm not sure how we can make the ontological turn until we study ontology and begin to think about various *onto-epistemologies* and the different methodologies that align with them. The point here is that no single methodology (i.e., conventional humanist qualitative methodology) can hold across different onto-epistemological formations, especially after postmodernism deemed epistemology problematic and scholars called into question the belief that knowledge could be pure and innocent, value-free. Butler (1992), for example, wrote that "the epistemological point of departure in philosophy is inadequate" (p. 8); Flax (1990) urged us not to continue asking the old knowledge questions; and Deleuze and Guattari seldom used the word *epistemology* in their texts. I would argue, then, that teaching and learning the history and politics of empiricism and of ontology, a focus on onto-epistemological formations, and less focus, if any, on methodology except as a historical phenomenon is necessary for the next generation of social science researchers.

Another critical factor for the next generation, one long overdue, is the proposed revisions to the Common Rule for the Protection of Human Subjects, which were recommended by a National Research Council committee of experts (2014) and supported by other groups, including the American Educational Research Association (see www.regulations.gov/document?D=HHS-OPHS-2015-0008-0001). As of this writing, (September 20, 2016), the U.S. Department of Health and Human Services' Office for Human Research Protection is considering over 2,000 comments submitted in response to the proposed revisions during the public comment period that ended December 7, 2015. The timetable in the docket folder in the Federal Register lists the final action as 09/00/16, so a new ruling governing the protection of human subjects in research should be available soon. In the proposed revisions, it appears that much conventional humanist qualitative research is exempt from Institutional Review Board (IRB) review, which is simply astounding given decades of lost energy and battles with IRBs, many of which just could not and/or would not understand qualitative research.

I believe the overreach of IRBs into research design helped shift the loose, emergent nature of first generation interpretive qualitative methodology to the current structure that requires a pre-existing research process driven by accepted, normalized methods rather than by encounters with the world that might require novel practices that do not exist ahead of the study and so cannot be approved in advance. More significantly, IRBs' necessary focus on the *human* – and a particular description of the human at that, the *cogito* – in their oversight of human subjects research inevitably narrows being to human being. How would one write an IRB proposal for a posthuman study or for a study that assumes human being is not prior to the world but always already entangled with it? The ethics of such a study require attention to the ongoing becoming, not of human being by itself, but of the assemblage. Because the structure of human subjects review assumes a particular kind of human being, it has legitimated *face-to-face* research methods like interviewing and observation that assume an intentional, agentive, knowing human being separate from the world, thus rein-forcing that particular description of human being. The proposed revisions ask questions for public comment about the definition of "human subject," about "activities that are deemed not research" (oral history, journalism, biography, and historical scholarship activities), including activities that most people consider more of less ordinary activities like interviewing and observation that would be unlikely to cause distress or injury. No longer inflating and elevating *interviewing* and *observation* to the privileged status of *research methods* makes room for other existing activities involving different kinds of human being – more-than-human, posthuman, nonhuman being – we might use and others activities we might invent during inquiry.

It appears to me that the playing field of the next generation of researchers is incredibly open, as (1) IRBs forgo their disciplinary, determining role that too often impoverishes inquiry; and (2) social science researchers reach toward phi-losophy and the humanities to invigorate the human sciences and perhaps to deconstruct those categories altogether. I strongly believe that clinging to any "methodology" invented to study a particular kind of being and human being will only limit the possibilities for new work after the ontological, material, and empir-ical turns that refuse both. Following postmodernism, post qualitative inquiry will always be suspicious of and prepared to refuse the entire methodological project. It does, however, encourage reading, writing, and "an experimentation in contact with the real" (Deleuze & Guattari, 1987, p. 12) in which anything can happen and does. We are limited only by what we cannot yet imagine, by what we cannot think and so do, by difference we cannot bear to embrace. I look forward to the radical work of the next generation.

Note

1   Thanks to Serge Hein for reminding me of this paper, in which the impossibility of "talking across differences" is evident.

References

Barthes, R. (1986). The death of the author. In *The rustle of language* (R. Howard, Trans.), (pp. 49–55). Berkeley, CA: University of California Press. (Original work published 1984.)

Braidotti, R. (1994). *Nomadic subjects: Embodiment and sexual difference in contemporary feminist theory*. New York, NY: Columbia University Press.

Butler, J. (1990). *Gender trouble: Feminism and the subversion of identity*. New York, NY: Routledge.

Butler, J. (1992). Contingent foundations: Feminism and the question of "postmodernism." In J. Butler and J. W. Scott (Eds.), *Feminists theorize the political* (pp. 3–21). New York, NY: Routledge.

Deleuze, G. (1994). *Difference and repetition*. (Paul Patton, Trans.). New York, NY: Columbia University Press. (Original work published 1968.)

Deleuze, G. and Guattari, F. (1986). *Kafka: Toward a minor literature*. (D. Polan, Trans.). Minneapolis, MN: University of Minnesota Press. (Original work published 1975.)

Deleuze, G. & Guattari, F. (1987). *A thousand plateaus: Capitalism and schizophrenia*. (B. Massumi, Trans.). Minneapolis, MN: University of Minnesota Press. (Original work published 1980).

Derrida, J. (1990). Some statements and truisms about neologisms, newisms, positisms, parasitisms, and other small seismisms. (A. Tomiche, Trans.). In D. Caroll (Ed.), *The states of "theory": History, art, and critical discourse* (p. 85). New York, NY: Columbia University Press.

Flax, J. S. (1990). *Thinking fragments: Psychoanalysis, feminism, and postmodernism in the contemporary west*. Berkeley, CA: University of California Press.

Foucault, M. (1979). What is an author? In J. V. Harari (Ed.), *Textual strategies: Perspectives in post-structuralist criticism* (pp. 141–160). Ithaca, NY: Cornell University Press.

Habermas, J. (1984). *The theory of communicative action. Volume 1. Reason and the rationalization of society*. (T. McCarthy, Trans.). Boston, MA: Beacon Press. (Original work published 1981.)

Haraway, D. J. (1988). Situated knowledges: The science question in feminism and the privilege of partial perspective. *Feminist Studies, 14*(3), 575–599.

Haraway, D. J. (1991). *Simians, cyborgs, and women: The reinvention of nature*. New York, NY: Routledge.

Harvey, D. (1989). *The condition of postmodernity: An enquiry into the origins of cultural change*. Cambridge, MA: Blackwell.

Hekman, S. J. (1990). *Gender and knowledge: Elements of a postmodern feminism*. Boston, MA: Northeastern University Press.

Jackson, A. Y. (in press). Thinking without method. *Qualitative Inquiry*.

Kuhn, T. S. (1970). *The structure of scientific revolutions*. (2nd ed.). Chicago, IL: University of Chicago Press.

Lather, P. (1991). *Getting smart: Feminist research and pedagogy with/in the postmodern*. New York, NY: Routledge.

Lyotard, J.-F. (1984). *The postmodern condition: A report on knowledge*. (G. Bennington and B. Massumi, Trans.). Minneapolis, MN: University of Minnesota Press. (Original work published 1979.)

Mazzei, L. A. (in press). Following the contour of concepts toward a minor inquiry. *Qualitative Inquiry*.

Morrow, R. A. with Brown, D. D. (1994). *Critical theory and methodology*. Thousand Oaks, CA: Sage.

Moss, P. A., Phillips, D. C., Erickson, F. D., Floden, R. E., Lather, P. A., and Schneider, B. L. (2009). Learning from our differences: A dialogue across perspectives on quality in educational research. *Educational Researcher*, *38*(7), 501–517.

Moustakas, C. (1994). *Phenomenological research methods*. Thousand Oaks, CA: Sage.

National Research Council. (2014). *Proposed Revisions to the Common Rule for the Protection of Human Subjects in the Behavioral and Social Sciences*. Committee on Revisions to the Common Rule for the Protection of Human Subjects in Research in the Behavioral and Social Sciences. Board on Behavioral, Cognitive, and Sensory Sciences, Committee on National Statistics, Division of Behavioral and Social Sciences and Education. Washington, DC: National Academies Press.

Reinharz, S. (1992). *Feminist methods in social research*. New York, NY: Oxford University Press.

Richardson, L. and St. Pierre, E. A. (2005). Writing: A method of inquiry. In N. K. Denzin and Y. Lincoln (Eds.), *Handbook of Qualitative Research* (3rd ed.). (pp. 959–978). Thousand Oaks, CA: Sage.

Sandoval, C. (2000). *Methodology of the oppressed*. Minneapolis, MN: University of Minnesota Press.

Scheurich, J. J. (1997). *Research method in the postmodern*. London: Falmer Press.

Smith, L. T. (1999). *Decolonizing methodologies: Research and indigenous peoples*. London: Zed Books.

Stanfield, J. H. II and Rutledge M. (Eds.). (1993). *Race and ethnicity in research methods*. Newbury Park, CA: Sage.

St. Pierre, E. A. (2015). Practices for the "new" in the new empiricisms, the new materialisms, and post qualitative inquiry. In N. Denzin and M. Giardina (Eds.). *Qualitative Inquiry and the Politics of Research*. Walnut Grove, CA: Left Coast Press.

St. Pierre, E. A. (2016a). The empirical and the new empiricisms. *Cultural Studies–Critical Methodologies*, *16*(2), 111–124.

St. Pierre, E. A. (2016b). A brief and personal history of post qualitative research: Toward 'post inquiry.' *Journal of Curriculum Theorizing*, *30*(2), 2–19.

St. Pierre, E. A. (in press). Untraining educational researchers. *Research in Education*. (Manchester, England)

Weedon, C. (1987). *Feminist practice and poststructuralist theory*. Cambridge, MA: Basil Blackwell.

Wolf, M. (1992). *A thrice-told tale: Feminism, postmodernism, and ethnographic responsibility*. Stanford, CA: Stanford University Press.

Wyly, E.. (2009). Strategic positivism. *Professional Geographer*, *61*(3), 310–322.

3

QUALITATIVE METHODOLOGY AND THE NEW MATERIALISMS

"A little of Dionysus's blood?"

Maggie MacLure

Introduction

I want to work through some issues that have been exercising me recently, around the turn, or return, to materiality in qualitative methodology. The new materialisms challenge the prerogative of the supposedly self-contained, coherent human subject, equipped to subdue the world with an armory of discursive and intellectual weapons – rationality, consciousness, creativity, intentionality, and language. A new materialist orientation would not suggest that these are fictions and should be abandoned, but rather, that they have traditionally been elevated to a status that occludes other capacities and connections, and diminishes the significance of matter and our human entanglements with it. New materialist thought challenges the notion of the world as the stage or background for the Big Human Adventure, and traces the many dire consequences of our chronic disregard for the agential and affective potential of matter. Not least of these consequences is the threat of human extinction. I will argue that the turn to materiality has powerful, but also powerfully dangerous, implications for qualitative research – and that these implications are not always fully recognized by those of us who have embraced, and been embraced by, the new materialisms.

What does method want?

It wants what Western philosophy, according to Deleuze, has always wanted: in short, to subdue difference. To confine its antics within the iron 'fetters' of *representation* (1994: 174), where identity and sameness regulate affairs, and difference emerges chastened and stripped of potential, as mere contradiction or opposition. That desire to control difference is easily seen in conventional qualitative method, with all its devices for reducing uncertainty and mining meaning from the ongoing flow of events. You can see it for instance in the sorting and subordinating practices of coding, or in strategies for controlling bias in interviews. You can see it in anxiety about data that block the route to propositional meaning: for example when jokes, reticence, or inconsistency surface in interview transcripts. Above all you can see it in the deep methodic aversion to materiality and the body when these irrupt into the linguistic economy of research: to tears and sneers and shifting in one's seat; to the currents of affect that might become fear, or disgust, or spite, or secret satisfaction, and disturb the equanimity of meaning.

However, Deleuze also argues that representation senses the presence of something else, something that it will always have failed to capture. Representation has a presentiment of the "chaos of potentials," as Deleuze calls it, on which its ordered hierarchies stand (Stivale, 2008, p. 20). This is the swarming groundlessness of difference-in-itself, which always escapes the iron fetters of reason, precisely by being beyond thought. Yet representation sometimes wants to incorporate or consume *that* too. It wants to seize the powers of "giddiness, intoxication and cruelty" (Deleuze, 1994, p. 262) that belong to difference, and render them fit for thought and reason.

But when representation becomes "orgiastic," as Deleuze calls it – when it tries to *devour* the excesses of difference rather than merely control them – it nevertheless wants to do that without getting its fingers burnt, or its self-assurance shredded. It's a question "of causing a little of Dionysus's blood to flow in the organic veins of Apollo" (262). Taking his lead from Nietzsche, Deleuze often associates difference with Dionysus, god of excess, intoxication, giddiness and cruelty; of madness, masks and theatricality, and contrasts him to Apollo, god of light, clarity, and good sense. But Deleuze notes that, so long as the iron rule of representation still covertly governs these adventures, we will continue to inhabit a world in which "one is only *apparently* intoxicated, in which reason acts the drunkard and sings a Dionysian tune while nonetheless remaining 'pure' reason" (1994: p. 264, emphasis added).

Is *this* what qualitative method after the material turn wants? In trying to free thought from the hierarchies of representation, and restore ontologies of difference, are we trying to get a little of that murky, impure Dionysian blood into the 'clear and distinct' veins of Apollonian representation? And if so, is this a matter of improper appropriation of materialist notions for old-school qualitative method – just acting the drunkard and whistling a Dionysian tune? Or should we think perhaps about judicious *dosage* – just enough Dionysian anomie to infuse life into a method that is increasingly exhausted, without killing the endeavor outright? I will not have a definitive answer to these questions. But I hope to be able to formulate some useful questions.

What, then, is new materialism, and what is it doing to qualitative research? New materialism is not necessarily the best term, though it is one of the most frequently used. I could refer instead to the new empiricisms. Or I could talk about turns: The material turn. The ontological turn. The posthuman turn. The speculative turn. The affective turn. It would be absurd to say that we are talking about a unified philosophical or methodological field here.[1] It should also be noted that new materialism has come in for critique from scholars who object to the colonial arrogance of announcing oneself as 'new' without due respect to other traditions, such as feminist theorisations of the body, and indigenous ontologies. As Alison Jones and Te Kawehau Hoskins (2016, p. 79) have recently remarked, "Indigenous ontologies never *had* a nature-culture dualism, never truly differentiated nature and culture." These are important issues and they deserve further attention, though I touch on them only in passing here.

For the moment, it may be useful to think of the term 'new materialisms' as a *'catachresis'* – a perpetually misused term, or a term without a stable referent. But nevertheless, a signal of *something* afoot: something that is zigzagging across these diverse fields or planes, pulling them together and apart in interesting ways. Let me brutally summarize some characteristics of new materialist work that I hope are relatively uncontroversial, before going on to consider the implications specifically for qualitative inquiry.

The material turn involves much more than a return to mundane empiricism. In the new materialisms, matter is agential, affective and self-differing. As Barad (2012, p. 59) famously wrote, "Matter feels, converses, suffers, desires, yearns and remembers." Agency and consciousness are not the prerogative of human subjects, and the bounded organism is not the unit of study. We are all produced from intensities and flows that far exceed and fall short of the contours of our bodies. Discourse does not discipline matter but tangles with it in shifting assemblages. Science and the social do not stand separate and opposed, and methodological virtue does not reside uncomplicatedly with one 'side' or the other. Lastly, experimentation is privileged over critique, at least where critique is construed as the exposure of error, the revelation of hidden circuits of power/knowledge, or the unmasking of ideology. Taken together, these characteristics raise an urgent question: does qualitative inquiry, as the transformative work of interpretive, intentional, critical human agents, still have a place in our theories and research practices? And if not, what shall we do?

Some possible answers: we would need to stop thinking of data as raw material for our own intellection. We would need to rethink our practices of interpretation and explanation, if these involve identifying 'what is really going on,' what something 'really means,' or uncovering something more significant (for example, more abstract; more general, more meaningful) beneath or above the surface messiness of talk or action. These customary understandings all assume a masterful human subject separate from the objects of her inquiry, which await her interventions in order to attain meaning. Analysis would become 'diffractive' – no longer a matter of magisterial interrogation by a human agent of her data, but an entanglement. We would need to develop forms of immanent critique – a matter of sensing and tweaking events as they unfold. We would need to think of thought as not intrinsically 'ours,' but as an impersonal force that exceeds us and catches us up. We would need to think of emotions, in a similar way, not as welling up from inside us, but as *affect* – pre-individual intensities that connect and disconnect bodies (see further, MacLure, 2015).

It is clear therefore that we are not talking about merely tinkering with the customary arrangements of qualitative inquiry. We are obliged to rethink the whole ontological and epistemological edifice, and this means thinking outside of the remit of thought itself. More than 20 years ago, Deborah Britzman (1995) spoke of the need for educational research to become *unintelligible* to itself, in order to free itself of its bad faith and its bad habits. This remains to be done. I want to explore further the question of how new materialist thought challenges qualitative inquiry, by considering two particular areas: firstly, the status of data in qualitative research; and secondly, the status of language.

Data

Taking data first: the status of qualitative data within the new materialisms has already received critical attention, including a recent special issue of *Cultural Studies⇔Critical Methodologies* (2013; eds. Koro-Ljungberg & MacLure) and a new chapter on data in Denzin and Lincoln's fifth edition of the *SAGE Handbook of Qualitative Research* (see Koro-Ljungberg, MacLure, & Ulmer, 2017). In conventional qualitative method, data are typically assumed to be mute until awakened to meaning by the interpretive prowess of the researcher and her specialist analytic tools. Their role is basically to nod in agreement with researchers' interpretations and thereafter to disappear – lifted up or subsumed under concepts or categories. But as St. Pierre (1997) reminded us years ago, data always has the potential to transgress the boundaries of coding and representation, and disrupt the whole research enterprise. Indeed, that is what qualitative method is *for*: to control those unruly potentials. New materialist research instead dwells with data's bad behavior – the ways in which it thwarts method's desire to tame it or make it disappear; its capacity to force thought; its queer agency.

This involves a loss of ontological security for the analyst, who can no longer exercise dominion over the data from the place of safety reserved for the intact, centered, humanist subject. Instead, researchers, participants, data, theory, things and values are mutually constituted in each 'agential cut' into, and out of the indeterminacy of matter, to use Barad's (2007, p. 178) terminology.

The task, then, is to be attentive to data's invitation; and alert to its capacity to force thought. The unruly potentials in data can be sensed, for instance, on occasions when something seems to reach out from the inert corpus of the data to grasp us – this could be a comment in an interview, a fragment from a field note, an anecdote, an object, a strange facial expression, or a feeling of déjà vu.

Moments like these confound the industrious search for meaning, and instead exert a kind of fascination. I have called this intensity that emanates from data a 'glow' (MacLure, 2013a).

It can be a long-lasting glow: Rachel Holmes (2016) describes how she has endlessly returned to a piece of video data that has continually clawed at her, and called her back to new thought. It is a short clip of a playground game of 'kiss chase,' in which two boys seize a young girl, who struggles to free herself. Such data, as Rachel points out, are easily available, in conventional critical terms, for multiple 'interpretations,' within discursive frames such as gender, play, creativity or desire. But the data always exceed these frames, without dismissing them or rendering them irrelevant. Holmes (2016) writes: "This film continues to de-compose my past, present and future encounters with this playground event. It attempts to multiply worlds, imbricating language, the human and the material on the surface, interfering with my educational gaze."

This is characteristic of data in the material turn – its capacity to reach and lead beyond itself, to a multiplicity of things and ideas not-yet-named; but without losing the *singularity* of the data itself. Holmes calls this relation to data "curiosity." I have called it, elsewhere, *wonder* (MacLure, 2013a), which was a synonym for curiosity for many centuries. We might think of wonder as an alternate concept in place of analysis in new materialist research. We would need to be wary however of its long, disreputable association with colonialism and orientalism.

At any rate, we are now seeing many creative interventions around data in qualitative research. We see data liberated from the page and the screen, taking strange forms and entering into unexpected assemblages with humans, who no longer merely read it or analyze it, but wear it, eat it, sculpt it, stitch it, walk it, breathe it, dance it. It is here indeed that the Dionysian spirit is perhaps most evident in post-qualitative research – in the displacements and metamorphoses of data.

It will be important, though, to keep asking the question, in each and every specific case, of whether we are caught up in a dance of difference, or just acting the drunkard and whistling the Dionysian tune. As long as we remain intelligible to ourselves as the orchestrators of data's adventures, it will be difficult to escape the fetters of representation, humanism, and anthropocentrism.

Language

We also need to talk about language. It is axiomatic in new materialist work that language has been given too much privilege in the dominant paradigms of 20th-century thought. It has rendered material realities subordinate to the discursive systems that supposedly mediate them, and stolen the agency of things. In new materialist ontologies therefore, language is typically displaced and demoted. Rather than sitting at the top of the tree of reason, dispensing categories and distinctions, it is forced to take its place as one element of assemblages that are always both material *and* discursive (e.g., Barad, 2007).

The demotion of language and discourse has been hugely productive, I would argue, in bringing about modes of critique that dissolve and remake the boundaries between matter and culture, science and the social. Nevertheless, I wonder if the displacement of language has actually gone far enough. In many accounts of material-discursive entanglement, the status and the mode of being of language is not *itself* interrogated (MacLure, 2013b). We are often left unclear about just how language tangles with matter; how words, bodies, signs, minds, and discourses intra-act and entangle. And the materiality of language itself is often not addressed – the fact that speech is formed from noises, breath, grimaces, and silences, and shot through with prelinguistic pulses of affect, while still being animated by something immaterial that somehow transforms it into a passage for meaning and ideas.

Deleuze, in his own work, and in his collaborations with Guattari, forms one notable exception to this lack of attention to language. In *Logic of Sense*, Deleuze identifies a "mad element" in language: something that exceeds propositional meaning – a Dionysian spirit in language. He called it *sense*. Sense works as a "mobius strip" – a double-sided surface between language and the world: it "happens to bodies and … insists in propositions" (2004, pp. 23, 142) allowing them to resonate and relate, and at the same time preventing language both from sinking back into the abject depths of the body or floating off as impotent "lofty ideas" (p. 150).

Deleuze and Guattari (1988) looked to figures that are able to *unhinge* conventional language from the bonds of representation – the child, the madman, the poet. These figures are able to make language *stutter* – to throw a spanner into its works by detaching words from their syntactic bonds and their freight of con-ventional meaning in order to play with them, and release the non-representing energies of sense. But as Deleuze and Guattari note, it's all too possible to get it wrong. We may think that we are assembling the forces and intensities needed "to make thought travel, make it mobile, make it a force of the Cosmos" – but end up "reproducing nothing but a scribble effacing all lines, a scramble effacing all sounds" (1988, p. 344). One may, in other words, just be acting the Dionysian drunkard again.

This is a cautionary message for those of us who are trying to respond to the Deleuzian call to make language stutter – to release its immanent powers of variation through experiments with form and meaning. We may fail to distinguish generative experimentation from the kind of linguistic play that was typical of some of our less successful experiments with 'postmodern' textual practices in qualitative research. I would definitely include here my own past efforts. Not stuttering but scribbling. Many of these postmodern textual experiments failed, I would argue, to effect any real change in the relations of power and authority that compose and are reflected in research texts (c.f. MacLure, 2011), and ultimately they left the authorial self intact. At best (or worst) they ended up reinforcing the identity of the postmodern author as jester or melancholic guide to the groundless abyss beneath language and discourse. But Deleuzian groundlessness is not the "indifferent black nothingness" envisaged by representation when it senses the abyss. Rather than comprising a total lack of differences, "it swarms with them" (Deleuze, 1994: pp. 276, 277). What would be needed therefore are (anti-)linguistic gambits that are genuinely capable of "unhinging" language and apprehending the fracture that runs through the self. "What, after all, are Ideas," Deleuze asks, rhetorically, "... if not these ants which enter and leave through the fracture in the I?" (p. 277).

It is rare however, outside of the Deleuze-Guattarian enclave, to find new materialist theory that strenuously engages with the problematics of language. It is certainly the case that many of the leading scholars wrestle with language in the attempt to express new forms of relationality among human and nonhuman entities. Take, for instance, this well-known quotation from Karen Barad, which I briefly alluded to at the outset. But read it this time with *the language* specifically in mind.

> I have been particularly interested in how matter comes to matter. How matter makes itself felt ... feeling, desiring and experiencing are not singular characteristics or capacities of human consciousness. Matter feels, converses, suffers, desires, yearns and remembers. (Barad, 2012, p. 59)

This is an exhilarating statement. But it is important not to be too seduced by its poetics. At the least, we need to be mindful that the materialist turn *over*-turns customary relations between words and things, propositions and bodies, with disconcerting implications for our understanding of how meaning consorts with the world. It is difficult, I suggest, to read language like this *outside* the conventions of a romanticised humanism that bestows upon matter the capacities that we so pride ourselves on having. Notions such as conversing, suffering, and yearning would need to take on an altered status, or sense, in new materialist ontologies, to disable the implication of bequest – perhaps to a point where such words came to hover or flicker on the edge of intelligibility.

I think the kind of language that Barad uses here reflects a certain stylistic tendency that is emerging within some versions of new materialist writing. Consider Jane Bennett's (2010, p. 112) description of matter as "vibrant, vital, energetic, lively, quivering, vibratory, evanescent and effluescent." For me, the language of these passages works, again, against the attempt to displace the centred, humanist self so that matter may speak. There is an expansive generosity in the language of quivering, yearning and suffering that conjures the anthropocentric, empathetic human subject behind its own back.

Clare Colebrook detects an *ultra*-humanism in theories such as these, which redistribute to all of nature, or life in general, the capacities for unmediated touch and connection that were once the prerogative of human subjects. She argues that this amounts to a new image of thought, which she calls "hypo-hyper-hapto-neuro-mysticism." She argues that this is, in fact,

> *not* a mode of thinking precisely because it operates less by way of statements, assumptions and values, and instead comes to a halt before a complex of mesmerizing images and barely thought-out figures. This orientation of pseudo-"thinking" is one in which a certain notion of the intellect as detached calculation is resented or accused in the name of a supposedly more primordial and proximate living ownness. (2013: pp. 1–2; original emphasis)

This new haptic image of thought therefore sets itself *against* thinking, at least according to Colebrook's definition of thought as "a comportment to the world that is without home, solace, identity or body" (2013, p. 1). Although Colebrook does not specifically pursue the issue of language, she envisages, in a footnote that is currently haunting me, "a form of *affectless* philosophical critique, at least in theory," and continues: "In addition to the world's 'murmurings' and 'patternings' [referring to a passage by Barad] I suggest that there is another world that is stony, white and silent" (2013: 10). This would indeed be a world in which methodology has become unintelligible to itself. At the least, it reminds me that, as Lyotard (1984: 81) urged many years ago, we may need to deny ourselves "the solace of good forms."

Conclusion

I started out by wondering whether new materialist methodology is genuinely engaging the Dionysian powers of difference, or just acting the drunkard. This is a complicated question, because Deleuze, in his own writing and in his collaborations with Guattari, has always been clear about the dangers involved in trying to harness the differential forces of the Cosmos. Taking his lesson from Artaud, he was aware of the risks of courting the mad element in language that might drag us back from the surface where sense plays, to the excremental depths of the schizophrenic body and its disarticulated language of cries and fragmented phonemes. Deleuze and Guattari (1998, p. 350) write of the risk of going too far in "opening the assemblage onto a cosmic force," warning that we may inadvertently collapse into "black holes and closures … cosmic force gone bad." They commend "an art of dosages" or "injections of caution" (p. 160).

It would be interesting to explore further how those dosages might be mixed, tested and administered. But for the moment, I think the danger is more one of failing to go far enough. It is difficult to think outside of the Enlightenment structures of the Cartesian self, and the stories it tells itself about progress, reason and the advancement of knowledge. So although we have come a long way in formulating cartographies for new materialist research, we are necessarily some way from the anticipated ontological transformations to our field. And this is not just because of institutional inertia or conservative methodology curricula in the neoliberal university. It is also because old epistemological habits tend to reinsert themselves behind our own backs. We may want to make language stutter and bring representation to its knees; we may believe that we are intra-acting, forming rhizomes, diffracting, mapping flat ontologies, and so on. And important studies are in fact emerging which do this – often by graduate students and early career scholars, precisely because they are intricately entangled with the materiality and the virtuality of the worlds they are researching. But I think we continue to underestimate the sheer difficulty of shedding the anthropocentrism that is built into our world-views and our language habits. We find it hard to *practice* critique and analysis on terms other than mastery. I know I do.

Overall then, I suspect that much new materialist research is still haunted by representation. But this time it's representation gone *orgiastic*. Or at least I would pose this possibility as a question – foremost of all for myself. I wonder if I am acting the Dionysian drunkard – mobilising all the uncanny machinery of new materialism, but still harnessing it to older narratives of empowerment, social justice, progressivism, or ideology critique. To make an example of myself: I have found the new materialisms, and Deleuze in particular, enormously productive in helping me to think differently about young children and pedagogy. I have been able to see how bodies, matter, and affect get tangled up with institutional discourses, history, policy, and memory; and I have experienced obscure glimpses of how things could be otherwise. But I fear that the ontological excitement of these new concepts is contained – bookended – by deeply ingrained, oppositional stances toward developmental psychology and certain notions of pedagogy.

But, if our new materialist work is framed and legitimated by familiar narratives of empowerment, emancipation, or social justice, how much of a problem is this? There may be very good reasons for continuing to use these investments as engines and purposes for our research. But we need to acknowledge that this is likely also to reinstall humanist notions of the self, and to invoke the superiority of the critic who undertakes to undo error and justice on behalf of subjects, and objects, that do not know what is good for them. Recalling that Dionysus is the god of wine, we need to ask: is this new wine in old bottles? Or perhaps it's old wine in new bottles? It's hard to tell. It is not that questions of emancipation and social justice are irrelevant: how frivolous would it be to say that? But perhaps it is a matter of learning to ask better questions: learning how to tap into the problematic structure of events, so that we can learn to be less guided by what we already think we know is important. Once we get better at doing that, we will be in a better position to experiment with dosages ....

Note

1   A range of new materialist work can be found in edited collection including Dolphijn and Van der Tuin (2012), Alaimo and Hekman (2008), Gregg and Seigworth (2010), Barrett and Bolt (2012), and Coole and Frost (2010).

References

Alaimo, S., and Hekman, S. J. (Eds.). (2008). *Material feminisms*. Bloomington: IN University Press.

Barad, K. (2007). *Meeting the universe halfway: Quantum physics and the entanglement of matter and meaning*. Durham, NC: Duke University Press.

Barad, K. (2012). Interview, in R. Dolphijn, R. and I. Van der Tuin (Eds.), *New materialism: Interviews and xartographies*. Ann Arbor, MI: Open Humanities Press.

Barrett, E., and Bolt, B. (2012). *Carnal knowledge: New materialism through the arts*. London: I. B. Taurus and Co.

Bennet, J. (2010). *Vibrant matter: A political ecology of things*. Durham, NC: Duke University Press.

Britzman, D. P. (1995). "The question of belief": Writing poststructural ethnography. *International Journal of Qualitative Studies in Education*, 8(3), 229–238.

Colebrook, C. (2013). Hypo-hyper-hapto-neuro-mysticism. *Parrhesia*, 18, 1–10.

Coole, D., and Frost, S. (2010). Introducing the new materialisms. In D. Coole and S. Frost (Eds.), *New materialisms: Ontology, agency, and politics* (pp. 1–43). Durham, NC: Duke University Press.

Deleuze, G. (1994). *Difference and repetition*. London: Continuum.

Deleuze, G. (2004) *The logic of sense* (C. Boundas, Ed. and M. Lester, Trans.). London: Continuum.

Deleuze, G., and Guattari, F. (1988). *A thousand plateaus* (B. Massumi, Trans.). Minneapolis, MN: University of Minnesota Press.

Dolphijn, R., and Van der Tuin, I. (2012). *New materialism: Interviews and cartographies*. Ann Arbor, MI: Open Humanities Press.

Gregg, M., and Seigworth, G. J. (Eds.). (2010). *The affect theory reader*. Durham, NC: Duke University Press.

Holmes, R. (2016). *Curious work: Using art and film to understand children differently*. Professorial Lecture, Manchester Metropolitan University.

Jones, A., and Hoskins, T. K. (2016). A mark on paper: the matter of indigenous settler history. In C. Taylor and C. Hughes (Eds.), *Posthuman research practices in education* (pp. 75–92). New York: Palgrave Macmillan.

Koro-Ljungberg, M., and MacLure, M. (2013). Provocations, re-un-visions, death, and other possibilities of "data." *Cultural Studies ⇔ Critical Methodologies*, 13(4), 219–222.

Koro-Ljungberg, M., MacLure, M., & Ulmer, J. (2017). Data and its problematics. In N. K. Denzin and Y. S. Lincoln (Eds.), *SAGE Handbook of Qualitative Research*, 5/e. Thousand Oaks, CA: Sage.

Lyotard, J-F. (1984). Answering the question: What is postmodernism? In *The postmodern condition: A report on knowledge* (Trans. Geoff Bennington and Brian Massumi). Minneapolis: University of Minnesota Press.

MacLure, M. (2011). Qualitative inquiry: Where are the ruins? *Qualitative Inquiry* 17(10), 997–1005.

Maclure, M. (2013a). The wonder of data. *Cultural Studies⇔Critical Methodologies*, *13*(4), 228–232.

MacLure, M. (2013b). Researching without representation? Language and materiality in post-qualitative methodology. *International Journal of Qualitative Studies in Education*, *26*(6), 658–667.

MacLure, M. (2015). The 'new materialisms': A thorn in the flesh of critical qualitative inquiry? In G. S. Cannella, M. Salazare Perez, and P. A. Pasque (Eds), *Critical qualitative inquiry: Foundations and futures*. Walnut Creek, CA: Left Coast Press.

St. Pierre, E. A. (1997). Methodology in the fold and the irruption of transgressive data. *International Journal of Qualitative Studies in Education*, *10*(20), 175–189.

Stivale, C. (2008) *Gilles Deleuze's ABCs: The folds of friendship*. Baltimore, MD: Johns Hopkins.

4

THE IMPORTANCE OF SMALL FORM

'Minor' data and 'BIG' neoliberalism

*Mirka Koro-Ljungberg, Anna Montana Cirell,
Byoung-gyu Gong, and Marek Tesar*

Abstract

Byoung-gyu: From my perspective, the relationship between data and neoliberalism has been under scrutiny, especially by some critical thinkers for some time now. The proliferation of research on neoliberalism and the rise of BIG data have incurred different terminology usages, which at least partially speak to the problematic role of data in neoliberalism. For example, scholars talk about informational neoliberalism (Neubauer, 2011), datafication (Chandler, 2015), dataphilia (Lambert et al., 2015), the society of metadata (Pasquinelli, 2015), the information society, and the data economy, among other things. Do we need various forms of expression, the power of lyric and poems, to move towards 'data' freedom? Could data function as a free entity that can be recognized as a form of relationality and as a force to resist governmentality?

Mirka: I wonder how qualitative researchers could work against dataphilia. How might small form, mundane, and minor data be important and transformative?

Anna: Wow. I just want to read the title over and over. The less and little is so much more. But shall you all go further and leave me behind, then please prepare for a bit of the potentialities and possibilities of data that might work to push beyond neoliberal data discourse. Smig!

Marek: I am intrigued by notions of resistance to BIG data. It does not have to be BIG resistance. Just a little one, with our daily encounters with all subjects and objects, is fine with me. I would like to see how data become subjects and subjects become data, to treat them with similar ethics and respect that they want to give to the individual subject under the neoliberal ideology.

A ('data'[1]) preface

Under the onion skin, neoliberal blanket and behind the Box: Foreshadowing some shadows of Academia

★★ Here onion skins, neoliberal blankets, and cardboard boxes are given different ontological status and as such elevated from the most mundane of objects to that of producing small form and minor data as ethereal cover and guard of nearly overcome doctoral student. Not only do they impart her academic security and safety from intellectual harm, but they mediate openings for critical perspective-taking on our current social shadows of academia (as data?)★★

if I simply shut my eyes for a really long time, can't I make the world go away? this worked for me last night in a dumpster. I hopped in and was excited to find it pretty empty with my feet planted firmly on solid metal. I stood up tall and steady admiring the cardboard boxes piled up haphazardly high making a brown chunky forest of the place. escaping a meaningless mash-up of endless hours of pouring overly dissertation revisions, I declared myself alive. but in this quiet volcano of solitude soon came the demons. separating out from the sound of my own beating heart and happily humming nerves came approaching voices amplifying to crescendo. I then saw the glowing shine of flashlights reflecting onto the opposite inside wall of the dumpster. times like these either call for a fearless and searching moral inventory of your every yuppified failing or the go-to reactionary impulse of every strung-out celebutante out there: run, fight, kill, plead innocence. yet, an impromptu plea was abandoned at the rememberance of my cardboard forest and the night cloaking us into one. so when the lookers came with their glowing flashlights to find me and re-chain me to my computer, I simply closed my eyes and hid. after a while, they threw out what they had to (onto me), finished their cigarette, and left. the sound of their dying voices relieved all tightness in my shoulders and my eyes opened to the peace and quiet of onion skins covering my own. but there is no hiding in academia. no one learns much behind a fort of cardboard. instead, you must enter this panoptic regime of sci-fi scholarship with eyes wide open and give the performance of a lifetime. your onion skins must be thick and ready to peel away at the first vulnerability. how else to grow new ones? reason tells you that things will never be easy or fair with pervasive morelocks dying to throw trash on you. for perspective, you transform weaknesses into strengths and define yourself by your "weaknengths" – which will soon be all you have left to give. and yet with onion skins all peeled away, will you even be human, when all is over … amid the semi-planetary existence of the cardboard-less ivory tower, I can only wield my every weaknength to climb up the escape ladder and story a less-viewed view of our neoliberal world. though escapism will soon fail me and I will then fall back into thieving my meaning from the stolen dreams of scholarly others, won't it be worth it to waste time in the telling of my eventual descent? yet, does it even matter how we fall if, in the end, we all break?

★★ I was sitting on the patio in a restaurant by the water. the table and chair I was sitting on were almost identical to the chairs and tables next to me, and to those that they have in other restaurants. my senses were transmitting the 'hard problem' of the neoliberal reality while the radio blasted some kitsch melody pop-rock music that they play in most eateries like this. I saw familiar advertisements of products on the walls, and the bathroom looked the same with its traditional male demeanour. above all, I was surrounded by young people who were similarly dressed, who drank familiar-looking drinks, and who behaved as casually as their contemporaries elsewhere. all of this can function as minor data. but somehow in this boredom of sameness and everydayness, of these encounters with minor data, I was in the centre of my 'hard problem', of merging empiric humanly shaped objects of boredom, and the discursive strive for the adventure of shapes, colours and stories. suddenly the need for minor methodologies and philosophies emerged, to puncture the ability to reveal and name all the events and objects in our limited scope of vision under this neoliberal blanket and the pursuit of BIG data.★★

Moving along neoliberal discourses and practices

Notions of data and methodological practices associated with data have been changing, and continue to change, as a result of the neoliberal forces, discourses, and market-driven decision making controlling today's higher education and scholarly practices. For example, Lambert et al. (2015) explained how the efficiency-driven neoliberal desire subsumes the education field by imposing quantification, measurement, and competition [of data]. According to these authors, neoliberal pursuance of efficiency incurred obsessive reliance on data, which they call 'dataphilia' or 'data-fetish', and resulted in the marginalization of human in that frame. The story of research became the narrative of the endless search for BIG data. These changes, amongst others, have been particularly nota-ble in the discourses and practices associated with qualitative and post-qualitative research (Denzin, Lincoln, & Giardina, 2006; Denzin & Giardina, 2009; Lather & St. Pierre, 2013; MacLure, 2013). Neoliberal-methodology-machinery has the unique and highly specialized task to produce a particular kind of knowledge, one that preferably reaches and covers all consumers constituting this knowledge enterprise. Data/knowledge enables coverage, coverage produces power, power produces data credibility, credibility leads to data effectiveness, effectiveness to research funding, funding to data/knowledge and so on. However, within this neoliberal-methodology-machinery running on fiscal austerity, only certain type of 'data' qualifies as meaningful, valuable, and desirable knowledge.

The liberal, market-driven focus on data and fast, efficient, transparent data pro-duction has actually morphed away from a jurisdictional emphasis and potential fairness toward a ruthless race toward data profit, toward the financial and productive value of data. As a result of this change, the contemporary, effective, and profitable generation of data dominates the market of higher education. Data have become the sources, target, and often the (only) possibility for competition and targeted marketing. Market forces such as data supply and demand, negotiable prizes for data, and data- and database-driven reports direct and stipulate scholars' and society's data production. Data are constructed as research capital and compose an important aspect of entrepreneurial scholarly self (see also Cannella & Lincoln, 2015; Foucault, 2008; Read, 2009). Rather than simply focusing on data exchange, neoliberalism creates an all-invasive governmentality associated with big-data that governs all small form, mundane, and minor data and knowledge production in the margins. This governing happens without governing through taken-for-granted and often internally established practices that protect and secure the role and functioning of big-data generators and big-data users, thus making big-data models, collaborative funding competition, and data–profits essential parts of the neoliberal data-systems.

Within neoliberal discourses, data often serve the interests of production. They are the core component of funded research, and they produce knowledge that are measurable and from which value can be calculated and reduced into productivity indexes. Data are likely to serve monetary benefits of researchers, funding organizations, and institutions of higher education. Furthermore, data in neoliberalism operate through their exchange value: data buy and create services and generate scholarly capital and privileges. Data sometimes produce themselves with and without oversight and sometimes in secrecy to stay uncontaminated, protected, guarded, individually or institutionally owned. Carefully guarded and protected data make possible both visible and invisible competition in all aspects of being and scholarly life. Many forms of data facilitate not only the values of competition but also completion especially when bigger and larger data banks are seen and used as moneymaking entities granting access to those who subscribe to them and are willing and capable to pay the fees required. Data transform themselves into self-regulated, self-directed, entrepreneurship and research capital. Data are being managed by data managers and project leaders. They are protected and secured by Institutional Review Board (IRB) regulations whereas software programs facilitate effective data management and data mining. Data depositories enable seeming democratic yet highly controlled access to knowledge and information.

Though all forms of data and knowledge are likely to service the neoliberal agenda privileging and protecting highly competitive scholarly competition, this is especially true with academic positions and funded research. Further, 'data economicus' is a vital partner in this facilitation of research competition, as new management strategies engage scholars to transform data into self-regulated, self-directed, data entrepreneurship that value big-data as the only profitable scholarly capital of scientific capitalism. According to Stronach (2009), "we have the ignoble dream of a 19th century 'scientific socialism' replaced by the parallel absurdity of a 21st century 'scientific capitalism'" (p. 261).

Researchers ponder these neoliberal methodologies and agenda, and dream of a 'scientific socialism'. In order to do so they activate philosophies that create a productive space to contest the BIG data. BIG data do approach researchers, as a need for their supply that cannot feed the demand. BIG data fill the empiric and discursive openings. How do we find cracks in the foundations of a technocratic society, how do we discover the deepest corners of the ruins of modernity, and how do we satisfy the need for methodologies and philosophies that allow us to face; if not resist, BIG data? How do we resist the free-market of BIG data? In his recent commentary on 'big social science' Torrance (2015; see also Torrance, this volume) traced the dynamic changes that have and are taking place in higher education production market: seemingly voluntaristic and increasingly effective system of knowledge producing global aims to produce "Big" social science through the production of big ideas, big grants, big schools, big knowledge enterprises, and of course through BIG data. It is assumed and also taken for granted that 'BIG' social issues of our time call for 'BIG' data, BIG plans, and larger and larger knowledge machineries. As Torrance (2015) noted, no singular scholar, no one research team, no one discipline can respond to these big problems.

In this sense, knowledge and scholarly activities need to be centralized. In this centralized system the power to produce acceptable and valid knowledge belongs only to those most competitive, productive, effective, and most worthy of public or private investment. As Torrance explains, "The overall operational milieu of social research is now infused with ideas of national economic competitiveness and the need for large-scale collaborations to secure resources for continuing intellectual work" (p. 278). However, it is puzzling that during the times of extreme global complexity, increasing diversity, and decreasing equity scholarly attention meanwhile is more and more drawn to big ideas, overly generalizing conclusions, regression to the means, sameness thinking, and knowledges of the masses. Far too frequently "risk-free sameness" (Davies & Bansel, 2010, p. 12) of data is celebrated and rewarded. These reproduced, fast, rapid, generalizable data reinforce the already known, and, as such, is unlikely to innovate, create newness, or generate a difference. Instead, productivity may be engendered through a focus on singularities, smallness and the minor, diversifying forces, and details of difference. And this alternative focus may better assist scholars, policymakers, and information users to tackle the global complexities and inequalities differently and from innovative, new angles. After all, can we afford our data and knowledge to be mass-produced or do scholars have some options?

Data/options/potentialities

It is time to problematize simplified understandings and controllable conceptualizations of 'data' as known, familiar, and inert objects often produced and governed within neoliberal discourses and practices and always already positioned as controllable and evidence-based. Too little attention has been paid to the alternative status of data *per se*: to the question of what data *do and how do they do what they do*; what kind of affect and difference can they produce and for whom? Or what might be some potentialities and possibilities of data that might work both for and against neo-liberalism or possible outside neoliberal discourses. In addition, data beyond neoliberalism call for ontological and epistemological scrutiny and ethical wonderings beyond the duty. As an ontological practice data pose questions of knowledge, subjectivity, relationality, politics, and power. Data are not one thing or somehow simplified production practice but they are connected to different political structures, discursive variations, and multitude of scholarly and linguistic assumptions and connections. Data function and multiply differently in different socio-political contexts.

If scholars were capable of departing from neoliberal practices or operating in the liminal spaces between neoliberalism and democratic responsibility they might be interested in different data questions. They might not ask what data are or how do they profit, but how they function beyond production and financial profit, how they resist, deconstruct, counter, transgress, transform, multiply, what they enable and disable, and how they meet the other, the unknown, the strange and yet becoming. Maybe data's different extensions function as discursive apparatuses that can regulate diverse effects of power (Foucault, 1980). Data may not be separated from truth(s), but can they be deliberated and released from the grip of normative science? Alternatively, data can be seen as a productive illusion or at least partially imaginative practice that can create movement in researchers, participants, data's surroundings and diverse political contexts. Data are, in other words, potentially illusive because they may produce themselves sometimes in unpredictable and provocative ways. Provocative data also hail for action, change, transformation, and for becoming something unanticipated and other since data are influenced and sometimes completely constituted through discursive practices and within networks of power.

We propose that by focusing our attention to the mundane, and minor, to small details, smaller nuances and the smallest differences qualitative researchers might be able to rethink their taken-for-granted practices, reconstruct normative discourses and attend to the Other (in its various and still unforeseeable forms). What happens when scholars stay attentive and sensitive to minor gestures, small differences, and mundane details also of the 'BIG'? Do we still have room for tailored suits, range free eggs, and small form or minor data?

Stronach (2009) offers concepts such as 'word-crashes' (e.g., small/big=smig), 'semantic collisions' (e.g., individualistic collaboration, organic methodology, singular plurality) (see Nancy cited in James 2006, 2012), and 'narrative near-misses' (e.g., narratives that are nonrelatedly related) to describe and potentially counter neoliberal spaces and discourses in contemporary/new world. These crashes, collisions, and near-misses might offer powerful counter measures also in relation to data especially focusing attention to ordinary particulars, productive mishaps, seemingly confusing yet prolifically disturbing contradictory details. It is possible, according to

Stronach (2009), that prepositions such as 'between', 'with', and 'against' can speak to the question of difference better than overly used nouns. Similarly, contradictory or opposing narratives can indeed mark the difference and create a useful and productive sequence. These narratives "oppose each other like an invisible, unwordable force, a discursive magnetism that at-tracts and dis-tracts the other" (p. 254). How would data function as a preposition such as between, with or against?

Smig!

Immanent, minor, 'small form' … data

Data beyond neoliberalism could be seen as a minor gesture (Deleuze & Guattari, 1986; 1987; Manning, 2016) or data in small form. As a minor gesture, small form and immanent data are always in relation to major (big) data. Manning (2016), mostly drawing from the work of Deleuze, Guattari, Whitehead, and Bergson, highlights the importance of minor gestures. For Manning, minor gestures (minor and small-form data) produce variation in the normative organization (e.g., in BIG data). Minor gestures' rhythms are not governed by the norm or pre-existing structures but they are in flux and continuously changing. Minor gesture or 'small form' data are not known in advance but they are produced in–act and in situ. They are activators, carriers, and allies of language in making and in action. Manning also proposes that minor gesture invents its own value and it does not claim a space (of BIG data) but "space-of-variation" (p. 2): "Minor gestures recast the field, open it to contrast, make felt its differential. They do so by activating, in the event, a change in direction, a change in quality" (p. 23). She continues, "Minor gesture is what *activates* the work under precise conditions, what makes the attunements of an emerging ecology felt, what makes the work work" (p. 65). Similar to major and minor, small and BIG data are not opposites but they are variabilities of co-composition. BIG data do not govern without small data. Minor data is not resistance against major/ BIG data. According to Manning the importance lies in the techniques that allow singularity to "open the work to its workings to come to the fore" (p. 66). Invention of techniques resist the small data's capture by the major/BIG data. Manning also refers to the usefulness and pragmatics of the useless. Data and its value are created in the act in doing and not inscribed ahead of time.

When moving beyond neoliberalism, data are no longer fixed objects but they can be conceptualized as practices with various different purposes. Similar to Nordstrom (2015), who views data as shifting moving assemblage, a moving line (a form of data-ing), we see data as a political and critical move, process, and practice – a practice with democratic attitude and differentiation within discourses of solidarity. Critical data practice relates to doing, knowing, inquiring, producing otherness, interacting, emancipating in ways that generate knowing differently and thus can address the alternative, foreign, and respond to the strange. Data practices do not repeat the same but they produce indefinite difference.

For example, in our recent work with undocumented students, data became a shifting and moving experiment with a variety of emerging sounds (Koro-Ljungberg, Hendricks, McTier, and Bojórquez, 2016). Sounds were recorded, found, compiled, and passed around and between authors, including one undocumented student, who then produced their own sounds in relation to those they had heard in the students' interviews and earlier sound encounters. Each iteration ended with a collective conversation that also began the next iteration. Some moments from these conversations gave a pause, created questions, and disrupted the flow of inquiry and exploration. Sometimes the authors produced sounds that they felt related very much to the experiences of the undocumented students (e.g., fabricated conversations between friends at a bar, dads at the park, or political rallies) whereas other times sounds were chosen that had more or less of a symbolic connection with students' experiences. There were also sounds that began to connect with undocumented students' stories and experiences in unexpected ways or that we expected to work in one way, but took another.

p. 23

It might also be productive to consider how data meet the other; other minor and mundane, and also the major. To 'truly' meet the other, data need to stay open and sensitive to diversity, difference, and becoming. When meeting the other, data extend their previous practices and current presences. Data practices such these are in flux and responsive. Drawing from Derrida (1993; 1995), we propose that when meeting the other data take responsibility, they react with immediacy and without knowing and hesitation even when the path is not given. This urgency of data obstructs the fixed horizon of anticipated knowledges and fixed forms. Data's responsibility cannot wait and this responsibility cannot be calculated. What happens to data, where, and when cannot be predicted but these data events must be lived. Living data, in turn, supposes rhythm, patterns, irregularities, and possible forgiveness of the offence of the other – unconditional forgiveness. Data practices indefinitely differentiate illustrating simultaneous spectrality (return of a ghost that is not dead or live) and survival (simultaneous continuation and suspension of life).

The simultaneous absence (of a small form data) and emerging presence of (immanent) data can be recognized in the work of Lucio Fontana. Fontana produced his first punctured canvases in 1949 by opening surfaces (of paintings) to the void beyond. His futuristic art indicated a move toward anticipation and waiting for the imagined future (and the other) presenting nothingness and illustrating the death of matter. Perforations or holes that Fontana called *Attese* (expectations) were cuts both in the expressive and narrative sense. These cuts signaled the absence of something in the major; mainly the absence of rhythm and temporality. Minor data relates to major. For Fontana cuts were infinite and they functioned as diverse and alternative dimensions of space that highlighted waiting, nullifying, and also building. Holes functioned as timeless void, or wormholes in artistic hyperspaces. Some of Fontana's holes were ornamentally and some regularly arranged, some holes were created from the front, and others from the back of the canvas (see Fontana, 2006b):

> The Cut is a decisive breach, that furrows and penetrates the symbolic purity of the monochrome, a kind of purifying gesture, and at the same time unambiguous symbol less of a romantic, instinctive or reckless gesture than of a conceptual, configured mental space … My cuts are above all a philosophical statement, an act of faith in the infinite, an affirmation of spirituality. (Fontana, 2006a, p. 23)

In his art, Fontana moved from philosophical space of cuts to material spaces. Space was no longer an abstraction but a human and material dimension that had potential to generate pain and terror among other things. Fontana attempted to give the form (cut) the sensation of pain and terror, and he aimed to place the observer at the center of the picture enabling the creation of herself through imagination. Fontana also introduced the trans–objectiveness of the painting; physicality of the painted surface and the hole that passes through it. The material behind the canvas was brought into the painting through the cut. Manning (2016) referred to operative cut of the minor gesture. This operative cut opens experience to its future and potential: "The affirmative cut of the minor gesture catalyzes a reordering. Cuts are not good or bad. It is what they *do* that makes a difference" (p.201).

Furthermore, we wonder what could be produced through the focus on uniquely quotidian occurrences or the small form that exist outside the regime of neoliberal scholarship. The new materialist or posthumanist data movement can offer some alternative possibilities assigning the smaller material details great weight in the construction of our social reality. Posthumanists ascribe purposeful action to nonhuman agents – no matter how minor or small in the detail or object (Barad, 2007; Latour, 1999; Pickering, 1995). Methodological implications of a posthumanist lens de–center and diffuse agency and thus data. Therein, no form of data is given more precedence or weight, as even the less 'prized' data could impart great impulse, transformational force to the research questions and problem at hand. Small, smaller, and the smallest data form and minor data gain momentum, increase speed, and transform from yeast, stones, laundry, to a clock's minute hand. From this lens, scholars acknowledge the rhizomatic and nonhierarchical relationality between data, which configure our complex network of human and nonhuman agents (Mazzei & Jackson, 2005).

Our necessary examination will then take up these posthumanist musings to unravel critical data fragments or narratives wherever they may lead like balls of yarn rolling quickly past us. Data produced through minor gestures, unexpectedly and even accidentally is no news. For example, Latour (1999) troubled common perceptions of Pasteur's lactic acid ferment by re-invigorating Pasteur's famous 1957 paper to the new tale of "Cinderella-the-yeast" (p. 115). Latour recounts the ontological blossoming of the everyday yeast as it evolves throughout Pasteur's paper from an inconsequential by-product to "a full-blown entity in its own right" (p. 116) to its final belle-of-the-ball status. The paper's beginning lens steeped too readily in assigned roles of dominating action and passive reaction could never notice the importance of the very entity that would soon stir up a whole bubbling chemical coup of possibility. In simpler terms, this indicates that the evolution of Pasteur's thinking about his data and his resultant breakthrough was dependent upon a de-centering from constraining conventions of privileging BIG data.

Similarly, in letting go of presumptions that carve linearity and logical neatness into our data through causal reasoning, scholars may more freely attend to illogical drivers of random data, encounters, and enactments. Freed from value claims, this permits qualitative researchers to ponder social practices as quotidian and seemingly unguided as children carrying stones (Rautio, 2013). Herein, scholars were allowed to also dialogue an interstice of non-opposing possibilities: the stones, in wielding a certain draw, invited their own carrying and thus problematized the human-centered orchestration of the child's ostensibly autotelic or self-serving aims (i.e., carrying stones simply for the sake of stone-carrying). Attention and openness to these minor data and smaller forms humbled the research agenda by dispelling illusions that anthropocentric part or type of inquiry is grander or more central than the nonhuman when enacting social practices (Rautio, 2013).

In posthumanist inquiry, the main vehicle for addressing larger questions, such as how home is made, is through interrogating the everyday, the understated, and the minute data. Taking up the very icon of ordinary, Pink, Mackley, and Moroşanu (2015) reshaped how we conceive of laundry in the social world to ask what its ever-presence can bring to the entangled experiences of the home. They examined the common social practice of laundry hung out to dry amid a larger cultural lens and the changing materiality of daily life. In doing so, they questioned how drying laundry indoors could immediately impact the home's built environment, sense of place, and flow of movement through the home as well as broader political issues of energy consumption, environmental conservation, and economic relations.

Still other scholars, such as Pacini-Ketchabaw (2012), put into discourse the smaller side of data by examining how we collude *with* clocks in classroom practices. Pacini-Ketchabaw underscored how a simple shifting of the clock's minute hand can shift the room into that next pre-ordained stage of time/space continuum. From tidy-time to storybook hour, the complex unspoken orchestration between the clock's face, the children's movements, and the teacher's gaze signify an implicit dance of shared rhythm and cohesive expectations (Pacini-Ketchabaw, 2012). Tensions, however, arose as educators experimented with better ways to engage *with* the clock (rather than being acted on *by* the clock) in ultimate pursuit of more effective clocking practices. In this rhizomatic relationality, a dynamic mangle of interwoven human/nonhuman contexts unveiled how individual variability (of children and teachers) intermingled nonhierarchically with embedded technology tools (clocks) and everyday practices to shape the ensuing learning and development (Barad, 2007; Latour, 2005; Pickering, 1995).

As illustrated in the previous examples, small form and minor data can enable complex, creative, and critical engagements with inquiry, participants, and our environments. Rather than providing answers to the fixed and stable 'data-concept' we wonder about possible ways in which minor or small form data may produce otherness, can differentiate the same, and diffuse the generalizable. Rather than seeing small forms and minor data might listen (see also Weaver & Snaza, 2016). Even though we acknowledge the powerful presence of neoliberalism in Academia and the role of productive resistance that data in various forms can offer we are hopeful that by challenging taken-for-granted data practices and by engaging with data in creative ways scholars might extend data into unthinkable yet critical dimensions that can speak to the policy and practice differently.

It has become clear that under the neoliberal ideology our treatment of various methodological and philosophical traditions allows a productive space within which every tiny branch of each sub-discipline and area of study cries out for its own independence and recognition, conference, society, or at least a special-interest group. And scholars passionately argue for it. Many of these philosophies and methodologies are struggling against the remains of the toxic ruins of modernity. Often, however, they carry on their struggle using means that were provided to them by the very methodologies and philosophies that they oppose under the neoliberal umbrella. Scholars thus employ all the rejected ways of thinking – and most of all the philosophies and methodologies that under the neoliberal agenda may be considered minor or even childish – and challenge all the dreadful, irrelevant commodities of the positivist and empirical philosophies and methodologies of the BIG data systems. Scholars become part of the global networks they oppose, often uniting under the very subjects, theories and claims that they simultaneously object. They appear as victims and supporters of the neoliberal systems in their institutions; at the same time, they can oppose and challenge these neoliberal structures and BIG data at the same time (Havel, 1985). Scholars thus contrast the technological inventions and methodologies that are employed to simplify if not to speed up the process and the outputs. Under the neoliberal ideology, some qualitative scholars are also compelled to tame and reject the very purpose of their inquiry. Some of the methodologies that scholars have worked through are still not accepted in many places in the world, and neoliberal thinking has become hostile to local traditions. Neoliberalism and its schemes of funding and focus on BIG data disregard the 'post' and 'new' turns in methodologies, as they need seductive BIG data, often in order to convince local and indigenous tribes that there is ONE useful, important, and correct pathway to govern the human subject. We crave for small form and minor data in our thinking and being, and in our turn to elevate the subjugated subjects, and thus we challenge the toxicity of BIG data.

Finally, rather than asking, Can you tell me about your data?, Derrida encourages us to ask questions about data – questions about data beyond neoliberalism and closure. The following data questions refuse to close, quote, punctuate, and structure language. Data are hanging, interacting, intra-acting, creating texts, readers, and themselves.

Borrowing from Derrida, Nordstrom, Deleuze, Manning, Foucault, Havel, and many others maybe

we could have *'immanent-uncertain-perhaps data'* which
would   transform   and
keep up not with the possible but with the impossible
    how do we live and meet data in ways that speak to our critical research goals and
collaborations around justice   difference ethics and equity could   differently
                    without defaulting into the sameness
the multiplicities within data create an academic
    community not of consensus but of dissensus puncturing perspectives how to
    provide and offer 'life support' to data and
rescue their pulsating muscle mass and beating heart   of the major

what if data's productivity is being calculated based on saved souls do data
    need more realism   sweat
tears   muscle pain   heart ache   smells of mulch and rotting fish
how can we break free from
    neo-positivist colonizing and/or oversimplified data practices as
well as uncritical forms of data production   power/knowledge
    how could qualitative researchers avoid creating power for themselves as the
    more "advanced/progressive" voice
for justice equity and decolonization
    whether using
        traditional, reconceptualized, or whatever is labeled "new" data
how   do
data address contemporary power contexts/material circumstances/lives and the
immediate need for transformations   and direct action
        how are forms of human privilege reinscribed within the
        small form and minor data
practices/acknowledgements/wants/entanglements historically
    is it   possible to decenter
data in research without creating an environment of post responsibility
    for justice socially   environmentally   and to the more-than-human Other
    and when
asks
who   from whom

what	from what
and	
how	from how

Note

1   The very notion, language, and practices associated with 'data' especially in (post) qualitative research have been questioned in various ways, and this chapter will extend the lines of these discourses (see, e.g., Lather & St. Pierre, 2013; Koro-Ljungberg & MacLure, 2013; Mazzei & McCoy, 2010).

References

Barad, K. (2007). *Meeting the universe halfway: Quantum physics and the entanglement of matter and meaning.* Durham, NC: Duke University Press.

Cannella, G. S., and Lincoln, Y. S. (2015). Critical qualitative research in global neoliberalism: Foucault, inquiry, and transformative possibilities. In N. K. Denzin and M.D. Giardina (Eds.), *Qualitative inquiry and the politics of research* (pp. 51–74). Walnut Creek, CA: Left Coast Press.

Chandler, D. (2015). *A world without causation: Big Data and the coming of age of posthumanism. Millennium–Journal of International Studies, 43*(3), 833–851.

Davies, B, and Bansel, P. (2010). Governmentality and academic work: Shaping the hearts and minds of academic workers. *Journal of Curriculum Theorizing 26*(3), 5–20.

Deleuze, G., and Guattari, F. (1986). *Kafka: Toward a minor literature.* Minneapolis, MN: University of Minnesota Press.

Deleuze, G., and Guattari, F. (1987). *A thousand plateaus: Capitalism and schizophrenia.* (B. Massumi, Trans., Original work published 1980 ed.). Minneapolis, MN: University of Minnesota Press.

Denzin, N. K., and Giardina, M. D. (2009). *Qualitative inquiry and social justice: Toward a politics of hope.* Walnut Creek, CA: Left Coast Press.

Denzin, N. K., Lincoln, Y. S., and Giardina, M. D. (2006). Disciplining qualitative research. *International Journal of Qualitative Studies in Education, 19*(6), 769–782.

Derrida, J. (1993). *Aporias* (T. Dutoit, Trans.). Palo Alto, CA: Stanford University Press.

Derrida, J. (1995). *The gift of death* (D. Wills, Trans.). Chicago: University of Chicago Press.

Fontana, L. (2006a). *Lucio Fontana: 1899–1968, "A new fact in sculpture."* Los Angeles, CA: Taschen.

Fontana, L. (2006b). *Lucio Fontana: Venice/New York* (L. M. Barbero, Ed.). New York: Solomon R. Guggenheim Foundation.

Foucault, M. (1980). *Power/Knowledge: Selected interviews and other writings, 1972–1977.* New York: Pantheon Books.

Foucault, M. (2008). *The birth of biopolitics: Lectures at the Collège de France, 1978–79.* Translated by G. Burchell. New York: Palgrave Macmillan.

Foucault, M. (1980). *Power/Knowledge: Selected interviews and other writings, 1972–1977.* C. Cordon, L. Marshall, J. Mepham, and K. Soper, Trans. Colin Cordon, eds. New York: Pantheon Books.

Havel, V. (1985). The power of the powerless. In J. Keane (Ed.), *The Power of the Powerless: Citizens against the State in Central-Eastern Europe* (pp. 23–96). London, UK: Hutchinson.

James, I. (2006). *The fragmentary demand: An introduction to the philosophy of Jean-Luc Nancy.* Stanford, CA: Stanford University Press.

James, I. (2012). *The new French philosophy.* Cambridge, UK: Polity.

Koro-Ljungberg, M. and MacLure, M. (2013) Provocations, re-un-visions, death and other possibilities of 'data.' *Cultural Studies⇔Critical Methodologies, 13*(4), 219–222.

Koro-Ljungberg, M., Hendricks, J., McTier, T., and Bojórquez, E. (2016). *Noise and Gossip: Sound Encounters and the Production of "Undocumented Students."* https://youtu.be/jD8cjvQRIlQ?list=PLoZ1K7VTPvrAGsURqNYKTNxLBjRPsO3LG

Lambert, K., Wright, P. R., Currie, J., and Pascoe, R. (2015). Data-driven performativity: Neoliberalism's impact on drama education in Western Australian secondary schools. *Review of Education, Pedagogy, and Cultural Studies, 37*(5), 460–475.

Lather, P. A., and St. Pierre, E. A. (2013). Post qualitative research. *International Journal of Qualitative Studies in Education, 26*(6), 629–633.

Latour, B. (1999). From fabrication to reality: Pasteur and his lactic acid ferment. *Pandora's hope: Essays on the reality of science studies.* Cambridge, MA: Harvard University Press.

Latour, B. (2005). *Reassembling the social.* New York: Oxford University Press.

MacLure, M. (2013). Researching without representation? Language and materiality in post-qualitative methodology. *International Journal of Qualitative Studies in Education, 26*(6), 658–667.

Manning, E. (2016). *The minor gesture.* Durham, NC: Duke University Press.

Mazzei, L. A., and Jackson, A. Y. (2005). *Thinking with theory in qualitative research: Viewing data across multiple perspectives.* New York: Routledge.

Mazzei, L. A., and McCoy, K. (2010). Thinking with Deleuze in qualitative research. *International Journal of Qualitative Studies in Education, 23*(5), 503–509.

Neubauer, R. (2011). Neoliberalism in the Information Age, or vice versa? Global citizenship, technology, and hegemonic ideology. *tripleC: Communication, Capitalism and Critique, 9*(2), 195–230.

Nordstrom, S. N. (2015). A data assemblage. *International Review of Qualitative Research, 8*(2), 166–193.

Pacini-Ketchabaw, V. (2012). Acting with the clock: Clocking practices in early childhood. *Contemporary Issues in Early Childhood, 13*(2), 154–160.

Pasquinelli, M. (2015). Italian operaismo and the information machine. *Theory, Culture and Society, 32*(3), 49–68.

Pickering, A. (1995). *The mangle of practice: Time, agency, and science.* Chicago: University of Chicago Press.

Pink, S., Mackley, K. L., and Moro anu, R. (2015). Hanging out at home: Laundry as a thread and texture of everyday life. *International Journal of Cultural Studies, 18*(2), 209–224.

Rautio, P. (2013). Children who carry stones in their pockets: On autotelic material practices in everyday life. *Children's Geographies, 11*(4), 394–408.

Read, J. (2009). A genealogy of homo economicus: Neoliberalism and the production of subjectivity. *Foucault Studies 6*(1), 25–36.

Stronach, I. (2009). Rethinking words, concepts, stories, and theories: Sensing a new world? In N. Denzin and M. Giardina (Eds.), *Qualitative inquiry and social justice* (pp. 248–277). Walnut Creek, CA: Left Coast Press.

Torrance, H. (2015). Investigating research power: Networks, assemblages, and the production of 'big' social science. In G. Cannella, M. Salazar Perez, and P. A. Pasque (Eds.), *Critical qualitative inquiry: Foundations and futures* (pp. 265–284). Walnut Creek, CA: Left Coast Press.

Weaver, J., and Snaza, N. (2016). Against methodocentrism in educational research. *Educational Philosophy and Theory.* doi: 10.1080/00131857.2016.1140015

5

BE CAREFUL WHAT YOU WISH FOR

Data entanglements in qualitative research, policy, and neoliberal governance[1]

Harry Torrance

'Data' is an increasingly contested term and concept in qualitative research, but its definition and use is also changing in social policy development and public service management. In this chapter, I will explore these parallel and apparently independent developments and argue that, while deriving from different fields and aspirations, these developments have elements in common and data is a term now as much applied to and used in political governance, as it is in (what used to be seen as) disinterested science.

Data in the natural and social sciences

The term 'data' derives from and is associated with observations and experiments in the natural sciences and continues to carry the implications and resonance of science for activity in the social sciences, including qualitative research. The Oxford English Dictionary defines data as "Related items of (chiefly numerical) information considered collectively, typically obtained by scientific work and used for reference, analysis, or calculation." (It further notes, for pedants, that in this definition it is "a mass noun" and can take a singular verb.) It goes on to elucidate various compound words and uses including data analysis, data handling, data mining, databank, and so on. Thus, classically, data is inert, passive, 'out there,' waiting to be discovered and collected, pre-existing and separate from the scientist who collects it. Moreover, data is not just collected, but categorized in various ways, so that analysis can aggregate and compare 'like with like.' Similarly, when variables are manipulated in experimental situations, data are, in effect, created, but are still regarded as being a property of the interaction of variables, external to the observer. The experimenter changes the independent variable to produce data pertaining to the dependent or outcome variable in question.

A similar set of assumptions seems to operate in much social scientific and qualitative research. Qualitative methods such as structured observation and even participant observation attempt to collect what we might term 'naturally occurring' data *in situ*. The implication and the assumption seem to be that the researcher can directly observe events without significantly interfering or intervening in them. Interviewing, focus groups, and so forth specifically try to elicit (create) data by directly interrogating participants. Clearly this involves intervening in social situations and setting up particular encounters, but still the assumption seems to be that this can be done without distorting the data collected in important ways. The texts produced – observational field notes and interview transcripts – are then regarded as the 'raw data' for conceptual categorization (coding), aggregation, and analysis. There is of course extensive discussion in qualitative research about the extent to which this can be done without interfering with and/or biasing the 'findings' of the research. However, with appropriate practices and protocols (immersion in the field, interview schedules, triangulation of data sources and methods, member checks, etc.) it has long been argued that the data can be collected, and that findings, which are relatively independent of the researcher, can be produced (Denzin, 1970; Hammersley & Atkinson, 1983; Miles & Huberman, 1994).

Furthermore with developments in digital technology and pressure for research to deliver better value-for-money and build knowledge across individual studies, archiving data is now becoming commonplace, implying that qualitative data can be removed from the circumstances of its production and aggregated and analyzed across contexts and over time. Such developments are not without critical discussion; as Flick (2015) asks:

> Can we use and re-use qualitative data in a meaningful way without really knowing the context of data collection … . To produce such decontextualized data is not really what qualitative inquiry is about. (p. 603)

Nevertheless, archiving is now well established and, taken together with the long-standing methodological injunctions noted above, we seem to be faced with a set of practices that St. Pierre (2011) has termed "conventional humanist qualitative methodology" (p. 611). St. Pierre (2013) also identifies what she calls the use of "brute data" in social research, including many approaches to qualitative research, which is regarded as "solid bedrock, building blocks of true knowledge that can be accumulated into regularities, generalities, scientific laws of the social world that emulate the scientific laws of the natural world" (p. 224). Joan Eakin (2016) has recently summarized these sorts of activities as

> post-positivist forms of qualitative research (PPQR) that operate more by positivist than interpretivist principles. PPQR uses qualitative data (e.g., words, texts) but analyses them through a realist objectivist lens.

Data are seen to be 'real' and ... conceptual categories ... are understood as 'findings' that reside in the data awaiting discovery ... At the core of PPQR is a conception of qualitative research as *method* or technique. (p. 111, original emphasis)

We might wonder why so much qualitative research has adopted the language and underlying philosophy of positivist natural science, given that its starting point and rationale is, ostensibly, very different; that is, to identify, describe, analyze, and report the perceptions, interpretations, and understandings of social actors from their own perspectives. But it can be argued that the very act of research implies the existence of some sort of additional external vantage point, some sort of privileged position from which to conduct the endeavor. Deriving from anthropology, and the very obvious powerful positioning of the (however benign) colonial observer over the 'native' or the 'other', qualitative research still assumes the position of observer, external to the culture, institutions and practices that are being investigated and reported on (of work, school, health care, youth, poverty, etc.). Moreover, given the increasing pressure for the findings of research to be immediately 'useful' in the context of (so-called) evidence-based policy making, the 'what works' movement, and 'scientifically-based research' (Torrance 2016), then it is perhaps not surprising that issues of sampling, coding, validity, reliability and generalizability have come to dominate discussions of both the quality and the teaching of qualitative methods (cf. AERA, 2006; Ragin et al., 2004; and many of the entries in the recent 2nd edition of Tashakkori & Teddlie, 2010).

Other approaches to social research have always been available of course, and other models of inquiry, policy development, and professional decision-making could have been more fully explored and developed in social science and social policy. Historical research, for example, has a much more sophisticated view of what counts as 'evidence' as compared with the 'what works' movement. Documents and artifacts are found, explored, compared, and contrasted, but are also recognized as social products in and of themselves, to be evaluated for warrant and veracity, rather than treated as objective 'data' per se. A high-status profession such as law, with very high-stakes consequences riding on what counts as admissible 'evidence,' grounds decisions in the examination of cases and the interrogation of individual witnesses. These processes are then deployed in the exercise of deliberation and judgment, and conclusions reached in the context of relevant precedents. Such observations about other models of inquiry have been made before (e.g., Stenhouse, 1978; Stake, 1995) but yet seem to be regularly eclipsed in the recurring 'paradigm wars' of social policy development. Social science has first and foremost appealed to the processes and practices of 'science' for its legitimacy, not history or the criminal justice system.

A linear model of research, policy and practice

Many philosophical issues are begged by whether or not we can observe data, isolate variables, identify cause and effect in social action, and so forth. They have been reviewed extensively elsewhere and I will not cover similar ground now (e.g., Howe, 2004; Maxwell, 2012; Morgan, 2014). However, a key empirical problem with the 'what works' call for scientifically based evidence is that the linear model which it invokes – of problem identification, intervention and application/dissemination – takes too long and, ironically, just doesn't work. The 'what works' movement seems to believe that the social world 'stands still' and waits for a solution to a problem to be found and implemented. The assumption seems to be that a particular issue can be identified as a topic of policy concern and solutions pursued in a relatively straightforward manner.

Take the issue of raising educational standards, for example, which is then broken down into ostensibly interrelated constituent parts, with a series of causal links or 'mechanisms' being posited and pursued: the underachievement of poor inner city children, the importance of early reading, the development of intervention programs to promote early reading in target groups. Curriculum materials and teaching strategies are developed, interventions designed and evaluated. If appropriately developed and effectively taught such interventions may make a positive difference for some children. Often, of course, they do not; often there is 'no significant difference' found between intervention and control groups (Viadero, 2009). But even successful interventions do not and cannot make a difference to all children in the target population – even positive results are only reported at the level of statistical probability, not individual certainty. Meanwhile large-scale replication and dissemination is difficult, demands additional and/or redirection of existing resources, and often creates as many problems as it solves. California's attempt to implement smaller class sizes off the back of the apparent success of the Tennessee "STAR" evaluation illustrates many of these problems. The Tennessee experiment worked with a sample of schools, whereas California attempted state-wide implementation, creating more problems than were solved as the policy created teacher shortages, especially in poorer neighborhoods in the state. There simply weren't enough well-qualified teachers available to reduce class size state-wide, and those that were available tended to move to schools in richer neighborhoods when more jobs in such schools became available (see Grissmer, Subotnik, & Orland, 2009). Furthermore, to return to the question of addressing underachievement and raising educational standards, the nature and the context of the problem changes over time, such that the relevance of the disseminated 'solution' diminishes. Large numbers of poor inner city children remain as underachievers but the social and educational milieu, and conditions of production of their underachievement, differs over time.

A much more open, dynamic, and iterative model of social action is needed in order to explore the ways in which research might make a difference to social problems. On the face of it, qualitative approaches to research ought to be able to encompass such a model, since social interaction is the core of a qualitative approach to research and the basis for the development of qualitative methods. But the issue of a linear and chronological approach to the relationship of research, policy and practice is not simply a product of the 'what works' movement. Social research more generally has experienced similar disappointments. Successive generations of social and educational researchers, including qualitative researchers, too often discover and rediscover social issues and problems rather than contribute to solving them. A significant illustration might be the cumulative work of researchers such as Hargreaves (1967), P. Jackson (1971), Willis (1979), McNeil (1986), McLaren (1989), Delpit (1995), and Lipman (2004), on the social organization of schooling and its impact on disadvantaged groups of students. These studies are exemplars of the very best of their kind, and constitute a formidable body of knowledge about the ways in which schooling privileges particular manifestations of middle class culture and behavior. The studies demonstrate how schooling contributes to the reproduction of social inequality, often despite the best intentions of teachers, administrators, and, sometimes, the researchers themselves as they have sought to feedback findings to promote change. However, while this and similar research has produced understanding and has documented the nature of the problem in terms of empirical evidence and the production of theoretical and analytic insight, it has not produced significant and lasting change to the nature of the problem investigated. Research-based understandings seem to have become an end in themselves, disconnected from processes of political and institutional change and, to reiterate, often despite the best intentions of the researchers themselves. Producing research is conceptualized as one thing, producing change is conceptualized as another. A better theory of how research might be linked to or implicated in social change is required.

Thus large tracts of social research, including qualitative research, still operates with a linear and chronological set of assumptions with respect to the relationship between research, policy and practice. The one (research) is assumed logically and necessarily to precede the other (changed policy and improved practice); thus: identify problem, investigate problem, propose solutions, evaluate solutions (including, often, with qualitative research designs as well as RCTs), disseminate solutions, solve problem. The sequence of linked activity involves and assumes a seamlessly connected chain of problem–research–data–analysis–policy–solution. Except, to reiterate, the problems generally persist. Something isn't quite right with the linear model or with adherence to the notion of "conventional humanist qualitative methodology" (St. Pierre, 2011), which mirrors the language, approach, and assumptions about 'data' of the natural sciences. Such endeavors may even seduce well-intentioned researchers into "the earnest advocacy that often leads to posturing and over-claims to make a difference" (Lather, 2016, p. 1).

New debates about the nature of data in qualitative research

Recently, considerable debate has been prompted in qualitative research about the nature of 'data', what counts as 'evidence' in debates over policy, and in what ways qualitative research might be able to dispense with the idea of data and embrace a more entangled, emergent, and intra-active notion of the role of the researcher in the creation of research activity and outcomes. As we have seen, St. Pierre (2011; see also her chapter in this volume) has been querying the limited and reductive nature of many teaching texts for some time now, along with what she sees as the desiccated nature of much qualitative research that is produced as a result. Denzin (2013) has written about the possible "death of data"; St. Pierre and Jackson (2014) edited a special edition of *Qualitative Inquiry* on "Qualitative Data Analysis After Coding"; Koro-Ljungberg, MacLure, and Ulmer (2017), are contributing a chapter on "Data and Its Problematics" to the forthcoming fifth edition of Denzin and Lincoln's *SAGE Handbook of Qualitative Research*. Further arguments about 'entanglement' are apparent in discussion of the "New Empiricisms and New Materialisms" (St. Pierre, Jackson, & Mazzei, 2016). The arguments are complex and not easily summarized. However, the core of the claims being made in these papers is that data are not inert, but created in and through the activity of the researcher, entangled in the material production of the activity. Moreover these claims go beyond what we might broadly term the well-understood idealist arguments about 'the social construction of reality' (Berger & Luckman, 1967). Rather these new arguments embrace ideas of material embodiment, emergence, and immanence; data are considered to be relational, emerging out of the assemblage of researcher, researched and the material conditions of the research act. Thus 'research' is not 'designed' and then, sequentially, undertaken, rather it is just 'done', emergent, produced in the moment along with other forms of social action: "There is no 'doer behind the deed'… the doer is produced either by or alongside the deed" (St. Pierre, Jackson, & Mazzei, 2016, p.7). The act of research is co-produced in the moment of its realization.

I will return to these arguments below. The point that I want to make for the moment, however, is that these critiques of the concept and use of the term 'data' in qualitative research relate to philosophical and methodological arguments within the qualitative research community. They are largely internal debates prompted, perhaps, by some of the engagements of qualitative inquiry with the demands of policy, and disillusionment with lack of educational and social change, but they are largely internal to the field nonetheless. The argument is about the philosophical basis and direction of qualitative research, and what theories and activities qualitative inquiry might encompass in the future. However, similar or, at least, parallel and somewhat comparable changes, can also be identified in the field of policy and governance and it is to this that I now turn.

Data in neoliberal governance

The definition and utility of 'data' is also beginning to morph and develop in the field of social policy and public service management. Data is now as much associated with the processes and procedures of accountability and 'governing at a distance' (Foucault 2009; Rose & Miller, 2008) as it is with the pursuit of 'research' or 'science.' This move transcends policy fields but can be particularly observed in health, social care, and education as governments seek to manage public services by setting targets for service delivery and render the individuals within them responsible for meeting the targets (Crawshaw, 2012; Ozga, 2009; Lingard, Thompson, & Sellar, 2016; Torrance, 2015). In education the move is perhaps exemplified and amplified, globally, by international comparisons of educational achievement such as the Trends In Maths and Science Study (TIMSS) and, particularly, the Programme for International Student Assessment (PISA) organized and orchestrated by the Organisation for Economic Cooperation and Development (OECD). The latest PISA program of tests was taken in 2015 by students in 72 countries. In order to produce comparable results for aggregation and analysis the tests cannot assess the content of 72 different national curricula so instead comprise assessments of general skills and abilities that are considered important for 15-year-olds to know and understand. The reference point for this transnational policy development then, is the skills and abilities that policymakers think are relevant and important for a global economic competition, rather than the content and cultural specificity of particular courses of study. The trend was critically reviewed in a recent special edition of *Teachers College Record*, and summarized very succinctly by the title of David Labaree's (2014) paper "Let's Measure What No-one Teaches." At the same time, however, national testing systems which should, in principle, reflect a wide range of local curriculum goals in their approach to accountability, are similarly narrow in the range of measures used, limiting the validity of the exercise and again focusing attention on a very restricted set of 'data.' In Australia, for example, the NAPLAN process focuses, as the acronym implies, on literacy and numeracy (National Assessment Programme – Literacy and Numeracy, Lingard et al., 2016). In England national tests at age 11 involve Maths and English, with 'English' deconstructed into distinct tests of Reading, Grammar, Spelling and Punctuation (Torrance 2016).

At first sight the setting and measuring of public service targets, and the construction of league tables and international rankings of countries' achievements in Maths, Science and Literacy, would appear to invoke the external and inert model of the natural sciences: data as "Related items of (chiefly numerical) information considered collectively" (OED). But these "items" are very specifically created and produced, manufactured, fabricated, in order to support policy and, in turn, political governance. Lingard, Thompson, and Sellar (2016) argue, furthermore, that such 'data' – league table positions across schools, districts, states and countries, targets which are met or missed – is now taking on a life of its own, *qua* data. The pursuit of 'good data' and the avoidance of 'bad data' drive behavior and public service activity, rather than inertly measuring it. Data has agency in and of itself, irrespective of the concerns and even resistance of individual social actors in particular situations. Pursuing the data (or perhaps being driven along by it) becomes far more important than simply doing what might ordinarily be thought of as a 'good job.' Peformativity dominates both the definition and the achievement of 'high quality' provision. Lingard et al.'s analysis derives from Australia, but similar observations can be made internationally, as the *Teachers College Record* special issue indicates. A recent paper on "The 'datafication' of early years pedagogy" in England (Roberts-Holmes, 2015), reflecting the narrowness of the measures deployed, and the intensity of the pressures produced, included several comments from teachers about the compulsion to produce 'good data':

> "We're totally data driven … We'll be punished if we have poor data so obviously it's a huge pressure to get the data looking good … it has really influenced thinking."
>
> "It's all based on data … the data is driving the pedagogy."
>
> "We have constant meetings looking at the data … you gotta play the game. If you're being judged on a score – teach to it – you're a fool if you don't. You must teach to the test." (Roberts-Holmes, 2015, p. 306)

Thus 'data' used dynamically in the policy sphere, renders actual definitions and manifestations of quality redundant. Rather the 'data' is taken as an absolute indicator of quality, a substitute for it, becoming as important if not more so in driving changes in behavior than static scientific data about 'what works.' Why wait for the (possibly unhelpful) results of the evaluation, when you can build policy implementation and behavior change into the instrument of evaluation itself?

Be careful what you wish for – entangled data

The debate about what counts as data in qualitative research might seem a little parochial then, even narrow and esoteric, in comparison to the pressure on teachers, students, and others involved in the provision of public services. Yet it may be that there are some resonances or echoes of the one in the other. Arguments about entanglement, immanence, and the emergent position of the researcher in the research process seem to have some parallels with the way in which the production of data to inform the management of public services has morphed into data servitude. Ljungberg, MacLure, and Ulmer (2016), reviewing the debate over data in qualitative research, argue:

> It is no longer possible to imagine the researcher positioned at arm's length from the data, exercising interpretive dominion over it … Equally however

data cannot be thought of as mere social construction with no material footing in the world … Instead, in new materialist thought researchers, participants, data, theory, objects and values are mutually constituted by each 'agential cut' into and out of the indeterminancy of matter … (p. 16)

St. Pierre (2013), drawing extensively on Deleuze, argues further that "Being in every sense is entangled, connected, indefinite, impersonal, shifting into different multiplicities and assemblages" (p. 226). Thus the key issue for research is to produce something new, rather than simply seeking to provide an account, however nuanced, of what is 'there.' As she writes:

For Deleuze, philosophy is fundamentally a matter of living rather than knowing … "instead of asking for conditions of possible experience … look for the conditions under which something new, as yet unthought arises." (p. 225)

Lather (2016) explores similar issues and ideas, seeking a possible reconciliation or rapprochement between the natural and interpretive sciences, even a new science: "the science possible after the critiques of science" (p. 1). She notes "post-humanist theories of agency" locate "agency within intra-active relational entanglements" (p. 2). Thus action, behavior, understanding, are immanent and emerge in situ. She further argues that, given this:

Another kind of theory of change is called for … a theory of change that is imminent rather than vanguard [involving] practice-based accretions rather than the 'big bang' of some new paradigm … that occur at a low level of visibility … as they remake through a network of mutual determinations. (p. 3)

There are resonances here with my earlier critique of much social research operating with a linear and mechanistic model of change. Change, rather, might arise out of "a network of mutual determinations" which includes the researcher. Lather goes on to deploy her argument with respect to policy development and implementation, noting that much qualitative inquiry demonstrates "the wild profusion of local practice" (p. 4, quoting Fenwick & Edwards, 2011).

However, to link back to the production and role of data in neoliberal governance, might not the individual responsibilization of teachers, students, health care workers, and the like, in their quest to "get the data looking good" be one example of such a "network of mutual determinations"? Isn't this exactly how neoliberalism insinuates itself into every aspect of our professional and personal lives? It seems as if neoliberalism already operates with a more sophisticated theory of change than empirical social science. Change has occurred in public institutions (and indeed in commercial organizations as well) in precisely this "immanent" incremental fashion – with "practice-based accretions" slowly 'bringing the frog to the boil,' so that almost without noticing it, everything has changed. Lather (2016) actually makes almost exactly the same interpretive point but draws different conclusions, seeing the slow accretions of neoliberal accountability as evidence of their fragility:

> How everyday material practices assemble and align with objects, ideas and behaviors involved in "new governing behaviours" particularly the over-reliance on "flows of data" as "calculating devices"… illustrate[s] the precarity of what looks so solid and immutable (p. 4).

Well, certainly, neoliberal "governing behaviors" are assembled and invoked in and through everyday practice, they are indeed neither "solid" nor "immutable", but they *feel* as if they are. This surely exemplifies the power of neoliberalism and the paradox of current theoretical thinking. Data are certainly not 'out there', waiting to be discovered. They are not inert, passive, manipulable. Quite the reverse, in neoliberal accountability they exercise "interpretive dominion" over us, we do not exercise dominion over them. They govern us, we do not govern them. Data, researcher, institution, and social actor are indeed entangled – but not in a good way!

Lather (2016) also wonders about whether or not the turn to a more relational ontology, to "something not containable, in excess of meaning" (p. 1) might produce an "incalculable subject … as a counter to neoliberal and 'Big Data' efforts to count and parse, capture and model our every move, a subject outside the parameters of the algorithms" (p. 2). But again, does this not invoke the same theoretical paradox? If we are entangled with data, implicated in both its production and use, we cannot stand outside of the process. We produce neoliberal data and governance even as we feel that it produces us.

Data then, are not inert. They are produced, but in turn become an agentic part of the assemblage that produces them. Thus theories of entanglement in qualitative research certainly address the problem of linearity in thinking about the relationship between research, policy and practice. Ideas of emergence and immanence locate the possibility of change in the here-and-now and the pursuit of change in the *practice* of research, rather than the findings of research. As such we might try to re-orient ideas about 'what works' towards ideas about what 'might work' if discussed, explored, and realized in situ, with research participants and respondents in particular communities addressing particular problems. Equally however it becomes clear that any claims for research must become more modest, and take their place in the larger assemblage. Data, once released from the Pandora's box of inertia and passivity, will not necessarily prove benign in its effects. The "incalculable subject" is currently very busy trying to calibrate itself. Even governments, pursuing better national positions in international league tables, come under pressure if a nation appears to perform worse than previously, and end up being as much subject to data as in control of it. Similarly however, it is apparent that we are indeed dealing with something that is "not containable, in excess of meaning" and as such will always provide the possibility of producing something new and, as yet, unforeseen.

Note

1   This chapter was originally presented as a paper to the plenary panel "The Concepts of Data: Challenges in Neoliberal Times," International Congress of Qualitative Inquiry, 19–21 May 2016, University of Illinois at Urbana-Champaign, USA.

References

American Educational Research Association. (2006). Standards for reporting on empirical social science research in AERA publications. *Educational Researcher, 35*(6), 33–40.

Berger P. and Luckmann T. (1967). *The social construction of reality.* London: Penguin Books.

Crawshaw, P. (2012). Governing at a distance: Social marketing and the (bio) politics of responsibility. *Social Science & Medicine, 75*(1), 200–207.

Delpit, L. (1995) *Other people's children: Cultural conflict in the classroom.* New York, NY: New Press.

Denzin N. (1970). *The research act.* Chicago: Aldine.

Denzin, N. (2013). The death of data? *Cultural Studies–Critical Methodologies, 13*(4), 353–356.

Eakin J. (2016). Educating critical qualitative health researchers in the land of the randomized controlled trial. *Qualitative Inquiry, 22(2),* 107-118

Fenwick, T., and Edwards, R. (2011). Considering materiality in educational policy: Messy objects and multiple reals. *Educational Theory, 61,* 709–726.

Flick U. (2015). Qualitative Inquiry – 2.0 at 20?. *Qualitative Inquiry, 21*(7), 599–608.

Foucault, M. (2009). *The birth of bio-politics: Lectures at the Collège de France, 1978–1979.* New York: Picador.

Grissmer, D., Subotnik, R., & Orland, M. (2009). *A Guide to incorporating multiple methods in randomized controlled trials to assess intervention effects.* Available at www.apa.org/ed/schools/cpse/activities/mixed-methods.aspx

Hammersley M. and Atkinson P. (1983). *Ethnography: principles in practice.* London: Routledge.

Hargreaves, D. (1967). *Social relations in the secondary school.* London: Routledge & Kegan Paul.

Howe, K. (2004). A critique of experimentalism. *Qualitative Inquiry, 10*(1), 42–61.

Jackson, P. (1971). *Life in classrooms.* New York, NY: Holt, Rinehart & Winston.

Koro-Ljungberg, M., MacLure, M., & Ulmer, J. (2017). Data and its problematics. In N. K. Denzin and Y. S. Lincoln (Eds.), *SAGE Handbook of Qualitative Research (5th Edition).* Thousand Oaks, CA: Sage.

Labaree, D. (2014). Let's measure what nobody teaches: PISA, NCLB, and the shrinking aims of education. *Teachers College Record, 116*(9), 1–14.

Lather, P. (2016). Top Ten + list: (Re)thinking ontology in (post)qualitative research. *Cultural Studies–Critical Methodologies,* 1–7.

Lingard, B., Thompson, G., & Sellar S. (Eds.) (2016). *National testing in schools: An Australian perspective.* London: Routledge.

Lipman, P. (2004). *High stakes education: Globalisation and urban school reform.* London: Routledge.

Maxwell, J. (2012). The importance of qualitative research for causal explanation in education. *Qualitative Inquiry, 18*(8), 655–661.

McLaren, P. (1989). *Life in schools.* New York, NY: Longmans.

McNeil, L. (1986). *Contradictions of control: School structure and school knowledge.* New York: Routledge and Kegan Paul.

Miles M. and Huberman A. (1994). *Qualitative data analysis.* Thousand Oaks, CA: Sage.

Morgan, D. (2014). Pragmatism as a paradigm for social research. *Qualitative Inquiry, 20*(8), 1045–1053.

Ozga, J. (2009). Governing education through data in England: From regulation to self-evaluation. *Journal of Education Policy, 24*(2), 149–163.

Ragin, C., Nagel, J., & White, P. (2004). *Workshop on scientific foundations of qualitative research.* Available at www.nsf.gov/pubs/2004/nsf04219/start.htm.

Roberts-Holmes, G. (2015). The datafication of early years pedagogy. *Journal of Education Policy, 30*(3), 302–315.

Rose, N., & Miller P. (2008). *Governing the present: Administering economic, social and personal life*: New York: Polity.

Stake, R. (1995). *The art of case study research.* London: Sage.

Stenhouse, L. (1978). The study of samples and the study of case. *British Educational Research Journal, 6*, 1–6.

St. Pierre, E. A. (2011). Post qualitative research: The critique and the coming after. In N. K. Denzin & Y. S. Lincoln (Eds.), *SAGE handbook of qualitative inquiry* (4th ed.) (pp. 611–635). Thousand Oaks, CA: Sage

St. Pierre, E. A. (2013). The appearance of data. *Cultural Studies–Critical Methodologies, 13*(4), 223–227.

St. Pierre, E. A., & Jackson. A. (2014). Qualitative data after coding. *Qualitative Inquiry 20*(6), 715–719.

St. Pierre, E. A., Jackson. A., & Mazzei, L. (2016). New empiricisms and new materialisms: Conditions for new inquiry' *Cultural Studies–Critical Methodologies, 16*(2), 99–110.

Tashakkori, A., & Teddlie, C. (Eds.) (2010). *SAGE handbook of mixed methods in social and behavioral research* (2nd Edition). Thousand Oaks, CA: Sage.

Torrance, H. (2015). Blaming the victim: Assessment, examinations, and the responsibilization of students and teachers in neoliberal governance discourse. *Studies in the Cultural Politics of Education*, 1–14. http://dx.doi.org/10.1080/01596306.2015.1104854

Torrance, H. (2016, September). Validity, or the lack of it, in English National Curriculum Assessment and School Examinations. Paper presented to British Educational Research Association (BERA) annual conference, University of Leeds, 13–15.

Viadero, D. (2009, April 1). "No effects" studies raising eyebrows, *Education Week*, available at www.projectcriss.com/newslinks/Research/MPR_EdWk--NoEffectsArticle.pdf

Willis, P. (1979). *Learning to labour: How working class kids get working class jobs.* Basingstoke, UK: Saxon House.

SECTION II

Ethics, politics, and resistance

6

FEMINIST POSTSTRUCTURALISMS AND THE NEOLIBERAL UNIVERSITY

Bronwyn Davies, Margaret Somerville, and Lise Claiborne

In this chapter, we enter into conversation with each other about what new modes of thought and being have emerged from feminist poststructuralist thought and how these modes of thought and being are positioned within the neoliberal university. Our discussion is oriented around these three questions: (1) how might we understand the neoliberal university?, (2) what is the position of poststructuralism in a neoliberal university?, and (3) how can they work together and/or apart?

How might we understand the operations of the neoliberal university?

Bronwyn: I first became aware of the creep of neoliberalism in the mid 1990s when I'd been appointed Professor and Head of School at James Cook University. Strategic Plans were the new thing and my School had to produce one. Conveniently, a consultant's name was provided by management, and, in good faith, she was appointed.

Meanwhile, although I didn't like the idea of a future limited by what we could imagine in the present, I initiated conversations with my new colleagues about what they wanted our future to look like; I sought an engagement in collaborative thought that would enable us to imagine a future that would be the very best future we were capable of, that would allow the things we were passionate about to flourish; that would allow new things we dreamed of, collectively, to flourish. When the consultant arrived with her bag of tricks for our two-day workshop, she explained to us that all we had been doing was irrelevant and inappropriate. We did not understand the genre of strategic plans. Furthermore, she made very clear that I was not to speak, as she was in charge. She got us to throw balls to each other to build up trust and produced a set of clichés that would form the basis of the very expensive plan we were paying for – probably identical to all the other plans she was the highly paid consultant for. We were in effect being normalized and regulated to produce a neoliberal scheme of things that was not of our own making. It was my first exercise in having creative and critical thought strategically switched off and responsibility handed over to this new player on our scene – the expert consultant whose grasp of neoliberal discourse and her expensive bag of tricks would apparently shape our futures.

In fact, the plan disappeared into a filing cabinet and wasn't seen again after its launch. No one had thought about its implementation.

There were many such initiatives in the ensuing months and years. We never knew which ones were going to come to matter and which would disappear. Each of these initiatives was apparently unconnected to the others and we were slow to realize they were part of a comprehensive program of globalization and neoliberalization that would transform the human species from *homo socius* to *homo eoconomicus* (to use Foucault's term).

This strategic transformation began with the *Trilateral Commission*, an alliance between a handful of political leaders and multinational big businesses (Sklar, 1980). They had decided that democracy was no longer unaffordable, and that people had to be made, without them realizing it, more manageable and more productive. Further, and without realizing it, workers must become complicit in increasing the flow of $$ toward the rich (Sklar, 1980). Rather than announce itself as a program for social change, it presented itself as the inevitable changes we must all engage in if we are to survive in a globalizing world. Vulnerability and fear were to be mobilized. The strategy of *piecemeal implementation* was adopted so none of us would realize what the tide of change was, and where it was coming from – or what it was we needed to resist.

To further disguise itself it appropriated terms that were vital to the world it was dismantling and gave them new managerialist meanings; 'ethics' and 'quality,' for example, would now be produced through regulation and surveillance. Collectivity was strategically undermined, and with it the capacity for resistance. A new hyper-individualism was installed. The erosion of collectivity was effected through a strategic assemblage of initiatives including:

Intensification of vulnerability through ever-increasing workloads and increased competition for reduced resources;
Transfer of responsibility from the social to the individual;
The creation of an the illusion of freedom through emphasis on choice;
The undermining of institutional/historical knowledges and allegiances through constant restructuring;
The de-valuing of critique and the demise of departments whose main purpose was to engage in critique, such as history, philosophy and gender studies;

The redirection of resources to administration, and to the production of regulations, of uniformity, and of surveillance, making accountability the new mantra for what would count as virtue;

The establishment of master's degrees in management that would teach new managerialism;

And, of course, the strategic weakening of unions and the demise of tenure as a job for life.

My horror at what was happening to universities led, finally, in 2009, to my 'Virginia Woolf moment'; I had an income, since I'd reached so-called retirement age, and I had a room of my own. I could create my own space, in which my work might continue without the requirement of dancing to the tune of the latest neoliberal madness. I am still a work in progress of de-institutionalization.

Margaret: I struggle with the neoliberal university as a daily reality but I also recognize that this university pays my salary and enables me to do the work I do. It helped when thinking about how it is possible to talk about the neoliberal university, in consideration of the ethics of this position, to scan a website hosted by Michigan State University. Its stated aim is to encourage public debate about the type of society we want, the direction neoliberal policies have taken society and its institutions, and to identify alternative paths that lead to a social order in which there is less poverty and greater opportunities for all. It invites public comment. (see http://futureu.education)

Analyzing the posts on this website makes certain universally common patterns visible. These include

- the rise and rise of college sports,
- difficulties for African American and other minority studies,
- the plight of contingent faculty staff,
- removal of staff who do not conform to neoliberal ideologies,
- increasing tuition fees – 'a public good has become a private matter,'
- lack of credentials of chief executives,
- the demise of social science and humanities,
- corporate sponsorship of universities, and
- and university branding and re-branding.

In reference to this last, the story of the re-branding of the University of Western Sydney, an occasion when I hit a wall of existential despair, has no ethical barrier that requires my silence, since it is specifically intended for a vast public audience. At enormous expense the University of Western Sydney has been re-branded as Western Sydney University. The re-branding required all signage, stationary, promotional materials, websites, business cards, name badges, even the Vice Chancellor's executive cars, to be replaced. Members of the university are required to use marketing templates and stock images of individuals produced by the marketing department in all documents and presentations. Not only does the new website feature individuals who represent particular marketized narratives, such as 'the successful refugee,' or 'the determined young woman from a low SES background,' but the overall catchphrase is 'Unlimited' with headings such as 'Discover stories of unlimited,' and 'Find your unlimited.'

This marketing catch-cry of 'unlimited' symbolizes the problem for me, articulated in Rosi Braidotti's Deleuzian analysis of advanced capitalism as a process ontology that codes and recodes the existing rules that construct our socio-economic relations. All possible emancipatory positions have been co-opted to the market economy, disconnected from the emancipatory potential of making a difference in the world.

"Animals, seeds, plants, and the earth as a whole" are subsumed into the market, she writes; "Seeds, cells and genetic codes" (Braidotti, 2014, np), all of our basic earth others, everything that lives, has become controlled, commercialized, and commodified. For Braidotti, the emancipatory gesture is seldom spectacular, involving a reconceptualization of the feminist politics of location, and of desire as lack, to desire as plenitude.

Lise: The examples above illustrate the ways that neoliberal discourses are ubiquitous in universities. These discourses create material demands on our bodies that sprout up, hydra-like, at every turn, since we are '24/7' workers constantly on call.

Recently, Monbiot (2016a; see also 2016b) suggested that neoliberalism is an ideology that needs to be named and shamed so that it can be routed. But there's the difficulty. If we are going to take theoretical insights from the whole poststructural project into account, a simple dualism – neoliberals versus those more enlightened 'not-neolibs' – will not work, since every dualism has within it the entanglement of presence and absence. The works of Bergson and Deleuze are helpful in pointing out the indestructible links between so-called opposites; their connection contradictorily affirms the dominant position under critique. Drawing on these theorists along with Colebrook, Dolphijn (2012, np) urges us to go beyond structure to "the establishment of a non-dualist logic of univocity," beyond the dualism and its two-dimensional expression towards splitting in time and space to create multiple differences. Here Barad's feminist poststructural project can assist by suggesting diffractive analysis that takes into account the complexity of discourses and material conditions that constantly propel our subjectivities towards expression within neoliberal norms.

Since being invited to participate in this conversation, I've been propelled down strange lines of ascent and descent as I have grappled with various subjectivities I have inhabited over my career as a senior university administrator. Initially this led me to feelings of hopelessness as the task of working on this paper became one of the many tasks I am constantly juggling, tasks that leave me depleted, exhausted, dissatisfied and always convinced I could have done more. Once I started to connect back to the feminist theoretical work I enjoy reading, though, my flow of energy started moving again, away from the stultifying confines of my "To Do" lists. Some troubling experiences provided a place for further analysis.

Last year I experienced, at a meeting of all staff in my faculty, a 'failure of indignation.' Someone from the floor commented that neoliberal ideas were a hegemonic force affecting the lives of all staff in the midst of the latest and most severe restructuring to date. Some time at the meeting was spent on the wording of a "strong yet fair" memo to be sent to senior managers at the university expressing a collective disbelief and subsequent sadness (given the presumed educational values we all share) at the unfairness of the announcement of the latest budget cuts. I was surprised by my own difficulty in generating energy for this task, something I could easily have mobilized a few years before. The whole project of writing the memo seemed a rhetorical act, part of a theatre of the absurd, with its touching faith in the power of logical argument and provision of information as a way to create a change in the operation of an institution that was already on a line of descent focusing on the altered flow of money and status. As I left the meeting I heard the comment, "we can't become cynical." Even the possibility of cynicism, with its glimpse of the individual body that is tired, overly experienced, and ultimately traitorous in its lethargy, seemed a fanciful figuration from another discursive era.

When searching for a new way to respond, I find Patricia Clough's (2012) analysis of possibility useful to consider. She also draws on Bergson and Deleuze to suggest that any supposed difference between what is possible and what is real is inevitably stuck within a commemoration of what was: "The possible anticipates the real or the real projects backwards to its possibility as if always having been" (p. 3). Such commemoration seems to underpin a complaint I have often heard at staff meetings, that "good education and care for students don't have a monetary value." Within the neoliberal discourses that dominate the university, this complaint is no longer intelligible (Butler, 2011), since value is defined by the financial. Taking a position in opposition to the neoliberal reaffirms the centrality of its importance. This leaves us without possibilities beyond a return to the familiar (resistance), stuck in a citational chain that holds the status quo in place.

Some senior administrators I know have refused to follow strongly worded suggestions about implementation of cutbacks. These managers can then themselves become sidelined, not asked to crucial meetings or having their main goals given little time in management discussions. This valiant resistance then becomes sucked into the vortex of the dualism, where to be 'non-neoliberal' is still a position defined in neoliberal terms as an aspect of the one reality, the same-old. Perhaps that is why administrators are now more likely to be sidelined from access to accurate financial information and hence to crucial decision-making. In my workplace, it is increasingly harder to get specific information about the institution's oft-mentioned straitened economic circumstances. There are general pronouncements about how important it is to save money and how drastic the actions have to be for the institution's survival. But the facts on which this argument is based are no longer transparent even to senior administrators.

Instead of staying within the possible-real plane, then, we could consider Clough's focus on the contrast between the virtual and the actual, where "[t]he virtual is 'never realized'; the difference creates a swerve, a divergence to the new or the future" (p. 3). That could take us fruitfully into new dimensions.

What is the position of poststructuralism in a neoliberal university?

Bronwyn: In thinking through the role of poststructuralist thinking in the new university I want to focus in particular on the contribution it can make to thinking about ethics; that is, to the recovery of 'ethics' from where neoliberalism has taken it. I want to trace a line here of how ethical thought has evolved from Foucault, through Butler, Cixous, Deleuze and Barad – from poststructuralist theory to new materialism.

The radical potential that Foucault offered us, as intellectuals, was through the analyses he undertook in order "to bring assumptions and things taken for granted again into question, to shake habits, ways of acting and thinking, to dispel the familiarity of the accepted, to take the measure of rules and institutions." (Gordon, 2000: xxxiv). He characterized the form of individualization under neo-liberalism as dangerous, saying that what is needed is de-individualization of our-selves and resistance to neoliberalism's impulse to make us isomorphic with itself; we must be able to position ourselves sufficiently outside its terms, he argued, in order to critique it.

Butler's work with performativity and responsibility has extended Foucauldian thought to elaborate how it is not only what those with power do to oppress us within neoliberal systems, or what the systems do once they take on a life of their own, but also what we do to ourselves and to others to gain power as autonomous and viable beings. Performances are not just of something that we repeat from an original that is external to us but the performance creates the thing itself that we perform. In Butler's sense we must transform ourselves into neoliberal subjects in order to have viable lives, and at the same time we must distance ourselves from it in order to critique it.

Through writing the body Cixous brought materiality to centre focus, not just the materiality of one's own body but of the other, and of the world of which the embodied being is part. It was through writing that she accessed the body. She too, like Foucault and Butler, was focused on the task of finding how to think the unthinkable in order not to be caught in the same old places, the same old crises:

> We go toward the best known unknown thing, where knowing and not knowing touch, where we hope we will know what is unknown. Where we hope we will not be afraid of understanding the incomprehensible, facing

the invisible, hearing the inaudible, thinking the unthinkable, which is of course: thinking. Thinking is trying to think the unthinkable: thinking the thinkable is not worth the effort. Painting is trying to paint what you cannot paint and writing is writing what you cannot know before you have written: it is preknowing and not knowing, blindly, with words. It occurs at the point where blindness and light meet. (Cixous, 1993, p. 38)

To dare to go where one is blind, where thought has not yet happened, where the unknown is yet to emerge and multiply, is, for Cixous, ethical writing (Williams, 2012). Ethics, in this sense, is an act of courage not to follow the lines laid down by neoliberalism, but to sink into the act of writing and to allow the body to take you to think the as-yet-unthought.

Deleuze offered us the concept of assemblage so that we could see how much more complex the system of our entrapment is – through discourse and discursive practices, through our bodies and our bodies' relations with others, through historical events and emotional commitments, and the repetitions that hold everything the same. Deleuzian ethics picks up the thread from both Butler and Cixous of the self's implicatedness in the other, and, like Foucauldian ethics, makes a break with moralistic judgment. He offers instead an ethics that is not so much spurred by the soul's own contradictions but by a radical openness to the emergent, multiple being of the other, where that other is both human and non-human, organic and inorganic:

> an ethics is completely different, you do not judge…. Somebody says or does something, you do not relate it to values. You ask yourself how is that possible? How is this possible in an internal way? In other words, you relate the thing or the statement to the mode of existence that it implies, that it envelops in itself. How must it be in order to say that? Which manner of Being does this imply? (Deleuze, 1980)

In such an ethics, the realization of one's identity, through establishing the moral values (or indeed measurements) with which to judge oneself and others, is no longer the point. The point is to become different from ourselves, to evolve creatively in the space that we open up between and among us. We do so through exploring the emergent intra-corporeal multiplicity that becomes possible in that space of Being (Fritsch, 2015).

Barad and the feminist new materialists again bring ontology, epistemology and ethics into focus, exploring their inseparability. As she writes:

> [Justice entails] the ongoing practice of being open and alive to each meeting, each intra-action, so that we might use our ability to respond, our responsibility, to help awaken, to breathe life into ever new possibilities for living justly. The world and its possibilities for becoming are remade in each

meeting. How then shall we understand our role in helping constitute who and what come to matter? (Barad, 2007, p. x)

In none of these ways of making sense of the world, of our place in it, and our ethical obligations, is ethics a matter of separate individuals following a set of rules as in neoliberal management of what it calls ethics. In postructuralist terms ethical practice requires thinking beyond the already known, being open in the moment of the encounter. Ethical practice is emergent in encounters with others, in emergent listening with others (Davies, 2014). It is a matter of questioning what is being made to matter and how that mattering affects what it is possible to do and to think.

The position of poststructuralism in neoliberal universities would therefore seem to be to challenge the reduction of ethics to a regulated, legalistic, and sometimes moralistic, process, the bottom line of which is to protect the university from being sued by research subjects who find themselves aggrieved. Poststructuralism's position in the case of ethics is to unsettle the certainties about what ethical practice is, and to make it relevant in every encounter. Since it is unlikely to unseat neoliberal 'ethics,' it must exist alongside it and also entangled with it.

Margaret: I have always worked against the grain of feminist poststructuralism, liberated into new thinking by its extraordinary possibilities but always struggling to reconcile its western ontologies with my theoretical origins in a world of Indigenous thought. In Bronwyn Davies' (2004) special issue of *International Journal of Qualitative Studies in Education* on feminist post-structuralism I wrote an article titled 'Tracing bodylines,' referencing feminist philosopher Elizabeth Grosz's *Volatile Bodies* (1994), in which she challenges philosophy from the perspective of the body. My contribution was to *emplace* those bodies. Collaborations with Indigenous communities have led to increasingly hybrid and complex onto-epistemologies expressed in a collaborative research framework of 'thinking through Country' in art and story (Somerville, 2013). Alongside this I theorized place and sought projects in sustainability education with children, a parallel attempt to bring western and Aboriginal epistemologies into conversation. It was not until a workshop about the Anthropocene in 2010 that there began to be a coming together of these two trajectories of research.

In contemplating Braidotti's analysis of advanced capitalism and the university's neoliberal practices I can easily become overwhelmed by a sense of inadequacy and self doubt, questioning whether anything we do in research can make a difference beyond the minutiae of the small local worlds we inhabit. It is the proliferation of scholarship mobilized by the global movement of the Anthropocene that gives me energy and hope. The concept of an age of human entanglement in the fate of the planet, named as the Anthropocene, has galvanized scholars across all disciplines to seek new ways to de-center the human as the sole focus of attention. This shift in understanding of the human subject and its relation to knowledge is profound. In the Introduction to her edited collection *Extinction: Framing the end of the species*, Clare Colebrook (2010) writes:

> It is as though what is facing extinction is not only the human species but also a certain mastery or image of the species: climate change is not only change of the climate but a change in the very way in which we think … Extinction is not only extinction of the species but also an extinguishing of the human animal's sense of humanity. (p. 15)

Anthropocene scholarship is way in excess of conventional academic forms; it lives in the virtual world of Facebook as well as in anarchic gatherings of researchers seeking new ways of being and knowing. Phematerialisms is just one of many Facebook sites with constant feeds of new materialist/post-human images and thought bites.

Barad's concept of entanglement in *Meeting the Universe Halfway* (2007) has been a starting point for me in the convergence of hybrid Indigenous onto-epistemologies and new materialist approaches. For Barad (2007), "To be entangled is not simply to be intertwined with another as in the joining of two separate entities, but to lack an independent self-contained existence" (p. x). Intra-action as a core operational concept offers new ways of understanding the mutual entanglements of different bodies of matter, each with their own force or agency. There is no prior existence for the individual subject, subjects emerge only through their intra-relating; time and space, like matter and meaning, come into existence iteratively reconfigured through each intra-action. For the first time there is a language for the fabric, the forms and elements of the earth, as well as all its living creatures, including humans that feature so strongly in Aboriginal onto-epistemologies.

I am in a state of wondering about my love affair with these new ideas and approaches. How do they relate to onto-epistemological work I have done in 'thinking through Country' that understands entanglement through collaboration with Australian Aboriginal knowledges? I wonder, too, about the trajectory from the materialist theories of the 1980s and 1990s, including Donna Haraway, Elizabeth Grosz, Vicki Kirby and others who have informed new modes of materialist thought. Ultimately, however, the diffractive move of Barad's theory, coming from quantum physics, has given me a new language through which to articulate an onto-epistemological position from a Western perspective that is resonant with this previous work but paradigmatically different.

Lise: My location in Aotearoa, New Zealand, is underpinned by a somewhat different historical engagement with Indigenous peoples and feminist poststructural ideas. In the 1980s, my attempts to introduce these ideas to ethnically diverse postgraduate classes relied on a critique of modernism to trouble the Eurocentrism of dominant theoretical models. The task was aided by a Fulbright visit from Patti Lather in 1989 at the height of conflict between feminist politics and 'obscure theories,' coming only five years after the publication of a hugely influential critique of colonization by a Māori lawyer (Awatere, 1984). Ironically, this Orwellian year was also the beginning of New Zealand's early embrace of radical neoliberalism (see Larner, 1996).

Despite New Zealanders' overall willingness to 'take the medicine' of neoliberalism as a survival strategy for a small country in a competitive world, the medicine has been bitter indeed. My institution has begun to implement a process of restructuring that shows little ethical sensibility. I am likely to lose contact with colleagues whose work I value greatly. Amidst all this, I am heartened by Bronwyn's reminder that ethics can be considered an intra-active (Barad, 2007) process that requires a bigger analysis of material forces within and beyond the human. As part of ethical engagement in this process, I have started to question my own tenacity in holding on to my job amidst the various cycles of change I've experienced. Now I question whether my work could be characterized not just as helpful to students and colleagues, but also compliant, because my experience indicates that perceived troublemakers are often the first to go. When recently I at first did not accept an administrative task 'offered' to me, I was surprised both by negative reactions from those senior to me, and by a feminist colleague's comment that I was 'incredibly brave' to say no. Before this, I had imagined I had volition in agreeing to work tasks, but then began to wonder at my own obtuseness. Did I have a rose-tinted view of collegiality as the foundation for my working relationships? This insight also led me to remind myself -- and the colleagues struggling around me – of Foucault's work on the disciplining of bodies. Senior staff are not simply duped agents of capitalist forces but are themselves (their bodies, their policies, their desires) cornered in positions that are discursively constrained. Agentic choices are illusory, yet I would argue, along with Braidotti, that collectively we are still accountable for the ethical implications of our work.

A specific embodied example may be useful here. A university administrator has emailed a group of employees to exhort them to behave in a particular way:

> *Attendance at the* [university event] *this morning was low from our group. I was disappointed. I saw that the powers-that-be noted who had not attended.*

These university events, of which there are several each year, are part of the institution's wider public face in the community. The email message could be seen as fitting well a neoliberal work environment, given its clear reference to surveillance of employees ("powers-that-be noted"). A question that could be asked is whether there could be a response that shows a reality beyond that of the neoliberal workplace.

Imagining responses by staff to this exhortation offers possibilities for poststructural intervention. A response about non-attendance at the event to other 'missing' colleagues could open a space for subtle critique. For example, a response might draw on Davies and Harré's (1990) use of positioning theory to identify the discursive moves in the message. The responder could point out to peers that the reference to 'disappointment' draws on an Oepidalised discourse that links the workplace to the nuclear family. Comments about surveillance could also be quite useful in support-ing the group collectively. Resistant humor could be expressed as congratulations to those who did not attend the event, positioning these staff as successful resisters of the neoliberal regime. But, as Deleuze, Dolphijn, and others have noted (see above), resistance does not unsettle the dualism with its dominant pole of neoliberalism.

In this situation a humorous response could be ill advised. A senior administrator at another university says that she never uses irony or humor in discussion with colleagues, since such texts are easily misinterpreted by those desperately seeking information about the precariousness of their jobs. This kind of discursive con-straint would also limit possible responses to the email above; any rejoinder would need to be performative of the speech of a worker in continuing employment.

Comments directly to the administrator would require more careful crafting of text. Discomfort about the experience of surveillance could be mentioned, per-haps humorously (since frontline employees – if not their managers – might still be able to use some forms of humor). A possible response to the administrator that takes the surveillance out a little further to absurdity, while also emphasizing the support of people in the group, might be a response such as, *Could I have the list of people who were able to make it to the meeting? I'd like to thank each and every one of them.*

While such a response performs an ironic Polyanna-ish (or even *Kimmy Schmidt*-ish) intertextual reference, it could also open a space for further group critique of our immersion in the neoliberal and possibilities for planning diver-gent responses together.

Despite the predominance of neoliberalism, other discursive flows and lines of flight are around us all the time. As mentioned above, invoking resistance to neoliberalism does not unsettle the power of the dominant term, since its other is nostalgic: the shadow of something more enlightened, from an earlier time ("the good old days"). Adding new materialist questions helps to keep the flow moving towards greater multiplicity and divergence beyond the limitations of resistance. While speech can be performative of compliance, it can also contain fragmented, alternative, less subjugated actualizations. Butler (2011) might point to the ways that administrators are subjugated to the disciplines of their jobs, yet there are also antic virtual moments that move beyond the constraints. Poststructural questioning helps us to work towards such becomings in the midst of seeming stasis.

Of great salience for extricating ourselves from this mire is Grosz's (2010) proj-ect of "[rethinking] concepts like freedom, autonomy, and even subjectivity in ontological, even metaphysical terms" (p. 140). Rather than considering freedom a matter of liberation or emancipation from particular social norms (such as neoliberalism), she develops "a concept of life, bare life, where freedom is con-ceived not only or primarily as the elimination of constraint or coercion but more positively as the condition of, or capacity for, action in life" rather than practices enmeshed in discourses around human rights (p. 140). Drawing on Bergson, she considers free acts as "those which transform us, which we can incorporate into our becomings in the very process of their changing us" (p. 146).

How can they work together and/or apart?

Bronwyn: Here I want to take an example of institutional engagement and poststructuralist theory working together:

In the early 1980s, before any of us knew about neoliberalism, I took my university to the New South Wales Anti-Discrimination Board. The dispute lasted for two years, at the end of which I was awarded a tenured lectureship. During that time I became actively involved in the union, and in negotiations with the university management over a range of policies, including for example, the establishment of sexual harassment policies and child care provision. I changed from being someone who was invisible in meetings, even when my hand was raised to bid for a turn to speak, to someone whose presence in meetings was not only visible, but audible. It was transformative for me to discover the power of collective discourse via the union work, to discover how I could become an entirely different person with agency when I positioned myself within specific legal discourses with reference not just to the Anti-Discrimination Act, but various acts that were mobilized through the union to ensure fair working conditions for workers.

A liberal humanist take on that transformative effect would be that I had become 'one of them' (the men, the managers) by adopting and becoming competent in the mobilization of their discourses.

There is a much more interesting analysis that can come from poststructuralist theory. I had become part of the institutional rhizome and it had transformed me from someone who was invisible and always completely vulnerable to the institutional sexism of that time, into someone who got how the rhizome worked and could use it effectively to bring about change. At the same time, I remember vividly my new sense of myself as researcher setting out to answer the question 'why does gender matter so much?' Having figured how to take on management and to contribute to significant changes to institutionalized practices of sexism, I felt no need to be bound by its preconceptions or by the preconceptions of conservative theory and theorists. I ignored the current developmental and role theories and launched myself with energy and excitement into the research that led to my first poststructuralist book *Frogs and Snails and Feminist Tales: Preschool Children and Gender*.

Deleuze and Guattari's discussion of the wasp and the orchid provides me with a quite different means of understanding the way in which these two quite different rhizomes, the institutional rhizome and the feminist poststructuralist rhizome could affect each other in ways useful to both, both of them playing themselves out on my body in the space-time-mattering of my academic life at that time. In their terms, institutional engagement and competence re-territorialized my body, turning it into an institutionally recognizable being. At the same time, my research – the lines of flight into new ways of thinking about gender de-territorialized my body, a multiple unfolding and refolding. In Deleuze and Guattari's metaphor of the wasp and the orchid, I could be the wasp and the neoliberal university the orchid. They ask:

> How could movements of deterritorialization and processes of reterrito-
> rialization not be relative, always connected, caught up in one another?
> The orchid deterritorializes by forming an image, a tracing of a wasp; but
> the wasp reterritorializes on that image. The wasp is nevertheless deterri-
> torialized, becoming a piece in the orchid's reproductive apparatus. But it
> reterritorializes the orchid by transporting its pollen. Wasp and orchid, as
> heterogeneous elements, for a rhizome. It could be said that the orchid
> imitates the wasp, reproducing its image in a signifying fashion (mimesis,
> mimicry, lure, etc). But this is true only on the level of the strata – a paral-
> lelism between two strata such that a plant organization on one imitates an
> animal organization on the other. At the same time, something else entirely
> is going on: not imitation at all but a capture of code, surplus value of code,
> an increase in valence, a veritable becoming, a becoming-wasp of the orchid
> and a becoming-orchid of the wasp. Each of these becomings brings about
> the deterritorializing of one term and the reterritorialization of the other;
> the two becomings interlink and form relays in a circulation of intensities
> pushing the deterritorialization ever further. There is neither imitation nor
> resemblance, only an exploding of two heterogeneous series on the line
> of flight composed by a common rhizome … an '*aparallel evolution* of two
> beings that have absolutely nothing to do with each other' (Deleuze and
> Guattari 1987, p. 10, emphasis in original)

Neoliberalism and poststructuralism/new materialism are, in Deleuze and Guattari's terms, completely separate rhizomes that have absolutely nothing to do with each other and at the same time they are engaged in territorializing and deterritorializing each other, temporarily forming a common rhizome, provoking and even fertilizing and reproducing each other. Both separate and together, inseparable and yet having nothing to do with each other.

Margaret: For me there is no final answer to this question, only a continual stammering of time, space, body and meaning between parallel worlds. There is the pre-dawn time of writing when time elongates with the coming of the light, there is the vibrant river of a daily walk, alive with life, and there is the body of the researcher always escaping the web that fixes energy within the everyday demands and specters of the neoliberal university. Ultimately the questions seem to be about how to nurture the lines of libidinous energy that lead to creation rather than despair, and how these lines of energy feed into more than just an individual self.

I turn here to a source of inspiration in Lather's (2013) blueprint for post-qualitative research. Over several pages and deep theorizing in her article

'Methodology-21: what do we do in the afterward?', she accumulates a set of propositions:

> Out of mutated dominant practices, through a convergence of practices of intensity and emergence, both practice and objects of a field are redefined and reconfigured … this is our critical project that is not about individual but collective procedure, a very social enterprise where we start where we are (p. 640).

For me the question of how neoliberal universities and new materialist research can work together or apart is linked to the last two elements in this quote. The project of the Anthropocene is a critical project, it is not about individual but collective procedure, it is a very social enterprise where we start where we are. It is a critical project because it is not a choice but a necessity, so whether it works with or apart from a neoliberal university is not really the question for me. It is more relevant to ask how can this work survive and flourish in the context of the neoliberalizing of university work. Where are the sites of possibility for this work to flourish? The question is not about how or where to change a system that is not possible to change but the fact that both within and outside of universities all over the world there is a growing body of people, research and practice that is connected and equally unstoppable. This growing body of research is not about individuals; it necessitates doing things together at all levels; it is a very collective procedure, a very social enterprise. It engages with the questions raised in the Michigan State University website: what sort of society do we want and how can we grow that literally from the ground up? To start where we are returns us to Braidotti's reconceptualized local, the only place we can speak from is where we are grounded, our feet on the ground, breathing the air around us, walking through and in our local places. In starting where I am I write from my everyday world to connect with yours:

> How can I capture the riverlands for you, the smell of wild fennel in sun after rain, tinkle of bellbirds, rise and fall of cicada call, and clip clop of gumboots through wet of last night's dew. Walk to river's edge in familiar dank air of river wetness, and settle against large sandstone rock on casuarina needles, overlooking deep part of river. Light breeze riffles olive green surface of water catching sparkles of sunlight. This place holds this self and this writing.

For me 'starting where we are' requires new forms of writing, writing that does not follow the existing language of universities based in logic and a linear sequence of cause and effect. In this writing that starts where we are, the world is reconceived through a different politics of desire, desiring to do good research, desiring that places and their life forms can thrive, desiring the sensory satisfaction that this everyday walk offers. It is a way of being and knowing that lives both within and outside of university structures supported by the growing tidal wave of researchers world wide that is far greater than the reach of any neoliberal institution.

Lise: And we might well want to keep walking through and beyond our local places, since at present there is great concern about the future of universities around the world. It seems degrees are no longer a predictor of future employment for many young people. The stampede of students away from universities creates even more economic pressure to cut staff and redeploy resources in superficially attractive ways. Yet perhaps, rather than fighting this flow and chancing the undertow, we might look for some new lines of flight out of the traditional institutional spaces.

What will it mean if degrees are no longer the credentials that signal a certain socially classed identity? In future each young adult may put together their own audio-visual-textual portfolio of experiences and skills to show to potential employers. What will it mean for research if higher education institutions are no longer the main players in the commodification of credible knowledge or the organization of viable funding of research? Further to this, how will new collective moves in community-based gathering of information, such as the citizen science studies, affect the divisions between the highly educated and the other? All these moves call out for complex critical analysis using the most creative theoretical tools on offer.

Braidotti (2006) calls for endurance in the ongoing search for *potentia*, a positive aspect of power, all the while realizing that there are limits:

> The nomadic ethico-political project focuses on becomings as a pragmatic philosophy that stresses the need to act, to experiment with different modes of constituting subjectivity and different ways of inhabiting our corporeality. (p. 133)

The task of turning the tide of negativity is an ethical transformative process. It aims at achieving the freedom of understanding, through the awareness of our limits, of our bondage. This results in the freedom to affirm one's essence as joy, through encounters and minglings with other bodies, entities, beings and forces. Ethics means faithfulness to this potentia, or the desire to become (p. 134).

This aligns with Bronwyn's proposal that we stay open to becoming different in ways that will evolve into new and emergent spaces. Such potentia will emerge in unexpected spaces and times, requiring openness to possibilities as well as vigilance. For me, vigilance includes looking at my own experiences over time as an academic in new ways, using more intra-actional analysis to consider how what once seemed possible might instead be viewed as virtual, as actualizable in divergence. Looking back at a virtual palimpsest of my teaching experiences, a potential assemblage emerges that links educational discourses of mastery with indigenous autonomy. This striated dualism eventually imploded in a deterritorializing openness to new directions. The assemblage could start with a formal tiered lecture theatre of the 1980s with its acoustic focus on the speaker at the front, a space where, as a new lecturer, I am interrupted by a Midlands English voice shouting from the back of the room that indigenous views cannot be considered to be theories of development. The sound of this voice in the room reterritorialized the euro-western knowledge I was working to interrupt.

The assemblage could proceed onwards in time to the complex social upheavals and policy changes that emerged a decade later after the 150th anniversary of the Treaty of Waitangi, the founding document signed by indigenous and colonizing peoples of the country. National education norms began to change, opening new spaces for indigenous knowledge in the university curriculum. Changed policies and social expectations had consequences for me as a teacher sitting in my little office in a prefabricated building. An indigenous student arrives at the door with a copy of the paper outline of my postgraduate course in her hand, saying that if the course did not begin with a discussion of the Treaty it was not worth enrolling in. That conversation and others like it changed the content of all I taught subsequently, albeit in a variety of surprising ways. And then, as this assemblage around Indigeneity and mastery fades across time, another space opens, this time in a small room within a large granite-faced building in the capital city where employment court cases are heard. Witnesses are waiting to speak on behalf of a former Dean of Education, a woman who has tackled the university's neoliberal regime by spending nights learning about accounting in order to be able to argue authoritatively with finance about biases in the 'virement' or transfer of funds. The dean, an advocate for Indigenous students and staff, is now being sued by the university for breach of contract, on charges that seem to me fanciful. We sit, side by side in the old fashioned wooden chairs, the former student and myself on the same line of ascent, supporting each other before, as individuals, we are led through the solid wooden door into the courtroom to stand in the witness box, turning our bodies to face the university's prosecution lawyers.

There is so much more of life than is contained in neoliberal discourses. The dualism collapses to show the virtual, the potentia of becoming. The potentia is already becoming but we need more time and space to talk together about how to move differently.

And what is the potentia to which we could be heading? Foucault might laugh and say discourses have never been something to be pinned down by an agentic individual. Barad might agree with Braidotti that there is potentia with each cut of reality, forwards and backwards. The old discursive lines of misogyny, homophobia, postcolonial alienation and neoliberal individualism are still there, whatever the current financial algorithms. We're used to these problems, but now we have some new theoretical tools to revitalize the analysis.

References

Awatere, D. (1984). *Maori sovereignty*. Auckland, New Zealand: Broadsheet.

Barad, K. 2007 *Meeting the universe halfway: Quantum physics and the entanglement of matter and meaning*. Durham, NC: Duke University Press.

Braidotti, Rosi (2006). Posthuman, all too human: Towards a new process ontology. *Theory Culture Society*, *23*, 197–208. DOI: 10.1177/0263276406069232

Braidotti, Rosi and Mura, Andrea (2014). Indebted Citizenship. www.opendemocracy.net/can-europe-make-it/rosi-braidotti-andrea-mura/indebted-citizenship-interview-with-rosi-braidotti

Butler, J. (2011). *Bodies that matter: On the discursive limits of sex*. Taylor & Francis.

Cixous, H. (1993) *Three steps on the ladder to writing* (trans. S. Cornell and S. Sellers). New York: Columbia University Press.

Clough, P. T. (2012). Feminist theory: Bodies, science and technology. In B. Turner (Ed.), *Handbook of the body*. New York: Routledge.

Colebrook, C. (Ed) (2010). *Extinction: Framing the end of the species*. Open Humanities Press.

Davies, B. (2014) *Listening to children. Being and becoming*. London: Routledge.

Davies, B. (Guest Ed.) (2004). Special Issue on poststructuralist theory in Australia. *International Journal of Qualitative Studies in Education*, *17*(1), 1–116.

Davies, B., & Harré, R. (1990). Positioning: The discursive production of selves. *Journal for the Theory of Social Behaviour*, *20*(1), 43–63.

Deleuze, G. (1980) 'Cours Vincennes 12/21/1980,' Available at: www.webdeleuze.com/php/texte.php?cle=190andgroupe=Spinoza andlangue=2) (accessed 10 February 2010).

Deleuze, G., & Guattari, F. (1987) *A thousand plateaus. Capitalism and schizophrenia*. (trans. B. Massumi) Minneapolis: University of Minnesota Press

Dolphijn, R., & Tuin, I. van der. (2012). *New materialism interviews & cartographies*. Ann Arbor, MI: Open Humanities Press.

Fritsch, K. (2015). Desiring disability differently: neoliberalism, heterotopic imagination and intracorporeal reconfigurations. *Foucault Studies*, *19*, 43–66.

Gordon, C. (2000). Introduction. In J. D. Faubion (Ed.), *Michel Foucault: Power* (pp. xi–xli). New York, New Press.

Grosz, E. (1994). *Volatile bodies: towards a corporeal feminism*. Sydney: Allen & Unwin.

Grosz, E. (2010). Feminism, materialism, and freedom. In D. Coole & S. Frost (Eds), *New materialisms: Ontology, agency, and politics* (pp. 139–157). Durham, NC: Duke University Press.

Larner, W. (1996). The "new boys": Restructuring in New Zealand, 1984–94. *Social Politics: International Studies in Gender, State & Society*, *3*(1), 32–5691.

Lather, P. (2013). Methodology-21: What do we do in the afterward? *International Journal of Qualitative Studies in Education*, *26*(6), 634–645.

Monbiot, G. (2016a). *How did we get into this mess? Politics, equality, nature*. London: Verso.

Monbiot, G. (2016b, 15 April). Neoliberalism: The ideology at the root of all our problems. *The Guardian*. Retrieved from www.theguardian.com/books/2016/apr/15/neoliberalism-ideology-problem-george-monbiot

Sklar, H. (Ed.) (1980). Trilateralism: The Trilateral Commission and elite planning for world management. Boston, MA: South End Press.

Somerville, M. (2013). *Water in a dry land: Place-learning through art and story*. London and New York: Routledge.

Williams, M. (2012) *Aspects of ethics on four plays by Hélène Cixous*. Unpublished masters thesis: University of Nottingham.

7

LEAKY PRIVATES

Resisting the neoliberal public university and mobilizing movements for public scholarship

Michelle Fine

In 1991, I began my counter-commute against the current of academic prestige: after twelve years at the University of Pennsylvania, I resigned a chaired position in this very private Ivy League to assume a faculty line in Psychology at the Graduate Center CUNY, a very public university. Friends and colleagues had serious "reservations" about my self-inflicted fall from grace, but CUNY was the site of historic struggle, where desires for public education were still seductive, in play, if contested.

The public university, and CUNY in particular, has long embodied the quintessential publicly contested space; the messy and degraded nexus where market logic, public struggle, intellectual and political chutzpa, democracy, settler colonialism, White supremacy, liberatory fantasies and Kroll security meet. In the 1930s, faculty and students at City College protesting fascism and capitalism received subpoenas; over 60 City College faculty were eventually fired (Chatterjee, P. and Maira, S. 2014). In 1940, the Rapp-Coudert Committee was created to track what were then called "subversive activities" and communist influence at public colleges throughout New York State.

Historically and today, public universities have thin membranes; are highly porous to State surveillance and corporate influence, and are intellectual and political carnivals of structural violence and radical possibility. This promiscuous mosaic has long been under assault, from within and outside.

In 1969, Audre Lorde, Toni Cade Bambara, June Jordan and Adrienne Rich were teaching at CUNY in the SEEK program, a space to support struggling students. In her notes on pedagogy, Rich sketched the sinewy contradictions of the public university classroom (Adrienne Rich, 1969, as cited in Savonick, D. [forthcoming]):

> *What we are part of – Adrienne Rich, 1969, teaching in SEEK, CUNY*
>
> *Classroom as cell—unit—enclosed & enclosing space in which teacher & students are*
> *   alone together*
> *   Can be prison cell   commune*
> *   trap   junction - place of coming-together*
> *   torture chamber*
>
> (Rich, "Interdisciplinary Program" 15).

Alexis Pauline Gumbs writes on June Jordan and Audre Lorde's CUNY class-rooms as "spaces designed in service of the colonial project to protest that same project, with varying levels of success" (2014, 242; Savonik, forthcoming). These contradictions are at the heart of Public.

Always a stew of contradictions and complicity, today the public university is being starved, Whitened, adjunctified in labor and intellectually surveilled and colonized, again, by/for corporate interests enacted by/through the State. If Sheila Slaughter and Gary Rhoades (2004) theorize "academic capitalism" in the United States, Boaventura De Sousa Santos (2010) argues that the academy, globally, is in crisis with respect to intellectual autonomy and academic freedom. Within the specific and precious space of the public university – dedicated at CUNY to educate "all of the children of the people of the city" – we see how neoliberal ideology, austerity practices and privatization have lodged themselves within, deepening the race/class stratification of the public university; accelerating the disinvestment in and degradation of human and intellectual culture of the public academy and fortifying our dependence on private resources and market forces.

And yet the embers of student/faculty/staff/labor protests, "repertoires of contestation" (Delgado & Ross, 2016) and radical public scholarship are ablaze globally and within the U.S., camping out on the main green landscapes of public universities, occupying presidents' offices, circulating on social media, tucked away as the radically provocative enactments of "civic engagement," popularized through digital scholarship, within and beyond what Robin Kelly might call "fugitive spaces" (2016).

These are, then, deeply contradictory and precarious times for the public university. Our financial bellies hungry, we are vulnerable to corporate seductions – predatory piercings of our integrity and our administrators will only rarely say no. And yet students and faculty are prepared to fight for the soul of the public institution, even as each of our radical interventions runs the risk of appropriation and commodification (see Daniels & Thistelwaithe on digital scholarship, and Hall, Clover, Crowther, & Scandrett, 2012, and Torre, Manoff, Stoudt, & Fine, 2016 on community based participatory research).

To begin this essay on the (ef)facing of public, and the fragile platforms for resuscitating/radicalizing the rhythms, commitments and solidarities with the public university, I open with an intimate autoethnographic moment when the walls of academic freedom surrendered too easily after corporate education reformers knocked on CUNY's doors to gather my personal emails.

* * *

Mid-November 2014, I left the YMCA after a great swim in Montclair, New Jersey, got into my car, checked my messages, and saw an email from a lawyer at CUNY.

> "When can we talk? We have received a FOIA request for your emails. See attached."
> My stomach dropped as I scrolled down.
> In some ways I had been waiting for this.

For the past year and a half I had been deeply embroiled in a multi-racial parent-union-educator movement in Montclair, New Jersey, a town long known for progressive education politics, almost 40 years of aspirational/not-yet-equitable desegregation and teacher driven educational creativity. We are – or were – the number one community for "integrated" families; we delight in the numbers of "queer" families in town. Montclair is also home to some of the major corporate education reformers –the names and financial backing behind high stakes testing, privatization, charters, teacher evaluation, data-driven decision making, contracting out. In 2012 a corporate dominated board hired a superintendent, without public input (unusual in our town), whom we learned was an Eli Broad Foundation trained superintendent and all hell broke loose, as has been the case in other communities (see "How to tell if your town has been infected by the Broad virus", Parents Across America, April 2011). Soon a number of under-qualified and overpaid "chiefs" were hired, straight out of the Broad/Gates/Walmart playbook and realigned the budget so that monies left the classroom into the pockets of consultants, technology firms, testing companies, and lawyers.

For two years, at first a trickle and then a growing, multiracial movement of parents, educators and labor activists took the mic at the board meetings: asking questions, hard questions, the kind considered "uncivil" to speak aloud in a suburban community known to be progressive and elite, even though half of the African American students in our strategically desegregated schools live below the poverty line. Questions like, "Are these new 'Chiefs' certified? Why are they being paid $150,000? Why are the legal and consultant budget allocations swelling while you are cutting and privatizing paraprofessionals who work with our most struggling students? Why is all professional development focused on test prep?"

We were piercing the edges of civility.

Over the first 18 months of the newly hired superintendent, the schools were pummeled with a number of "disruptive corporate innovations" – the imposition of quarterly assessments on schools distinct for their magnet themes; a contagious chill of intimidation winding through the schools; online attacks designed to discredit the African American woman president of the teachers union; attempts to recover the IP addresses of critical anonymous bloggers and an active subpoena hanging over the head of the one Black male board member, and a "conflict of interest" charge against the African American town councilor who sat on Board of School Estimate because he is a union official. There are courses on "disruptive innovation" taught in every Ivy League School of Business in the country.

At Board meetings, the public space for debate, the mic grew hot. The teachers union was no longer invited to open each meeting with an update, as they had been for years. They were now restricted to 3 minutes like the rest of us. School board sessions were highly contentious, as we learned was typical of districts "infected with the Eli Broad virus."

MCAS – Montclair Cares about Schools – evolved, as did the Montclair 250 – a group of teachers in the district who are also parents. Both groups were outraged at the depth and velocity of corporate penetration of what had been a relatively progressive, integrated district with great respect for teacher autonomy. MCAS developed a rich and provocative website to bring the reform opposition movement into our sleepy, relatively self satisfied, "progressive" suburb. We were accused, early on and throughout, of being a "union front," and I of being a "union operative."

In May 2012, we heard that the board was about to approve an invoice for thousands of dollars to have our public school teachers professionally "developed" by the teachers from a corporate charter school in Newark. The husband of a board member had political, if not financial, interests in this school. While the school's oft-repeated college going data were "impressive" their persistence/graduation rates, especially for Black boys, were dismal. As Black boys were pushed out/dropped out, the school selectively "back filled" with those likely to be successful. Eventually the graduation class was filled with college going seniors. I approached the mic:

> I see an invoice suggesting we are sending teachers from our public schools to X charter in Newark. Recently I calculated the 6th–12th grade persistence rates for Black boys, which is approximately 28%. In contrast the persistence rate for Montclair public schools is more like 92%. Yes they send most of their seniors off to college, but what percent of those seniors were at the school since 6th grade? From the available data it seems that most Black male students leave prior to graduation. Perhaps the teachers at X charter should come to Montclair public schools for professional development.

I handed the seven board members the relevant data.

As I returned to my seat, the husband of the president of the board, quite active in his local synagogue, turned to me angrily: "Why didn't you just call us (wife and husband) at home to discuss the issues about the superintendent, or how we are spending money? Why raise them in public?" I answered that I didn't believe these were quiet conversations for elite Jews to have in private, but public conversations for broad based, cross-class, race and zip-code deliberation. I should have known: this was not going well.

This was one of many cues that civility for elites insists on privacy. We learned quickly that as much corporate reformers seek to privatize the finances and labor of education, they also seek to privatize the politics – and hold conversations only behind closed doors, using pseudonyms on blogs, distributing monies to buy off defunded community based "allies" and launching Freedom of Information Law (FOIL)[1] requests anonymously. In the dialectics of public and private, the more they tried to privatize democracy with back door deals and secret meetings, the more "uncivil" the parents and teachers appeared to be.

A few months later, a very wealthy, well-known (as a "character") community member who had been working with the Superintendent on her public relations approached me, after a Board meeting, introducing himself as the "campaign manager for Cory Booker, Hilary Clinton." He wanted to have coffee, because he was doing some work for the superintendent. We talked much, searching for common ground. He tried to get me, and our MCAS members, to stop speaking in public and meet with her one on one. We did. As you can imagine it was a disaster. One evening after I spoke, questioning some district data that pointed to the miraculous closing of the achievement gap because of all the testing (they removed the Black special education students from the calculations, and – miracle – the gap closes), he approached me at the back of the auditorium, "You are a liar." I was standing next to a friend; the president of the NAACP was as surprised as I. "I am rich as fuck and I will ruin you." So much for civility.

Within weeks (remember, we are a small town), two activist parents overhead a "short, white man" in Dunkin Donuts talking on the phone, instructing someone to "start to collect opposition files on the union leaders and the parents." Doing a bit of our own reconnaissance, we learned this man was on the Board of a major NYC charter network a local leader in the very small Montclair Republican party.

At about the same time, the Montclair Schools Watch appeared; an online blog that ran anonymous clips of the union president's 1989 tax records, assaults on critical education scholar Ira Shor (who also lives in Montclair and was involved with MCAS) and a White parent who worked for an education labor union, accusations that two African American women who spoke up at the Achievement Gap meeting were "Michelle Fine's lieutenants." Classic corporate smear tactics – opposition files gone viral.

And then in November 2014, *my emails were FOILED by someone using the pseudonym Mark Smith.*

Indeed, I was the White woman, at the public university, who was the portal to the emails of 28 (and then 38) activist parents, courageous educators who refused to be intimidated, a series of Black activists and political figures. And, I think, a race-traitor in the eyes of my corporate [White, investment banking/hedge fund] neighbors.

Montclair is a progressive, racially integrated community – with desegregated schools that are not-quite-as-good-as-we-wish, still-fraught-with-enormous-gaps – that tries to do what most of the country has walked away from. We are also what popular blogger Jersey Jazzman/Ph.D. candidate Mark Weber calls "Reformyville" – dedicated to high-stakes testing and major investments in technology; hostile to teachers' unions, pensions, and health care; hungry to privatize paraprofessionals and standardize curriculum; and wealthy, White, and dedicated to "anonymous" strategies for "reform."

The anonymous FOIL request specified that CUNY turn over "all emails to and from Michelle Fine", over a two year period, from a list of what I call the *FOIA 28*: three Black elected politicians in town who have probed, responsibly and publicly, the finances and governance of the district; five journalists who have written about educational politics in town; eight activist parents; the president of the Montclair Education Association and other trade unionists; a few bloggers (including AssessmentGate, who had the subpoena issued last year – s/he was cleared by the intervention of the NJ-ACLU) and the superintendent, some of her Chiefs, the communications assistant and members of the Board of Education.

I went public with the FOIL request immediately, contacting the FOIA 28, presenting at the School Board and expressing regret for getting them "entangled" in this collective witch hunt, nodding to the ghosts of McCarthy. AssessmentGate wrote to the CUNY lawyer that s/he considered this an extension of the earlier subpoena; the parents from Montclair were outraged that their personal emails to me were subject to a FOIL request; the journalists were surprised that they were not immune.

The CUNY lawyer asked "Mark Smith" of SOSCAMDEN.ORG – all fictitious – for a name and address so she could send the requested documents, at an expense of 25 cents/page. "Mark" responded:

> The request I made of the University has been *publicly showcased* by a representative of the University [*that would be me*]. While my request is legal, the actions taken but [sic] your University representative has [sic] been disruptive and intimidating. Based on the specific actions witnessed by Dr. Fine, I do not feel safe … Dr. Fine decided to make this a *public event*…. It was never my intent for *this private request to become a public matter.*

The perverse twisting of public/private deserves a moment of analysis to unpack the weird inversions of corporate logic: what's public and what's private;

who is vulnerable and who is innocent. I made a private matter public; he feels unsafe and violated. Corporate reformers seem to believe that all matters – financial, political, and educational should be private; even public schools, democracy, and governance.

Without putting up much resistance at all, CUNY moved forward on the FOIL request; they gathered and prepared to send over 1100 emails to and from me to the lawyer, whom the corporate group hired.

I contacted friends at the New York Civil Liberties Union, who were surprised that CUNY was complying with the request and sent a lengthy memo to the CUNY Counsel, specifying why CUNY should not simply comply with the full request. CUNY rejected the advice.

The evening before CUNY was set to send the 1100 emails (the list had now been expanded from 28 to 38 persons), I emailed the CUNY Chancellor, Graduate Center president and the president of the Professional Staff Congress. I briefly tried to argue that:

> *Two years ago I worked with then-President Kelly and Provost Robinson on a large Ford Foundation grant for moving public scholarship into the public square. Indeed I left my Chaired position at the University of Pennsylvania to be at a public university that took seriously our roles as public intellectuals. I recognize the Internet has complicated the work; I recognize that parents and teachers from around the country email me at the GC because that is my public email; I realize that perhaps I should always rely on GMAIL for public scholarship - but the soul of CUNY lies in our obligation and intellectual debt to move from the ivory tower into local school board meetings, town councils and bring our craft into public issues of urgency.*
>
> *This FOIL request is simply harassment – increasingly a strategy by the Right and corporations directed at public university faculty. This is of course ironic that those who seek to privatize public education are relying upon a public interest law to undermine the public scholarship of public intellectuals. No one said they aren't clever.*
>
> *In Montclair as a parent, I have been vocal about statistical errors in the town's achievement data; a large group of parents and educators have raised questions in public about privatizing paraprofessionals and where the budget has gone, and why so much is being spent on technology – hence the "key search words." The FOIL against me is an attempt to chill the dissent in town.*
>
> *I ask that you respect the parents/educators who have corresponded with me, and my rights to speak. Again I agree that many of the documents should be forwarded - but this process is a bit of a witch hunt, and I am uncomfortable facilitating the hunt.*
>
> *I appreciate your time, appreciate the goodwill of the lawyers, and hope we can come to an agreement within the university about how to defend institutional transparency, the public's right to know, academic freedom, and our right/obligation to be scholars in the public square.*

CUNY's chief counsel conveyed to the president of the Graduate Center that because "Michelle Fine used State machinery" to circulate "political" messages, CUNY had to comply with the FOIL. I tried to explain these exchanges reflected the very public scholarship they were "branding" as distinct to the GC; the questions posed and debates engaged grew from my research and scholarly expertise; this was why I came to CUNY; this was the grey zone of public intellectual project. I also indicated that if I had known that CUNY would enact a narrow, technical, corporate response I could have stayed at Penn – a real corporate entity – which would have treated me "as if" they owned me, like a "good" corporation, and protected my interests.

Of course, Penn couldn't be FOILED.

CUNY administrators insisted that as a public university they were obligated to respond in full to the request. I wrote to the chancellor that I understood their position, disagreed and would write no more to them about the matter. The president of PSC (our union), Barbara Bowen, was outstanding and insisted we all meet.

Management never responded.

Within a week, CUNY sent all of the requested emails to an anonymous corporate reform group Montclair Kids First, through their lawyers; they have posted all of them, including my correspondence with private citizens, parents, students, activists, educators, lightly redacted with cheap Magic Markers, CUNY style; anyone can read through (feel free – mostly boring, no conspiracy, some profanity).

The following week, I attended an unrelated session of civil rights activists considering a race-based class action suit against CUNY, contesting the declining admission rates of Black and Latino freshmen into the most competitive four-year colleges. In 2008, on the wave of the foreclosure bubble and financial crisis for middle and working class families, CUNY raised the requisite SAT score to 500 on language arts and quantitative at a number of the flagship four year colleges. As a result, more White, wealthy, and higher-scoring freshmen were admitted to the four year flagship institutions, with larger ratios of Black and Latino NYC high school graduates re-directed to the community colleges for inadequate SAT scores. After a strategic discussion by lawyers and activists, someone from the NAACP LDF mentioned, with a sense of exasperation: "You know, we have FOILED the information from CUNY about the racial profile of their incoming students at community colleges and four-year colleges, but they delay, claim it's a violation of privacy, and deny us the information."

I drafted another email to the chancellor, the university lawyer, and the Graduate Center president, asking them why they comply with FOIL requests when my reputation is swinging in the breeze, and yet refuse FOIL requests when their institutional integrity is vulnerable.

Two years later, I await a response.

Following the online posting of my emails, newspaper articles appeared in the *Montclair Times*, scouring my emails, a new attack video was distributed on YouTube, splicing misquotes from the emails, with decontextualized clips of public comments over the past two years as ominous music and subtitles warn that MCAS is violating the town, that Michelle Fine is a Divider, Destroyer and Hater. Within a few weeks, an international petition, initiated by friends and colleagues, circled the globe, accumulating more than 3,000 signatures gathered in my "defense." The photo they used in the YouTube was copyrighted by Feminist Voices in Psychology, and was eventually removed.

In reality, I was not wounded; was unbelievably touched by the community of support; and somewhat taken aback at the lengths corporate reformers would go to silence criticism. *But the behavior of the public university administrators was most shocking.* They didn't have to do what they didn't have to do; it was a small gift to their corporate predators; just enough evidence that they are willing to play "bottom" in the *dialectic S/M of academic philanthrocapitalism* and complicity with *corporate interests.*

In a short time I have learned much and spoken to many – about ALEC's (American legislative exchange council) commitment to exploiting FOIA for public university faculty as the "portal" to silence, expose and gather intelligence on progressive critics; about the vulnerability of those of us who teach at public universities and believe naively that we have academic freedom on our institutional accounts *or* other email/text accounts that are linked to our university accounts; about the importance and rarity of courageous administrators who stand by faculty despite the corporate challenge, but mostly about how widespread is the fully funded, prefer-to-be-anonymous strategic attempts to silence those in public universities who dare to question the corporate agenda.

People who seek to privatize public education are exploiting a significant public interest legal tool (FOIA is our law!) against public university faculty who position ourselves as public intellectuals to induce a sense of surveillance, silencing and chill. As a teacher at a board meeting explained, "Some hide behind sheets; others behind anonymous blogs, Super PACS and money. But we are not fooled."

* * *

But enough about me. I want to pause to think aloud about "what is left" of the construct Public as it has morphed, been contaminated and/but was always rooted in settler colonial soil as a mosaic of contradictions?

This is a moment when the public assemblage is being dismantled and recalibrated; when the construct of "public" needs to be assessed.

Those of us working in public institutions bear witness and are complicit, even as we may resist, the reconstitution of public. We struggle for social justice within the colonial project of the University, at precisely the nexus where, drawing on Melanie Klein and Pierre Bourdieu, the good state and the bad state meet. The state is neither hollowing nor disinvesting wholesale; it is realigning with the interests of global capital, elite Whiteness and logics of privatization and the project of racialized securitization. Pierre Bourdieu (1992) reminds us that the state always had a left and right hemisphere; the former comforts some while the latter controls and contains Others. The public university is a petri dish where these dynamics are at play. And as Adrienne Rich noted, the public university unfolds as the commons and encloses as a torture chamber.

And yet when "public" danced off the tongue of Hannah Arendt (1958), she conjured *la vita activa*, a life of engagement, dialogue, dissent, participation. For Arendt, Public constitutes a space of engaged and contentious deliberation.

Today, and again, we are in the tumultuous spin of oscillating constructions, constrictions and expansions of Public. As Gramsci argued in the *Prison Notebooks*, "The **crisis** consists precisely in the fact that the **old** is dying and the **new cannot be born**; in this interregnum a great variety of morbid symptoms appear" (p. 275). The morbid symptoms flash off my smart phone.

In the name of *public* safety, police routinely hunt and kill Black men and are almost never held accountable; mayors close black schools; the U.S. government sends drones, deports immigrants and feeds the beast of mass incarceration in the perverse name of human security. In the U.S., as in the UK and dripping across the globe, in the name of public accountability, we generate metric madness for K–12 and now higher education, undermining the sanity, humanity, integrity, accessibility, and sustainability of public institutions once dedicated to the collective good. In the darkest communities, public translates to police with drawn guns in unlit stairwells, crappy schools with metal detectors and military recruiters.

The word is promiscuous and the affects are racialized/classed. Public has been colonized, invaded and penetrated so to speak by corporate interests and the jaws of securitization. Historian Robin Kelley has vividly detailed how the very same public spaces/buses have signaled freedom and mobility for Whites, and surveillance, capture, vulnerability for Blacks. Public has perhaps always been the body through which capitalism and empire traveled, and my White privilege has kept me from seeing.

Always classed and raced, U.S. public institutions have, of recent, endured a doubled loss: material loss in the form of radical disinvestment/austerity, and ideological saturation of public institutions by leaky private interests – sometimes even with good intent. (You may recall that in New York City, actress/singer Bette Midler had to buy a series of city parks to keep them public.)

The notion of "public" has become a hologram, clever, deceptive, and imaginary; contaminated, complicit, a borderland. With no accountability, we must ask:

- *Was the lead poisoning of children in Flint, Michigan, contaminated by corporate dumping and ignored by the state, a public act?*
- *Are the publicly funded school vouchers in Milwaukee, provided to parents of children who attend Catholic schools, public?*
- *Are the religious cyber charters in Pennsylvania, managed by private education management organizations, public?* (In the 2003–04 school year, 6,832 students were enrolled in state cyber charter schools. Today, nearly 37,000 kids are enrolled, according to a Pennsylvania Department of Education spokesman, STATESCOOP, 2-2-15).

- *In 1960, state support accounted for 78% of the University of Michigan general fund; in 2015, state support accounted for 16%, with tuition and fees paying for 71% of the general fund. Is the University of Michigan still a public institution?*

Below I consider how we might slow down the curdling process of disruptive innovation and privatization in higher education; to take in the landscape, strategies and consequences of privatization and confront the existential question – (how/with whom/under what political and ethical conditions) can we resist from within but also reimagine Public, when public institutions are so fully contaminated by the voracious and punishing logics of capital, greed, White supremacy and anti-labor commitments? And borrowing from Leigh Patel, to whom are we, as public university faculty/staff/students, answerable?

Market creep

The radical edges of the Public University, at moments bold if always controversial, have begun to fray. The defining adjective "public" has come to be a lite metaphor, a wink, as levels of state support decline, open access to racial/economic diversity shrinks, academic freedom is patrolled and the right to protest/challenge/research/teach counter-hegemonic topics is under attack from within and without.

My colleagues Mike Fabricant and Steve Brier write, in their new book *Austerity Blues*:

> We fear for the future of public higher education, both nationally and close to home at the City University of New York (CUNY). Year after year, we witness the steady withdrawal of state funds and, in turn, restricted access for "the children of the whole people" (CUNY's original mission, as stated in the mid-nineteenth century) to a quality public higher education. Conversely, we have seen tuition at CUNY increase by 25 percent at the same time that about $500 million of public money has been withdrawn. Over the past forty years at CUNY, the ratio of tuition paid by full-time students to public funding has shifted from zero to about 50 percent for students, many of whose annual family incomes are below $30,000. Within that same time frame the proportion of classes taught by full-time faculty has diminished from almost 100 percent to less than 50 percent. We also see the continuing disappearance of young males of color, especially African Americans, in undergraduate education, with black women outnumbering black men in CUNY's community and senior colleges by a ratio of 2 to 1. These are not merely local but rather national trends.

And yet and still as these three faces of "public," efface – state support, broad racial/class access and unfettered academic freedom to write, teach and protest – the wild expansion of critical public scholarship and activism explodes from within, and beyond, the walls of the public university.

The changing face of the public university

As if shoplifting from the littered landscape of the neoliberal public university, below I review varied dynamics through which the construct "public" is undergoing dramatic reconstruction within higher education. I won't spend enough time talking about proprietary institutions, Massive Open Online Courses (MOOCs), the adjunctification of labor, student debt – and for that I apologize. The review is neither comprehensive nor deep but is intended to be provocative, making legible the multiple fronts upon which privatization seeps through public academic membranes seriously compromising the race/class project, the intellectual project, labor relations and the ethical answerability (Patel, 2015) of the public university to the public good.

To begin: in terms of state support, public universities have suffered substantially in the past decade, with far more of general fund dependent on rising tuition, transferring the cost of public education to private students, and therefore rising student debt. Second, in terms of broad public access, we witness flagship public universities altering admission policies by jacking up SAT scores and cutting financial aid (even as over 800 elite private universities are now SAT-optional) with the effect that fewer students of color and students of poverty are gaining admission to flagship institutions. Third, the curricula, values and areas of research pursued within public higher education are undergoing strategic transformation via both the soft side of philanthrocapitalism and the harsh forms of corporate assault on academic scholarship critical of dominant political and/or financial interests (e.g., research that critically investigates fracking, climate change, corporate education reform, scholars engaged in anti-Zionist/pro-Palestinian scholarship or activism, researchers investigating Republican and/or Tea Party tactics, e.g., the American Legislative Exchange Council). Fourth, higher education institutions are increasingly militarized, with police and cyber-security firms incorporated into the general fund budget (note the contentious hiring of Kroll Security at both University of California-Davis, and CUNY). And yet fifth, provocative public scholarship and activist coalitions – via digital scholarship and activism, blogs, participatory research with communities, public journalism, deep research–based coalitions have been sutured with local and global social movements – have been mobilized by/on/with public universities across the nation.

Public funding

Thomas Mortenson (Winter 2012) of the American Council on Education estimates that: "Based on the trends since 1980, average state fiscal support for higher education will reach zero by 2059, although it could happen much sooner in some states and later in others. Public higher education is gradually being privatized."

Fabricant and Brier concur (2016): "The universities of Minnesota, Illinois, and Washington, and Ohio State University, for example, presently receive less than 10 percent of their total operating budgets from tax levy or public dollars. The rest of their budgets must be raised largely through tuition; private fundraising; income derived from copyrights, patents, and "tech transfer" fees; and grants" (p. 92).

While almost all states are trending downward in terms of tax levy support for higher education, they vary in speed and depth of their retreat from higher education. While Wyoming (up 2.3 percent) and North Dakota (up 0.8 percent) have managed to maintain their fiscal 1980 investment through 2011, all other states have reduced their support from 14.8 percent to 69.4 percent. A few examples:

- Colorado has reduced its support for higher education by nearly 69.4 percent, from $10.52 in fiscal 1980 (and a peak of $13.85 in fiscal 1971) to $3.22 by fiscal 2011. Colorado state appropriations are expected to hit zero in 2022.
- Minnesota has reduced its higher education investment by 55.8 percent, from $14.17 in fiscal 1980 (and a peak of $15.08 in fiscal 1978) to $6.27 by fiscal 2011. State funding for higher education could reach zero in 2037.
- Virginia reduced higher education funding by 53.6 percent from 10.47 in 1980 (and $11.37 in FY1979) to $4.86 in 2011. State funding could reach zero in 2038. Loss of state support provokes a rise in tuition and spikes in student debt.

With the loss of state support, public institutions raise tuition rates, and creatively invent fees, provoking a spike in student debt. In December 2014, the U.S. Government Accountability Office calculated that from 2003 to 2012, state funding for all public college decreased by 12 percent and median tuition rose 55 percent. According to their analysis, 2012 marked the first time in recent history when a greater percentage of public college revenue derived from student tuition than all state sources combined. The state disinvestment in public higher education parallels a rise in the growth and reach of the for-profit sector of higher education. While enrollment for all public colleges increased by approximately 20 percent from 2002 to 2011, the for-profit college sector swelled from 817,156 enrollment in 2002–2003 to 2,047,844 in 2011–2012, a rise of 250 percent. A 2016 analysis published by the National Bureau of Economic Research finds that on average associate's and bachelor's degree students experience a *decline in earnings after attendance at for profit institutions*, relative to their own earnings in years prior to attendance" and a *significant rise in student debt* (www.nber.org).

These students – disproportionately low income, African American or Latino and female – are also saddled with relatively high loan defaults, as demonstrated by Adam Looney of the U.S. Treasury Department and Constantine Yannelis of Stanford University (2015):

> drawing on a unique set of administrative data on federal student borrowing, matched to earnings records from de-identified tax records, [m]ost

of the increase in default is associated with the rise in the number of borrowers at for-profit schools and, to a lesser extent, 2-year institutions and certain other non-selective institutions, whose students historically composed only a small share of borrowers. These non-traditional borrowers were drawn from lower income families, attended institutions with relatively weak educational outcomes, and experienced poor labor market outcomes after leaving school. In contrast, default rates among borrowers attending most 4-year public and non-profit private institutions and graduate borrowers—borrowers who represent the vast majority of the federal loan portfolio—have remained low, despite the severe recession and their relatively high loan balances. Their higher earnings, low rates of unemployment, and greater family resources appear to have enabled them to avoid adverse loan outcomes even during times of hardship. (www.BPEA.org, July 5 1026)

Cuts in public sector spending on higher education create the grounds for the expansion of the for-profit sector, sucking the monies and dreams of desperate low income students hungry to be educated and credentialed, carving open spaces for predatory lending and the branding of desire.

Access: The whitening of flagship public institutes

According to a report by Hechinger Institute, only 5 percent of students at flagship public universities are Black, a smaller percentage than was true a decade ago (Kolodner, 2015). Note the wide variation between percent Black freshmen in flagship public institutions and percent Black high school graduates at, for instance, Universities of Virginia (5 percent vs. 22 percent), Delaware (5 percent vs. 30 percent) and Georgia, (7 percent vs. 34 percent). In 2010, The Education Trust found that "America's most prestigious public universities are decreasing representation of low income students and spending more institutional aid on students from wealthier families." Reducing aid and spiking SAT admissions cut scores are two strategies that have effectively diminished enrollment of students of color. At CUNY, my own university, SAT cut scores were raised at the moment of the fiscal crisis, at the top senior colleges for incoming freshmen such that thousands of Black and Latino graduates from NYC schools who would have previously been accepted to Hunter, Brooklyn, City or Queens were being demoted to the community colleges for admission. Drawing from Fabricant and Brier again, consider the following:

> The difficulties poor students face in successfully completing college are not entirely explained by academic challenges. The *New York Times* and other media have, for example, reported that the crushing pressures of accumulating debt and the growing need to work while attending college

have disproportionately affected poor and working-class students, stalling and "dead-ending" movement toward degree completion by even the most gifted students. These economic stresses, when combined with academic challenges, have produced a seismic shift in the proportion of poor students earning college degrees. Martha Baily and Susan Dynarski, economists at the University of Michigan, have reported that "thirty years ago there was a 31% difference between the share of prosperous and poor Americans who earned bachelor's degrees ... Now the gap is 45%" (DeParle, 2012, p. A-1). Greg Duncan, an economist at the University of California, Irvine, notes that "on virtually every measure we have the gaps between high- and low-income kids ... widening" (p. A-1). These data also contain a critical subtext. As the gap in academic achievement between poor and affluent students grows by race and class, it is accompanied by ever-widening income and gender disparities, especially of young males of color. For example, black women undergraduate students at CUNY's senior and community colleges, according to a 2005 Inside Higher Education report, "outnumbered [black] men 2 to 1 (a ratio that is quite common nationwide)" (p. 113).

The moves of slow privatization affect not only who attends public universities, but who teaches and under what labor conditions.

Faculty: Adjunctification of higher education – particularly for the poor

Don Edmonds writes in *Forbes* magazine, "More than half of college faculty are adjuncts: should you care?" (2015), noting that more than 75 percent of American professors are contingent faculty. While 31 percent of faculty were part-time in 1970, by 2011, that figure rose to 51 percent part time, 19 percent non-tenure track full time – constituting almost 75 percent who are NTTF (non-tenure track faculty, full or part time). These faculty are of course less experienced, less secure, less available and less reliable over time for students; they reflect an underpaid and exploited contingent labor force. Many/most are fantastically dedicated mentors and teachers, but the conditions of their labor make it impossible for them, and their students.

The impact of a largely adjunct faculty on students is now well documented. The Delphi Project reports that students who work with contingent faculty are less likely to graduate and less likely to transfer from a 2- to a 4-year institution than their peers. From 2000 to 2012, while public research universities full-time faculty ranks remained flat, part-time faculty/instructors/grad assistants rose by 12 percent. At public community colleges, full time faculty dropped by 8% and part time faculty dropped by 7 percent. At private research universities, full-time faculty rose by 16 percent and part-time by 21 percent (Desroches and Kirshstein, 2014). Hunter College at CUNY is listed as having 34 percent full-time teachers.

Curriculum: Philanthrocapitalism, academic containment, and corporate bullying of the public university

Market creep affects not only who attends and who teaches, but the values and logics that permeate the curriculum, university response to dissent/protest, and how much corporate interests penetrate the foundational values of the institution. For purposes of discussion I will distinguish the passive/aggressive dynamics of *philanthrocapitalism*, which may be viewed as a "generosity project" and *corporate assaults* on, challenges to and ethical charges posed against progressive scholars who contest corporate-bought science.

Philanthrocapitalism/The generosity project: With a flat lining of full-time faculty and spikes in contingent labor, it is perhaps no surprise that the labor-walls, and knowledge-walls of public universities are increasingly porous to monied interests. This turn takes a variety of forms: a rise in philanthrocapitalism (Rogers, 2013) which attaches to what is called "catalytic giving" – the pernicious influence of elite "givers" to determine who teaches, what is taught, what values and ideologies are featured for instance in Economics or Middle Eastern Studies Departments (Cassidy, 2015). *Chronicle of Philanthropy* reports (1/27/16) that U.S. colleges raise $40 billion in philanthropy, with Stanford leading the pack with 1.6 billion. Almost 30 percent of the philanthropy went to six colleges – 7.6 percent above last year. Of the top 20 receiving institutions, five are public – four in the UC system – USC, UCSF, UCLA, UC Berkley, and Michigan.

The country is littered with stories of universities receiving grants, contracts, and gifts that overreach: influencing who will, and will not, be hired, and what will and will not be taught. A 2012 story from Florida State University has all the imprint of Koch money and curriculum colonization: "The Koch Foundation has been quietly influencing universities across the country for years; its own list of funded programs for 2011 includes 187 colleges and universities."

There is much that can be learned from events as they have developed in Tallahassee. The foundation proposed a donation of nearly $6.6 million, with a $1.5 million initial grant to hire staff and fund fellowships and new undergraduate programs. An agreement was reached, and the program got off the ground without much publicity in its first years. By spring 2011, however, some muttering about outside influence on academic matters could be heard on campus and in town. The two of us knew no one in the economics department, but because we have long-term ties with FSU, we decided to take a look at the donor grant agreement and memorandum of understanding between the Charles Koch Foundation, the FSU Foundation, and the FSU economics department.

The provisions called for the appointment of five professors as well as other staff members, the establishment of a Program for the Study of Political Economy and Free Enterprise and a Program for Excellence in Economic Education, and the development of educational programs for undergraduates. The money had strings attached: the major one was the appointment of an advisory board chosen by the Koch Foundation. The board would determine which faculty candidates would qualify to receive funding, review all publicly provided material submitted by applicants for the professorship positions, and review the work of the professors to make sure it complied with the "objectives and purposes" of the foundation. Several clauses made clear that the Koch Foundation could pick up the marbles and go home if dissatisfied (www.aaup.org6/2012).

In "Spreading the Free Market Gospel," David Levinthal (2015) documents the 2013 Koch Brothers' contributions of $19.3 million to 210 campuses in 46 states and DC according to Center for Public Integrity analysis of IRS filings. Koch dollars lubricate the ideological privileging of free market economics in the curriculum. And provide an EZ pass for further indoctrination. At College of Charleston in South Carolina, Koch Foundation sought names and emails of students who participated in Koch-sponsored classes, reading groups, clubs, or fellowships, and insisted that the College not speak to the media about Koch funded programs without prior consent from the foundation. The funding teaching aligns with libertarian economic philosophy and the foundation maintains partial control over faculty hiring and often graduate student funding. According to Levinthal, "nowhere is expanded Koch involvement in higher education more evident than at George Mason University," the site of the recent controversy over the Scalia law School: $14.4 million in 2013 alone where the Mercatus Center has become a primary "source" on Obamacare – which claims to be a stand alone nonprofit: "George Mason University and its students do receive millions of dollars in annual financial benefit from the Mercatus Center, according to federal tax filings. That alone is a major incentive for a public university in Virginia, where state funding of higher education is dwindling, to host a privately funded operation on its campus." At George Mason, the Mercatus Center spent $3.64 million to support graduate students and $1.82 million for communication of research to "media and opinion shapers" – which has met resistance from a national campaign UnKoch my Campus.

Academic containment/The silencing project

In dynamic relation with the corporate funding of neoliberal academic values, faculty and courses, universities – often under external pressure - are weighing in against some faculty who are accused of crossing the [always shifting] line. In *The Imperial University*, Chatterjee and Maira (2016) document what they call academic containment of scholars who "cross the line" as "too political" (p. 22). They trace the shifting contours of what constitutes political, and too political, over time, only to note that some areas of research and/or engagement are more likely to provoke administrative or extra-university challenge, including activism/scholarship on Palestinian justice, climate change, fracking, corporate education reform, campaign finance and the tactics of the American Legislative Exchange Council, to name a few. They recognize that "If one speaks from already dangerous embodiments, structured historically, then that speech risks always being seen as a threat" (24). And that "the neoliberal structuring of the university is also a racial strategy of management of an increasingly diverse student population.... Well funded, neoconservative organizations and partisan groups, such as ACTA, David Horowitz's Freedom Center and Campus Watch have placed ethnic studies, feminist and queer studies and critical cultural studies in their bull's-eye" (p. 25).

In the same volume, V. J. Prashad argues that *cultural vigilantes* police teaching, scholarship and university activisms to narrowly constrain what can be taught, who can teach and what issues can be mobilized. Likewise, Steven Salaita, in his chapter "Normalizing state power," writes that the term *political scholarship* "when used to describe another person's scholarship, functions as polite denunciation because of its ability to signal a disapproval that need not be articulated.... The adjective 'political' an imputation disguised as a descriptor, is both accusatory and exclusionary" (p. 221).

I would add here that the corporate sponsorship of FOILs, Ethics Complaints and threats to academic freedom are further enactments of chilling strategies.

There is a growing list of academics engaged in research on fracking, climate change, corporate education reform, Republican and/or ALEC tactics, philan-throcapitalism or lead paint who have been targeted by legal assaults that have come to be known as Strategic Lawsuits Against Public Participation, or SLAPPs. The Public Participation Project describes SLAPPS as

> Strategic Lawsuits Against Public Participation. These damaging suits chill free speech and healthy debate by targeting those who communicate with their government or speak out on issues of public interest. SLAPPs are used to silence and harass critics by forcing them to spend money to defend these baseless suits. SLAPP filers don't go to court to seek justice.... To end or prevent a SLAPP, those who speak out on issues of public interest frequently agree to muzzle themselves, apologize, or "correct" statements. (www.anti-slapp.org/your-states-free-speech-protection)

Others who have engaged with BDS organizing, or Students for Justice in Palestine have been censured, or, if contingent labor, not rehired.

You will remember the case of Bill Cronin, renowned historian at University of Wisconsin, when he was attacked by then Governor Scott Walker. In 2011, the Republic Party of Wisconsin sent a request to University of Wisconsin Madison legal office requesting all emails into and out of professor William Cronin's state email account referencing Republican, Scott Walker, recall, collective bargaining, AFSCME, WEAC, rally, union, and so forth.

On March 25 and 28, the Mackinac Center for Public Policy made a FOIA request for email correspondence of professors at three labor studies programs (PSC CUNY, 4/12/11, FOIA, academic freedom and use of university email and computer resources). In response to the Cronin controversy, Chancellor Carolyn Biddy Martin offered a quite narrow response, arguing that "private email exchanges among schools that fall within the orbit of academic freedom and all that is entailed by it" should be excluded. Martin recognized academic freedom was placed in peril, threatening the "processes by which knowledge is created."

That same year, Wayne State, University of Michigan, Michigan State, and University of Virginia received FOIA requests for faculty emails. The year before, in 2010, the American Tradition Institute, an environmental think tank, FOIAed the research records of Michael Mann, director of Earth System Science Center at Pennsylvania State University. Mann's research had documented patterns of climate change for past 1,000 years, displaying dramatic increases in global temperatures in the 20th century. The University resisted, and provided only one quarter of the 12,000 requested emails.

More recently, at Rutgers University, Professor Julia Sass Rubin, nationally recognized for systematic research on charter school selection biases and achievement outcomes, received an Ethics Complaint from the New Jersey Charter School Association alleging that she misused her academic affiliation to promote the legitimacy of her findings. To date her University, and union in particular, have defended Sass Rubin's scholarship and refused to require an institutional disclaimer on her work.

And then in the Summer of 2014, Dr. Steven Salaita, having resigned his tenured position at Virginia Tech, accepted a tenured appointment as Associate Professor in the Program of American Indian Studies at the University of Illinois at Urbana-Champaign. The appointment still needed final approval by the Board of Trustees of the University of Illinois, but Professor Salaita and the AIS faculty had reason to believe the appointment was secure. At the same time, tensions and violence were escalating between Israel and Gaza. Professor Salaita expressed his outrage in a series of impassioned tweets on Twitter. On August 1, Chancellor Wise wrote to Professor Salaita that his appointment would not be recommended because the University would not tolerate what were considered words or actions that conveyed disrespect and incivility.

The AAUP investigating committee of Henry Reichman, Joan Wallach Scott and Hans-Joerg Tiede reviewed the case and found that both the administration and the trustees acted in violation of the 1940 Statement of Principles on Academic Freedom and Tenure and the university's institutional policies on the subject.

With dangerous similarity, in March 2016, members of the NY State Senate threatened to slash CUNY funding because of "inaction on anti-Semitism" – the rising presence of and protests by Students for Justice in Palestine and faculty support from four CUNY campuses. The move came after the Zionist Organization of America urged CUNY Chancellor James B. Milliken to prevent the harassment of Jewish students at Hunter College, John Jay College, Brooklyn College, and the

College of Staten Island by members of the pro-Palestinian Students for Justice in Palestine.

All of these incidents reveal how porous are the membranes of public institutions; long heralded as the site for critical democratic dialogues, always filled with contradiction and colonizing commitments, these institutions are today hungry for money, vulnerable to criticism and fiscal punishment, and undoubtedly highly responsive to conservative pressures. These institutional instincts are neither new nor surprising, but they are quite pronounced, ironically (or not) at a moment when critical public scholarship is flourishing within and beyond the academy.

And yet ... Critical public scholarship

In defense of public we must be vigilant about these three faces of Public where we witness erosion, blockage and cooptation: the rise of tuition and debt, and the swelling of administrative budgets and salaries, accompanied by a slashing of state funding; the strategic realignment of admissions criteria that limits access for students of color and/or poverty, undocumented students or those with criminal justice records; the deep penetration of philanthrocapitalism and our universities' submissive response to corporate containment of scholarship, activism and dissent.

On these fronts we must be relentless and defensive.

And at the same time, we must engage unapologetically in teaching/research/ public performances/political mobilizations with communities, social movements for justice, challenging the dominant stories of science being told by corporate funding and instead aligning the public university with the interests and struggles of those who own the public university – the people. We must contest the slippage to the Right of what constitutes "political" or "advocacy" work; we must trouble why some "partnerships" (e.g., with the military, police, Department of Homeland Security, Big Pharma) are considered well funded policy/research partnerships while other collaborations (with social movements, with communities under siege, with social justice policy organizations) are considered advocacy or suspect. And those of us at Public Universities must dare to host the "dangerous" conversations worthy of debate.

Indeed, as tax levy dollars and bodies of color leak out of public higher education, as there are calls for the Scalia Law School at George Mason and the Koch Brothers donate and inseminate public higher education to reproduce neoliberal market ideologies, silence critics and narrow the gaze of inquiry, there is, at the same time, a virtual explosion of public scholarship, community-based research, activist-scholarship coalitions, blogs, radical archiving projects, protests and critical participatory science with social movements in local communities, across the country and with global solidarity movements.

In his essay "Practically Socialism," Gar Alperovitz (2016) chronicles a series of "innovative experiments with public ownership" that "point the way toward a more just and sustainable economy," including worker owned cooperatives, neighborhood land trusts, and decentralized municipal corporations (pp. 19–20). Alperovitz notes that communities in Philadelphia and Santa Fe are developing municipally owned banks; in Boulder, Colorado, climate change activists have municipalized local utilities, and more than 250 community land trusts have been established to prevent gentrification. Bioregional efforts "anchor economic, social and environmental development in national regions" and Food Solutions New England, for instance, seeks to develop a sustainable and equitable regional food system by 2060. Alperovitz asks us to imagine a "pluralist commonwealth" rooted in participation, collectivity, and sustainability. To this list, let us add democratic and participatory production and ownership of critical inquiry by and for communities under siege (De Sousa Santos, 2010). A form of public oriented and cooperative science, like worker-owned cooperatives, community land trusts, municipal corporations, and the massively expanding practices of participatory budgeting, critical public scholarship challenges the hegemony of elite interests as the dominant lens of science, and insists on social inquiry theorized, practiced, and collectively owned by and for particularly those communities enduring State violence. This must be the project of the public university.

We are now flooded with a landscape of radical possibilities seeded within/ beyond/despite the academy; the "fugitive spaces" Robin Kelly (2016) describes; transgressive engagements across our campuses and within our classrooms as Lorde, Jordan and Rich reveal; the building of movements with campaigns within and beyond the academy (e.g., BlackLivesMatter, Black youth project, The Dreamers project, UndocuQueer, Inside/Out Coalition for Banning the Box); and the explicit commitment to progressive, community-based research coalitions (e.g., in the critical social sciences Congress of Qualitative Inquiry; Rouge Forum; Participatory Research in Asia (Rajesh Tandon); JustPublics and the Center for Human Environments, Center for Place, Culture and Politics at the CUNY Graduate Center; the Next Gen Project for community-based research and social responsibility in higher education at University of Victoria, developed by Bud Hall, Walter Lepore, Rajesh Tandon, and colleagues; URBAN at CUNY, directed by Celina Su; the Global Assembly for Knowledge Democracy 2017, borne within the Action Research Network in the Americas, in the United States; the ALICE project: and "Strange Mirrors, Unsuspected Lessons for Europe," drawing on epistemologies the South organized by Boaventure de Sousa Santos, 2016.

We are of course at a crossroads when market logic and radical academic possibilities sit side by side under the sprawling academic tent – the latter always vulnerable to being colonized by the former. Public universities are quite vulnerable, and yet by virtue of the radical commitments and chutzpa of faculty/staff/ students we are perhaps best prepared to resist the assault. We now know that public scholarship/civic engagement/digital humanities/democratic knowledge will be advocated and branded by our administrations until we "cross the line." And then our institutions may well abandon. Particularly for junior faculty, faculty of color and otherwise marginalized academics. As Tressie McMillam Cottom has written (2012):

> The inequalities women and minorities face in traditional academic models only exacerbates the potential risks of contributing to public scholarship. That is potentially devastating to those who would benefit most from the kind of visibility, credibility, and network building that public scholarship can provide. I am clear about these risks. I am also clear that, for me, the risk of not speaking in these spaces is far greater. I am deliberate in how I engage conversations that matter to me. That I make that choice is not a reason for accolades and neither should it be a reason to shame those who make a different risk analysis. However, when women and minorities shy away from public scholarship from fear of retribution I am reminded of Audre Lorde who said, 'Your silence will not save you.'

Public scholarship spins with a doubled thread: radically rooted beyond the academy, and firmly stitched into the neoliberal brand of the "responsive" public university. Jessie Daniels and Polly Thistlewaite address this conflation when they write on digital scholarship:

> Surveying the landscape of the neoliberal war on higher education, many observers mistake the rise of digital scholarship with the neoliberal impulse to commercialize the university. While it is tempting to dismiss the rise of digital scholarship as just another victory for the forces of neoliberalism, or, to get swept away by the rhetoric of the disruptive potential of digital technologies to transform all of higher education "with just one click." both views are too facile. Understanding the complicated landscape of what it means to be a scholar now requires a more sophisticated appreciation of both the shift from legacy to digital scholarship, and the struggle between the forces of commercialization and democratization. (p. 17)

With such rich proliferation, we can not be naïve. History teaches us that progressive educational praxis (open admissions, no tuition, ethnic studies, technology, college in prison, the Free University, Affirmative Action, etc.) advanced *solely* within the walls of the academy is fundamentally vulnerable, always susceptible to full retreat and/or commodification (becoming institutionalized and "acceptable"). These moves of institutionalization, domestication and the metaphoric circumcision of the radical tip of vibrant movements on campus, speak to the predictable curdling of the radical education imagination, as Rich and Audre Lorde warned 50 years ago (for important counter story, see McCann, 2016).

Thus it may be naïve to say: each engagement, lodged at the periphery and the center, swirls as an assemblage of contradictory vectors. Those of us still fighting for the highly compromised space called the Public University must press to evoke and cultivate the critical public strands, resist the neoliberal and be in solidarity with movements/activists/communities/artists beyond the academy focused on economic and racial justice. We now know that the possibility/likelihood of academic complicity runs high.

And as we build these fragile solidarities, even from within, we must also be bold in our critique of the very institutions in which we are situated, as Norman Denzin and colleagues have done through the Qualitative Inquiry Congress website:

> The 2016 Congress of Qualitative Inquiry is devoting a town hall meeting to the topics of the academy, freedom of speech, tenure, faculty appointments and academic boycotts. In 2015, we held a town meeting in response to actions taken by the administration at the University of Illinois regarding their decision about Professor Steven Salaita. Though the matter has been resolved legally, legal resolutions often do not restore what becomes lost when there is a need to litigate. It is in this spirit, the need to heal and reestablish a confidence in the institution as a credible and ethical place of intellectual inquiry within the academy, that we feel the importance of ongoing discussion.
>
> Since its founding, ICQI has been a forum for critical conversations about the role of scholarship in advancing qualitative inquiry as a democratic practice. The tenets of freedom of speech and academic freedom are integral to these discussions. We stand by our mission to be leaders in fostering research and pedagogy that engages the pressing social issues of our time. Our university community has mobilized to support the tenets of academic freedom and intellectual integrity that form the DNA of higher education.

* * *

We can not look at educational or political leaders to advance Public as the collective intellectual, political and ethical project; but those of us on faculty – in full-time and contingent tracks, on tenure or short-term lines, must link arms across status, with students, progressive labor unions, community members, activists, those engaged with environmental justice, prison abolition, K-12 education, and racial justice/immigration/queer activists, demanding equitable, anti-Racist, decolonizing and democratic education, as allies in the struggle to resuscitate the Public as a solidarity project, as if our lives depended on it – because of course they do.

Note

1   FOIL, or Freedom of Information Law, is a law enacted in New York State to "ensure public access-by-request to records held and produced by or on behalf of state governmental agencies, including the legislature." FOIA, or Freedom of Information Act, "is the federal equivalent and precursor to FOIL" (http://researchcenter.journalism.cuny.edu/2013/03/06/foil-and-foia-faqs/).

References

Alperovitz, G. (2016, February 11). Socialism in America is closer than you think. *The Nation*. Retrieved from www.thenation.com/article/socialism-in-america-is-closer-than-you-think/

Anderson, M. (2016, March 3). The ongoing battle over ethnic studies. *Atlantic*. Retrieved from www.theatlantic.com/education/archive/2016/03/the-ongoing-battle-over-ethnic-studies/472422/

Arendt, H. (1958). *The human condition*. Chicago: University of Chicago Press.

Bourdieu, P. (1992). The left hand and right hand of the state. Variant, 32 (interview by R. Droit and T. Ferenczi). Retrieved from www.variant.org.uk/32texts/bourdieu32.html

Brodkin, K. (1998). *How Jews became white folks and what that says about race in America*. New Brunswick, NJ: Rutgers University Press.

Cassidy, J. (2015, December 2). Mark Zuckerberg, the rise of philanthrocapitalism and implications for democracy. *New Yorker*. Retrieved from www.newyorker.com/news/john-cassidy/mark-zuckerberg-and-the-rise-of-philanthrocapitalism

Chatterjee, P., & Maira, S. (2014). *The imperial university: Academic represession and scholarly dissent*. Minneapolis, MN: University of Minnesota Press.

Chatterjee, P., & Maira, S. (Eds.). (2016). *The imperial University: Academic repression and scholarly dissent*. Minneapolis: University of Minnesota Press.

Cottom, T. M. (2012). Risk and ethics in public scholarship. *Inside Higher Ed*. Retrieved from www.insidehighered.com/risk-and-ethics-public-scholarship

Daniels, J., & Thistlethwaite, P. (2016). *Being a scholar in the digital era: Transforming scholarly practice for the public good*. London: Policy Press.

De Sousa Santos, B. (2010). The university in the twenty-first century. In M. W. Apple, S. J. Ball, & L. A. Gandin (Eds.), *The Routledge International Handbook of the sociology of Education* (pp. 274–282). Abingdon: Routledge.

Delgado, S., & Ross, E. (2016). *Students in revolt: The pedagogical potential of student collective action in the age of the corporate university*. Unpublished manuscript. Vancouver: University of British Columbia.

DeParle, J. (2012, December 22). Poor students struggle as class plays a great role in success. *The New York Times,* p. A1.

Desroches, D., & Kirshstein, D. (2014). Delta cost project: Labor intensive or labor expensive? American Institutes for Research. Retrieved from www.deltacostproject.org/sites/default/files/products/DeltaCostAIR_Staffing_Brief_2_3_14.pdf (accessed July 12, 2015).

Edmonds, D. (2015, 28 May). More than half of college faculty are adjuncts: Should you care? *Forbes*. Retrieved from www.forbes.com/sites/noodleeducation/2015/05/28/more-than-half-of-college-faculty-are-adjuncts-should-you-care/#11d14cb71d9b

Fabricant, M., & Brier, S. (2016). *Austerity blues: Fighting for the soul of public education*. Baltimore: Johns Hopkins University Press.

Giroux, H. A. (2010). Bare pedagogy and the scourge of neoliberalism: Rethinking higher education as a democratic public sphere. *The Educational Forum, 74*(3), 184–196.

Gramsci, A. (1971). *Selections from prison notebooks*. New York: International Publishers.

Gumbs, A. (2016). Nobody mean more: Black feminist pedagogy and solidarity. In P. Chatterjee and S. Maira (Eds.), *The imperial University: Academic repression and scholarly dissent*. Minneapolis: University of Minnesota Press.

Hall, B. L., Clover, D. E., Crowther, J. & Scandrett, E. (2012). *Learning and education for a better world: The role of social movements*. Rotterdam: Sense Publishers.

Haney, F., & Moten, F. (2013). *The undercommons: Fugitive spaces and black study*. New York: Minor Compositions.

Jones, O. (2014). *The establishment and how they get away with it*. Brooklyn/London: Melville House.

Kelly, R. (2016, March 7). Black study, black struggle: The university is not an engine of social transformation. Activism is. *Boston Review*. Retrieved from https://bostonreview. net/forum/robin-d-g-kelley-black-study-black-struggle

Koenig, R. (2016, January 27). U.S. colleges raise $40 billion; Stanford tops list at $1.6 billion *Chronicle of Philanthropy*. Retrieved from www.philanthropy.com/article/ US-Colleges-Raise-40/235059

Kolodner, M. (2015). Black students dramatically underrepresented at flagship institutions. *Hechinger Report*. Retrieved from http://hechingerreport.org/black-students-are-drastically-underrepresented-at-top-public-colleges-data-show/

Levinthal, D. (2015, October 30). Spreading the free-market gospel. *Atlantic*. www.theatlantic .com/education/archive/2015/10/spreading-the-free-market-gospel/413239/

Looney, A., & Yannelis, C. (2015, September 10). A crisis in student loans? How changes in the characteristics of borrowers and in the institutions they attended contributed to rising loan defaults. Brookings Papers on Economic Activity Conference, Washington, DC.

McCann, M. (2016). Labor scholarship and/as labor activism. *Perspectives on politics, 14*(2), 432–441.

Melamed, J. (Winter, 2006). The spirit of neoliberalism: From racial liberalism to neoliberal Multiculturalism. *Social Text, 89*, 1–25.

Miller, K., & Bellamy, R. (May–June 2012). Fine print, restrictive grants and academic freedom. AAUP. Retrieved from www.aaup.org/article/fine-print-restrictive-grants-and-academic-freedom#.V_WNsoftJeU

Mortensen, T. (2012). State funding: A race to the bottom. *American Council on Education*. Retrieved form www.acenet.edu/the-presidency/bolumns-and-features

Opotow, S. (1990). Moral exclusion and injustice. *Journal of social issues, 46*(1), 1–20.

Parents Across America. (2011). How to tell if your town has been infected by the broad virus. Retrieved from http://parentsacrossamerica.org/how-to-tell-if-your-school-district-is-infected-by-the-broad-virus/

Participation Project. (2016). State anti-SLAPP laws. Retrieved from www.antislapp.org/ your-states-free-speech-protection/

Patel, L. (2015). *Decolonizing educational research*. New York: Routledge

Rich, A. (2016). Teaching at CUNY, 1968–1974 (Part I & II). Lost & Found: The CUNY Poetics Document Initiative. New York: Center for Humanities. Retrieved from http:// centerforthehumanities.org/lost-and-found

Rogers, R. (2013, July 14). The price of philanthropy. *Chronicle of Higher Education*. Retrieved from www.chronicle.com/article/The-Price-of-Philanthropy/140295

Ross, E. W., & Vinson, K. D. (2013). Resisting neoliberal education reform: Insurrectionist pedagogies and the pursuit of dangerous citizenship. *Works & Days 61/62, 31*(1–2), 27– 58.

Savonick, D. (forthcoming). *The promise of aesthetic education: On pedagogy, praxis and social justice.* New York: CUNY Graduate Center.

Sedgewick, E. (2002). *Teaching feeling.* Durham: Duke University Press.

Slaughter, S., & Rhoades, G. (2004). *Academic capitalism and the new economy: Markets, state, and higher education.* Baltimore: Johns Hopkins University Press.

Torre, M., Stoudt, B., Manoff, E., & Fine, M. (2016). Critical participatory action research on state violence: Bearing wit(h)ness across fault lines of power, privilege and dispossession. In N. Denzin and Y. Lincoln (Eds.), *SAGE Handbook of Qualitative Research* (5th edition). Thousand Oaks, CA: Sage.

Truth and Reconciliation Commission of Canada (2015). Ottawa, Canada. Retrieved from www.trc.ca/websites/trcinstitution/index.php?p=3

U.S. Government Accounting Office (2014). Higher education: State funding trends and policies on affordability. Retrieved from http://gao.gov/products/GAO-15-151

8

ASSEMBLING A WE IN CRITICAL QUALITATIVE INQUIRY

Stacy Holman Jones

Anywhere and anytime

In January 2015, I saw Judith Butler speak on the idea of 'we the people' and public assembly at CalARTS in Los Angeles. In that talk, and in her subsequent book *Notes Toward a Performative Theory of Assembly* (2015), Butler considers what happens in the invocation of 'we the people' and the performative act – the expression of the 'speech' of an assembled we – that precedes and exceeds the vocalization or inscription of these words.

Butler's premise is that in the very act of assembling – of gathering our bodies in space – 'we' performatively enact a claim to the political. That is, in standing together, we invoke a relation and take an action. She begins her argument about how this happens – how this is so – by invoking the words (and the embodied relation they create in space) of Hannah Arendt (1958), who writes, "action and speech create a space between participants which can find its proper location almost anywhere and anytime" (p. 198).

Arendt's words and Butler's treatise help us answer the question of how critical qualitative inquiry might be a powerful instrument for fighting against attacks on freedom of speech, such as those leveled against Native American Studies professor Steven Salaita following posts on his private social media account about the Palestine–Israel conflict and the subsequent revocation of a job offer from the University of Illinois at Urbana-Champaign (Chandler, 2015). Although the university was censured by the American Association of University Professors for violating the principles of academic freedom, the firing of Salaita demonstrates the "insidious nature of the censorship" in the academy and beyond (Kimberly, 2015) and underscores the importance of gathering together to speak in the wake of such injustices, large and small. Borrowing from Arendt, I believe it is important to consider critical qualitative inquiry as action and speech that creates a space between participants – between

> we, as a community of scholars, artists and teachers
>
> we, as a collective body of speakers who bring, as writer Raymond Carver (2001) would have it, 'news of the world' (p. 89) of others to our readers, audience members, students, and communities
>
> we, as a privileged and ethically responsible assembly of human beings who must struggle to support other beings who are subject to precarity, inequality, and injustices.

In other words, I am proposing that we think about how critical qualitative inquiry might be an act of assembling a 'we.' That we consider our work in critical qualitative inquiry as a relation of the *freedom to speak* that enables us to act ethically (and equitably, supportively, persistently, and resistently) with and toward one another. In the balance of this brief chapter, I will consider each element of these ideas in turn.

Assembling a we

Butler (2015) writes that the statement 'we the people' is "first and foremost a speech act" (p. 175). Assembling a 'we' in critical qualitative inquiry is a performative – when we say 'we,' we seek to create an *us*, to, "bring about the social plurality" we name (p. 175). In other words, saying 'we the people' does not describe our collective, but rather "gathers that group together" through the act of speaking (p. 175).

Critical qualitative inquiry is, I would argue, invested in assembling a 'we.' While other research modes and practices are rightly and very capably interested in *describing* the world (a collective), our scholarship is – and should be – invested in gathering people together to create an us: one that brings about a plurality that is invested in one another. A collective which does not speak for an other, but instead speaks *with* one another. Butler also reminds us that our 'we' – our assembly – is "already speaking before it utters any words" (p. 156). It is already an enactment of a collective or popular 'will,' something quite apart from the way a "single and unified subject declares its will through [the] vocalized proposition 'I am'" (p. 156).

As a critical qualitative researcher who has spent many years doing and writing about the methodological practices of autoethnography (see, e.g., Adams, Holman Jones, & Ellis, 2014; Holman Jones, 2005; Holman Jones, 2016; Holman Jones, Adams, & Ellis, 2013), Butler's words speak clearly and passionately about what I believe the purpose of autoethnography research – as a practice of critical qualitative inquiry – to be. Autoethnography is not, as some assert, 'me-search,' nor is it a means for a "single and unified subject [to] declare its will" (Butler, 2015,

p. 156). Autoethnography does not speak through an individual or isolated voice, saying 'My story, my experience, my self, the end.' Rather, autoethnography is interested and invested in assembling a we – a clutch of listeners and speakers – who, before uttering any words, are already enacting (and speaking) a collective and popular 'will.'

In this view, autoethnography becomes an affective force, where the affective is as Kathleen Stewart (2007) puts it, "a surging, a rubbing, a connection of some kind that has an impact" (p. 128). Affect in autoethnography is not quantifiable or mutually shared emotion. It is not, as some critics would have it, the elusive search for the 'evocative' in our writing or the effort to move others to tears in hotel conference rooms. It is "not about one person's feelings becoming another's" at all, "but about bodies literally affecting one another and generating intensities: human bodies, discursive bodies, bodies of thought" (Stewart, 2007, p. 128). It is the will to connect, to be in conversation with each other and in the world, to embody a relation of freedom.

A relation of freedom

A relation of freedom is just that: a relation. We do not have freedom to act upon or apart from one another. Instead, freedom is created in and through human relation and need. Butler, reading Arendt, writes: "Freedom does not come from me or from you; it can and does happen as a relation between us, or indeed, among us" (2015, p. 88). What does this mean for critical qualitative inquiry, or for autoethnography for that matter?

Firstly, it means that we cannot write or work isolation; instead, we must support and be supported by a community, a *we* and an *us*. It is support – bodily, emotional, material, and intellectual – that enables us to act (Butler, 2015, p. 72). As critical qualitative scholars, we must ask: What kinds of supports do we provide or deny one another in our work as researchers, artists and teachers? What kinds of supports do we provide or deny the others with whom we are in relation in our work?

Secondly, if we are to create or to experience freedom, we must act together, in relation. Not for or in the name of an other or in the absence of the other, but between and among. Autoethnography is rich with stories that create, name, and perform a relation of freedom (see, for example, Boylorn, 2012; Chawla, 2013; Cunningham, 2016; Ellis & Rawicki, 2013; Gingrich-Philbrook, 2015; Harris, 2016; Holman Jones & Harris, 2016; Johnson, 2014; Spry, 2016; Tillmann, 2014). Our work is not to 'find the human dignity' in a person or group of people or a story or group of stories or to show or speak or enact that dignity for the education or benefit of others. Instead, our work is to "understand the human as a relational and social being, one whose action depends on equality" (Butler, 2015, p. 88). Our work, in critical qualitative research and in autoethnography, is to articulate a relation of freedom that *speaks* the "principle of equality" (p. 88).

To speak

What does speaking a relation of freedom sound like? Look like? Feel like? Butler (2015) says, "Showing up, standing, breathing, moving, standing still, speech, and silence" are all parts of a "political performativity that puts livable life at the forefront of politics" (p. 18). The performative power of a 'we' does not only or firstly "rely on words" (Butler, 2015, p. 174). It relies foremost on bodies gathering and connecting; the "speech acts that unfold from there articulate something that is already happing at the level of the plural body" (p. 174). It relies on what happens when we connect the singularity of one person's experience in meaning and in time to what Brian Massumi (2002) describes as a "vital movement" that can be "collectively spread" (p. 250).

When we gather and connect in the pages of journals and books or in person at conferences such as the International Congress of Qualitative Inquiry, we become a plural body, one that speaks, thinks, moves, and together, if not in concert, then in conversation, dialogue, dissent. More than this, as a community, we must remember that bodies can and do gather and connect in the work we make, in the places in which we choose to share that work, in the silences and gaps that that gathering and connecting makes. Our work is not our own – a singular statement spoken into a void. It says something; it signifies something about us – who we claim ourselves to be and what we stand for. It also creates a motor for movement, an embodied unfolding of how not only our ideas, but also our actions in the world, might be shared collectively with and toward one another.

Acting ethically with and toward one another

One of the things Butler asks us to remember is that the speech (vocalized or not) that happens out of 'official' and 'sanctioned' public spaces – whether in 'ranked' or 'unranked' journals or at conferences or in hallways or classrooms or in the absent presence of those who take a stand by not placing their bodies in the spaces in which human equality or relational freedom does not seem possible – our gathering must, to borrow Butler's phrase, make a "call for justice" (Butler, 2015, p. 18).

That call for justice is the call to act ethically – equitably, supportively, persistently, and resistantly – with and toward one another. It is calls us to remember that the embodied performativity of our 'we' is "marked by dependency and resistance" (p. 18). It asks those among us who have the power and the privilege of speaking (because of tenure, because of institutional support, because of race and gender and class and age and ability and religious privileges (among others) to assume the responsibility of supporting and acting ethically and justly toward those of us who do not have such privileges.

Butler (2015) writes that

> when we ask the basic ethical and political question how ought I to act, we implicitly reference the conditions of the world that make that act possible or, as is increasingly the case under conditions of precarity, that undermine the conditions of acting. (Butler, 2015, p. 23).[1]

We only need to think of the events in Nice, Istanbul, Baton Rouge, St. Paul, and Orlando to understand the precarity of certain people and lives. "What does it mean to act together when the conditions for acting together are devastated or falling away?" (Butler, 2015, p. 23). And what might critical qualitative scholarship and activism gain from working in and through precarity's 'positive qualities' – "leaning away from habit, stepping outside of comfort zones, chancing the speculative and uncertain act of critical thinking" that might lead to "actions of resistance and change" (Ridout & Schneider, 2012, p. 9)?

If our gathering itself – especially under conditions of precarity – is an act of both persistence and resistance, then answering the ethical question of how we ought to act in critical qualitative inquiry must exhibit its values and its freedom in the work itself. We must remember that critical qualitative inquiry is always a claim to the political (Butler, 2015, p. 18). More than this, it is an investment in collectivity, in support, and in a commitment to creating "durable and livable" lives together (Butler, 2015, p. 85).

> For a relation of freedom to speak and act ethically with and toward one another.
> For an assembling we.

Note

1 [A] struggle for "employment and education, equitable food distribution, livable shelter, and freedom of movement and expression ..." (Butler, 2015, p. 72)

References

Adams, T. E., Holman Jones, S., and Ellis, C. (2014). *Autoethnography*. London: Oxford University Press.

Arendt, H. (1958). *The human condition*. Chicago: University of Chicago Press.

Boylorn, R. (2012). *Sweetwater: Black woman and narratives of resilience*. Walnut Creek: Left Coast Press.

Butler, J. (2015). *Notes toward a performative theory of assembly* (Vol. 1). Cambridge: Harvard University Press.

Carver, R. (2001). On writing. In W. L. Stull (Ed.), *Call if you need me: The uncollected fiction and other prose*. New York: Vintage Contemporaries.

Chandler, A. (2015). A six-figure settlement on campus free speech. *The Atlantic.* Retrieved from: www.theatlantic.com/national/archive/2015/11/a-six-figure-settlement-on-campus-free-speech/415680/

Chawla, D. (2013). Walk, walking, talking, home. In S. Holman Jones, T. E. Adams, & C. Ellis (Eds.), *Handbook of Autoethnography* (pp. 162–172). Walnut Creek, CA: Left Coast Press.

Cunningham, S. (2016). A lonely discourse. *Departures in Critical Qualitative Research, 5*(1), 8–22.

Ellis, C., and Rawicki, J. (2013). Collaborative witnessing of survival during the Holocaust: An exemplar of relational autoethnography. *Qualitative Inquiry, 19*(5), 366–380.

Gingrich-Philbrook, C. (2015). On Dorian Street. In D. Chawla & S. Holman Jones (Eds.), *Stories of home: Place, identity, exile* (pp. 199–214). Lanham, MD: Lexington Books.

Harris, A. (2016). *Creativity, religion, and youth cultures.* New York: Routledge.

Holman Jones, S. (2005). Autoethnography: Making the personal political. In N. K. Denzin and Y. S. Lincoln (Eds.), *SAGE handbook of qualitative research* (3rd ed.) (pp. 763–791). Thousand Oaks, CA: Sage.

Holman Jones, S. (2016). Living bodies of thought: The critical in critical autoethnography. *Qualitative Inquiry, 22*(4), 228–237.

Holman Jones, Adams, T. E., & Ellis, C. (Eds.) (2013). *The handbook of autoethnography.* Walnut Creek, CA: Left Coast Press.

Holman Jones, S., and Harris, A. (2016). Monsters, desire, and the creative queer body. *Continuum: Journal of Media & Cultural Studies, 30*(5), 518–530.

Johnson, A. (2014). Doing it: A rhetorical autoethnography of religious masturbation. *Departures in Critical Qualitative Research, 3*(4), 366–388.

Kimberly, M. (2015). Palestine and free speech: The University of Illinois' decision to fire prof. Steven Salaita on behalf of the Israel lobby. *Global Research.* Retrieved from: www.globalresearch.ca/steven-salaita-palestine-and-free-speech/5469012

Massumi, B. (2002). *Parables for the virtual: Movement, affect, sensation.* Durham, NC: Duke University Press.

Ridout, N., and Schneider, R. (2012). Precarity and performance: An introduction. *TDR, 56*(4), 5–9.

Spry, T. (2016). *Autoethnography and the other: Unsettling power through utopian performatives.* New York: Routledge.

Stewart, K. (2007). *Ordinary affects.* Durham, NC: Duke University Press.

Tillmann, L. (2014). *In solidarity: Friendship, family and activism beyond gay and straight.* New York: Routledge.

9

TRICKSTER AS RESISTANCE

Impacts of neoliberalism on Indigenous research and Indigenous methodologies

Roe Bubar and Doreen E. Martinez

Introduction

Those of us engaged in qualitative research, ethics, and methodologies "face the complex challenge of attempting to body the invisible, give voice to the silent, mediate without violating, and, above all facilitate an awareness that [knowledges and research] we call [Indigenous] is indeed an 'other' [knowledge] that nonetheless – in keeping with tricksters' ubiquitous and uncontainable presence participates profoundly" in the production of knowledge we call qualitative inquiry (Owens, 1995).[1]

In writing *Grave Concerns, Trickster Turns*, Chris LaLonde (2002) suggests that Louis Owen, a Native American scholar, uses trickster activism as his personal approach to encourage the world to change and challenge outsider imagining and ideas about Native Peoples. Tricksters are often tribal specific and most are represented in stories as supernatural mischievous creatures with an array of unconventional behaviors whose purpose may be oppositional or resistant in nature to reinforce tribal values and beliefs or act as a check for balance. Owens employs trickster and trickster discourse in his novels to reimagine the figure and economy in a way that will free us and compel us to reexamine the world in which we live as a way to integrate cultural traditions while being contemporary evolving and responding cultures. It is an activism responding to neoliberalism that seeks to push – that is, assimilate – as well as an activism embodying Indigenous consciousness of economies.

In reference to the novel *Wolfsong*, LaLonde says Owens was trying to "[help] us to re-examine the world regarding the troupe and vanishing [Native] both of which are key to resistance and affirmation of true identity" (2002, p. 27). This framing thus uses Indigenous knowledge as a trickster by engaging the unexpected and acting upon the spiritual as knowledge origins.

In this chapter we consider the trickster as a way to resist neoliberalism in research processes and ethics, particularly those involving Native Nations and Peoples. To this end, we gesture to a reimagining of notions/practices of Native sovereignty as a way to consider ethics in academic research and in Indigenous knowledge making with Indigenous Peoples. We begin with a discussion of the unique relationship that Native nations have with the United States and the trust responsibility that flows from that relationship. The politics of how students, scholars, and others remain unaware – and uneducated (willing and unwillingly) – on the status of tribes increases the vulnerability of how Native nations are currently positioned within the academy. These relationships, structures, and concepts are technical and involve analysis of the legal status of Native nations and the duty owed to them by the United States and, therefore, federal agencies. We then consider how academic research, and specifically research ethics, bound within a Western paradigm and couched within neoliberal academic contexts, aggravates Indigenous knowledges systems that arise from Native belief systems and are intimately tied to tribal sovereignty and daily lifeways. We suggest a re-centering of tribal sovereignty and respect of Indigenous knowledges as mile markers to cover the distance that must be overcome in the academy in order to embrace Native nations as political entities rather than simply as human subjects. The invisibility of tribal sovereignty and thus Native nations' ability to provide protection of Native citizens, knowledges, and resources speak volumes and traverse many miles to the ways in which notions of whose humanity is in the crosshairs of neoliberal interests in the academy and whose knowledge and lives are worth protecting.

The trust responsibility

Trickster enters to remind us: Indigenous Peoples have a unique status of nations that is often silenced and ignored in favor of neoliberal efficiencies such as statehood or local municipalities that support, contradict, and challenge Indigenous sovereignty. Indigenous sovereignty and relationship and tensions to the nation-state has had a long history. This imperialistic history originates from the reasoning and articulation in treaties, statutes, agreements, court decisions, Executive Orders, and the framing of Native Nations within the U.S. Constitution and the extraconstitutional status of Native Nations upon which inherent sovereignty originates and yet is frequently denied.

Initially institutionalized through varying agreements or protocols, the "trust relationship," upon which a "trust responsibility" is based, emerged from the sovereign status of Native Nations and a nation-to-nation relationship between the federal government and Native nations. The initial concept of the trust responsibility was first articulated judicially in the case of *Cherokee Nation v. Georgia* (1831). "*Cherokee Nation* was an original action filed by the tribe in the Supreme Court to enjoin enforcement of state laws on lands guaranteed to the tribe by treaties" (Cohen, 1982). The United States was found to owe a trust responsibility, to enforce treaty relationships, to all federally recognized Native Nations.

One could argue the principles of research ethics are also intended to hold scholars to the highest standard of conduct since it compels justice, respect for persons, and beneficence in academic standards for research (*Belmont Report*, 1979).

This responsibility developed over time via the courts and nation-state-local agreements, and obligates the United States to protect the status and rights of Native Nations while respecting and supporting their tribal sovereignty that is rights of self-governance. The duty the United States owes to Native Nations is ongoing and entails moral, sacred, and legal obligations to protect and act responsibly to the greatest extent toward Native Nations (Cohen, 1982; Getches, Wilkinson, Williams, & Fletcher, 2011; NCAI Policy Research Center, 2012). This means promises associated with treaties obligate the United Sates to protect tribal sovereignty, resources, health, and ensure education is made available to Native Nations (Getches, et al., 2011). This obligation applies to all federally recognized tribes, not just those tribes with treaties signed prior to 1871. These early nation-to-nation legal agreements are the pillars of liberalism (freedom, justice, and democracy) that neoliberalism masks (independence, cooperative agreements) and to which the trickster must attend (racism, violence, and ongoing threats to sovereignty, e.g., resource use, water rights).

Calling upon trickster

Year after year, former Advance Placement and International Baccalaureate students (the exceptional ones) show up in our college classes completely unaware of the status of Native nations as sovereigns and the trust duty owed to them legally and morally by the United States. The politics of how Indigenous issues and contemporary challenges are rendered invisible adds to the pushback we must contend with year after year. We must conjure up trickster-like stories complete with historical references to a history non–Native students (and some Native students) did not study. From there, contemporary examples invisible in mainstream media coverage are integrated to encourage an oppositional reading to the imagined Native no longer relevant in their lives. After all, the impact of colonization is "to render invisible the successes of Indigenous science and knowledge while simultaneously infusing public discourse with images of Indians as intellectually inferior" (Walters, Stately, Evans–Campbell, Simoni, Duran, Schultz Stanley, Charles, & Guerrero, 2008, p. 148). Today's neoliberalism is seen when Indigenous resource knowledge is sought to address disproportional climate change catastrophes or ways to return to nature when nature has virtually been decimated.

Furthermore, "The trust doctrine is viewed today as a source of federal responsibility *to* [Natives], creating two sets of commitments, one broad and the other more narrow" (Pevar, 2004, p. 33, emphasis original). Broadly, the trust responsibility is a *duty owed* to all federally recognized Native Nations to support tribal sovereignty and economic prosperity. In a narrower sense and in conflict,

Congress has placed Native lands and resources under the control and protection of federal agencies. This type of legislation and regulation requires Native Nations to obtain approval from federal agencies for any actions involving tribal resources. Typically, when Congress delegates this type of authority to provide a level of supervision over Native resources Congress is expected to act with "the most exacting fiduciary standards" (Getches, et al., 2011; Pevar, 2004). It essentially means that the United States must be held to the standard of a trustee and to act in a morally, ethically responsible manner. Historically, illegalities, immoral personnel, failure of resources, mismanagement, and absent accountability have marred these relationships. Additionally, there are numerous federal policies that have caused significant and long-lasting harm to Indigenous Peoples here in the United States: relocation, allotment, removal, and forced boarding schools are all examples of past federal policies resulting in significant levels of trauma (some genocidal). The resulting trauma is passed along and continues into the present with ongoing generational impacts, most notably access to criminal justice, education, health, behavioral health, and employment, particularly for Native youth (Yellow Horse Brave Heart & DeBruyn, 1998; Executive Office of the President, 2014). Similar lapses of trust have occurred in academia with respect to Institutional Review Boards and in breaches of Human Subject protocols and research integrity practices. These breeches, whether of the trust duty or research integrity, will always require an extraordinary dedication to restore mutual trust in order to repair relationships. It is here where the trickster may be called upon to work its magic.

Tribal consultation

In 2000 President Clinton signed Executive Order 13175, Consultation and Coordination with Indian Tribal Governments, which essentially reaffirmed the trust responsibilities doctrine. In the United States, arising from the trust relationship, there are now clear tribal consultation processes that require federal agencies with regulatory responsibilities to consult consistently with Indigenous Nations, particularly if regulatory changes will impact Indigenous Nations.

In spite of a gridlocked political environment, President Barack Obama directed federal agencies and officials to take action via presidential memoranda and executive orders in their work with Indigenous Nations. In 2009, President Obama supported and reinforced his commitment for Tribal Consultation efforts by directing Heads of Executive Departments and Agencies to "regular and meaningful consultation and collaboration with tribal officials in policy decisions that have tribal implications including, as an initial step, through complete and consistent implementation of Executive Order 13175" (Executive Office of the President, 2014).

Obama essentially amended Executive Order (EO) 13175 in 2010 to make clear the Executive Order "applies to any federal 'agency,' including any executive department, military department, government corporation, government controlled corporation, or other establishment in the executive branch of the federal government" (NCAI Policy Research Center, 2012). The Executive Order requires each agency to develop a tribal consultation policy and plan (NCAI Policy Research Center, 2012). Furthermore, the National Congress of American Indians (NCAI) pushes the ethical considerations and encourages all regulatory agencies even those that are independent to engage in tribal consultation. Again, we call upon the trickster.

The trickster goes to university

Native Nations maintain nation-to-nation relationships with the United States. As discussed, this relationship provokes (the trickster teases and flashes its appearance) an obligation to engage tribal consultations with regard to regulatory impacts, changes, and so on. But universities are not considered extensions of the federal government, even though they receive federal dollars for their institutions. There is federal legislation that applies to universities when they accept federal funding to attain, produce, and disseminate ethical knowledge.

Specifically, in the university research environment there is tremendous inconsistency in how universities acknowledge tribal sovereignty, provide informed consent, consider data ownership, and behave ethically with Native Nations. We argue here that universities must ethically be held to consultation standards with tribes and Indigenous Peoples regarding research protocols and Institutional Review Board (IRB)–related challenges. It is these protocols and guidelines that determine knowledge allowance, presence, acknowledgement, productions, and responsibilities. Therefore, what is at stake for Native Nations in research is at least as significant as consultation, which has been recognized federally. Two examples that occupy both federal trust responsibilities and academic research efforts are historic preservation issues and Native American Graves Protection and Repatriation Act (NAGPRA).

University human subject research is governed by a set of uniform federal regulations. Those federal guidelines (i.e., 45 CFR 46) rarely consider or incorporate the specific interests or status of tribes as sovereign nations. These regulations are set up to protect, as a guardian, Indigenous Peoples but are absent of Indigenous ethics and consciousness. Federal regulations fail to provide sufficient protection for Native communities involved in research. The recent Havasupai case (*Arizona Board of Regents v. Havasupai Tribe*) is a prime example of Western desire of knowledge for discovery superseding any trust responsibility and complete denial of Indigenous knowledge as sacred (see below; Harmon, 2010). If the point – the neoliberal point – of tribal consultation with federal agencies is to listen to tribes on regulatory issues that impact them, it should follow that federal regulation over human research in universities must include the voices of Indigenous Peoples and Native Nations. The trickster can liberate those voices, while the universities must never be exempt from these policies and requirements.

Consider the following: as a result of research abuses of psychiatric patients and prisoners, the federal government organized a group of policymakers and scholars to draft an ethics code published as the *Belmont Report* (1979). Three principles were included to guide academic research in that report: respect for persons, beneficence, and justice. These three principles often form the bases of IRB protocols and human subject research regulations. However, scholars and advocates for Native communities believe the *Belmont Report* fails to go far enough in protecting Indigenous knowledge and Peoples. The three principles assume cultural competence that relies on *Western* definitions of respect, beneficence, and justice. Sahota (2008) has written about how the principles are set up to protect individual interests. We demonstrate how these precepts facilitate and place a focused lens on individualism rather than community lifeways, beneficence of humans over cultures, and justice embedded with treads of monetary worth. All these delineations discriminate against and subjugate Indigenous ethics, knowledge, and practices.

At the very least federal rules regulating academic research, for example, need to include a tribal consultation process to ensure tribes have a right to articulate and assert their interests and concerns. Tribal consultation with any amendments to current federal research regulations must ensure protections for Native communities and knowledge systems. Although tribes act in the fullest regard possible as sovereign entities, many nations lack funding and resources to fully protect and advocate for themselves. In addition, various research projects and entities pursue Indigenous knowledges, which actively raises the stakes and need for protection. We are advocating for clear and enforceable processes not an elimination of research involving Indigenous knowledges. This could include a requirement for universities to incorporate Native communities (urban and reservation) interests and compliance with other much needed regulation around Indigenous research efforts.

To recap, although 567 federally recognized Native Nations are considered sovereign governments, universities (that accept federal funds and rely on federal legislation to guide human research) engage Native communities only randomly, at best, reflect just and ethical nation-to-nation relationships. In addition, there is a lack of consistent treatment of tribal engagements with universities in the same state or across the country. This allows scholars to work from individual neoliberal and individualistic stances that place tribes and Indigenous scholars at risk. Current policies and practices are inadequate to protect Indigenous knowledges and Peoples.

The trickster whispers.... We know that when those whom are most marginalized are realigned to the center of the analysis, the analysis itself shifts and transforms how we understand knowledge processes particularly those of privilege and oppression (Crenshaw, 1997; Hill Collins, 2000). Transformation is what is needed. Trickster is dancing.

Re-centering tribal sovereignty

In U.S. universities, knowledge production is centered on the researcher as an "individual" who extracts data. The university and principle investigator (PI) are owners of data, which continues to privilege an individualistic neoliberal Western worldview of property, rights of ownership, and notions of discovery. These cornerstones are largely patriarchal, colonial, and capitalistic, and subsequently problematic for Native communities seeking to engage and collaborate with university partners. This idea of property ownership raises significant implications for conducting research in a manner congruent with tribal sovereignty and the duelling (Western or Indigenous) research ethics that flow from it. Thus, it matters substantially that we critically think through the intersections between tribal sovereignty and contemporary approaches and methodologies in academic research.

As mentioned, the academy exists to a large extent outside of the regulatory and legal grasp of federal agencies (and the problematic fulfillment of them). Yet, federal regulatory and legal parameters of tribal–state relations do intersect with academic research. Academic research should engage those intersections, particularly in a milieu with increasing demands on individual production of research as a commodity. In reflecting upon an increasing efficiency culture within higher learning, Margaret Kovach (2015) offers this perspective:

> For many scholars with a genuine interest in Indigenous research and methodologies we are increasingly taking up this approach to research within the constraints of a corporate culture of post-secondary institutions that is built upon the meritocracy of an individual orientated society. Modern western philosophy has laid the foundation for a doctrine of individualism and the rise of the "solitary self." This belief (and value system) in concert with the advent of industrial capitalism in the eighteenth century has led to a situation in which western society continues to privilege an individualism that feeds upon an economic system requiring the exploitation of natural and human resources for capital gain. Within this economic system, commodities are the blood that pumps the system. Knowledge is one form of commodity within this system that is becoming increasingly important and thus exploited. (n.p.)

Kovach (2015) goes on to say,

> As Mark Spooner (2015) points out, this has contributed to an audit culture within post-secondary institutions. "Academic 'outputs' are accounted for by tabulating publications and research grants" (p. 217). Within an audit culture system, the focus becomes metrics, outcomes, indexing, and efficiencies. As a result, our post-secondary institutions are increasingly attaining the feel

and function of corporate entities where we are positioned to participate as settlers in a continuing colonial approach to knowledge production. In today's post-secondary environments, the quantification of achievement is the method by which worth is measured and daily the language of metrics assaults us. On a practical level, rampant individualism couched in an audit culture of post-secondary landscapes poses a number of risks for Indigenous research, methodologies and for Native Nations. As active Indigenous researchers and allies, we have been confronted with academic research processes that privilege such individualism at the expense of a collaborative collectivism. (n.p.)

Neoliberalism contrasts with traditional values found and practiced within Indigenous knowledges, contradicts sovereignty, and places Indigenous peoples at risk. When there is a continuing expectation in the academy to produce and secure research funding and use limited evidence-based criteria or other preferred positivist protocols from Western research paradigms with Indigenous communities (Carjuzaa & Fenimore-Smith, 2010), Indigenous Peoples, communities, and cultures are placed at risk, endure violence, are silenced, and become the visible–invisible (Martinez, 2014.)

Untrained scholars and IRB expectations that ignore the rights of Native Nations and short cut principles of engaging Indigenous communities and knowledges are allowed to surface in this environment. Controlling, owning, and extracting Indigenous knowledges becomes a continued form of territoriality, one that smacks of settler colonialism. Universities are sites to carry out colonial notions of appropriation and the owning of knowledge production, particularly when Indigenous knowledge is at risk to be commercialized in different ways. Indigenous scholars are concerned with the commercialization of Indigenous language, culture, art, and knowledge, and how lack of Indigenous consent and benefits to the community allows further extractive methods to continue (Battiste & Henderson, 2000; Martinez, 2012).

IRB approval alone is only one piece

Often IRB or an ethics committee approval is simply a piece or fraction of practicing ethical and just methodologies. Since U.S. IRBs rarely if ever address intellectual property issues and methodological choices, such approaches are positioned to ignore Indigenous voices and privilege researchers who are at risk to eclipse meaningful inclusivity and authentic multiple perspectives (Carjuzaa & Fenimore-Smith, 2010). Once projects receive IRB approval, Western notions of access to knowledge open the door to potential abuse(s). Once knowledge is shared, it is understood in a Western context to be free to all. Once knowledge is shared, Indigenous cultures have acknowledged it becomes real (Martinez, 2014).

Which is also why, in an Indigenous context when knowledge is communally shared, knowledge keepers decide with whom and when sharing with others is appropriate. When outside experts come and extract or take knowledge, it becomes particularly problematic if Native communities aren't fully informed about what it is they are consenting to and how universities operate.

As an element of sovereignty Native Nations are entitled to a detailed informed consent standard in addition to separate consent processes for individual Natives sought out or recruited to engage as participants in the research (Harry & Kanehe, 2006; NCAI Policy Research Center, 2012). These issues might be articulated in some university or state contexts or perhaps covered in particular MOUs, agreements, or legislation. However, often these documents are written and offered using neoliberal language and practices based on hierarchal and linear data collections techniques. If Indigenous principles are employed these very documents must take on a framework of respect, relationships, humility, and responsibility (e.g., pipeline protestors are understood and presented as water protectors).

Furthermore, continuous and ongoing abuses of obtaining and sharing Indigenous information presents serious challenges, since there is a lack of specific and consistent regulations or protocols explicit to obtaining information and publishing that require tribal approval, edits, or inclusion of Native members in publications. IRBs simply require inadequate training or acknowledgement of tribal sovereignty; they do not incorporate nation-to-nation principles or an Indigenous consciousness. Agreements with Native communities must cover a number of points, particularly given the rights of sovereign governments to protect their resources, which includes Indigenous knowledges and Indigenous Peoples. Agreements must also be honored and accountability of them secured.

Under the federal legislation referred to as NAGPRA, for example, tribes have rights to gain access to and repatriate their funerary objects and cultural patrimony. This is a federal legislative process that articulates what happens after cultural or funerary objects and patrimony have already been taken often times inappropriately or illegally. This example can highlight current university collections and processes in which objects have and/or are currently being held. In addition, university personnel can become advocates and facilitate the return processes, acting as bridges between academic entities, public and private holdings, and nation artifacts, ceremonial items, and ancestors.

Certainly, we need to ensure ways in which Native Nations are included in the first instance to protect their peoples and knowledge from being taken inappropriately in the first place. These stories, practices, cultures, and knowledges are part of a tribe's resources, their wealth and thus their futures. The United Nations definition of genocide and the United Nations Declaration on the Rights of Indigenous Peoples (UNDRIP) have illustrated what happens when these cultural elements are taken/stolen/destroyed.

Detailed informed consent in the language and framework of those participating is critically necessary given the increasing complexity of research. There is a real need to clearly explain, provide relevant examples, and clarify explanations by illustrating them for what will occur, when, for how long, and what all the implications are for this consent. Participants must know how the data, themselves, will be utilized. Coercion, whether by omission or commission, must be attended to in a methodical manner. Academic access to participants, data, data ownership, analysis, interpretation, results, authorship, and having control over the dissemination of findings continue to reflect ongoing colonial practices, struggles for power (Lomawaima, 2000) and neocolonial aspirations, and demands of profit-driven prestige associated with published research.

Tribal sovereignty and Indigenous knowledge

Sovereignty, ethics, and data sharing remain some of the most critical areas to consider when working with Indigenous Peoples while at the same time resisting the neoliberal seduction of success currently defined by the audit culture within the academy (Harding, Harper, Stone, O'Neill, Berger, Harris, & Donatuto, 2011). Tribes as sovereign nations must be positioned to determine which universities and scholars are best suited as institutions of higher learning (those accepting federal funds may offer more spaces to achieve such) to address their research needs from a nation–to–nation arrangement. If universities were accountable to Indigenous nations much like they are to federal funders or engage formal consul-tation processes, perhaps this shift would concurrently shift the power dynamics as well. Feasibly, then, we would see real change in protocols, processes, and ethics. After all, Indigenous nations and Peoples are in the prime position to identify adverse outcomes, appropriate Indigenous methods, and appropriate data sharing, ownership, and desired benefits in the research process (Hardin et al., 2011).

Native nations and national Native organizations across the country have engaged a variety of strategies for protecting cultural property and asserting their tribal sovereignty in research that occurs with their members and their communities (Harry & Kanehe, 2006; NCAI Policy Research Center, 2012; Sahota, 2008). In 2000 the Development of the Indigenous Peoples Council on Biocolonialism (IPCB) provided a model tribal law to assist Native nations in the protection of their citizens and resources. This model law came about as a result of unauthorized research conducted on the Havasupai Tribe in which tribal members consented to give blood for diabetes research and later learned second-ary data analysis occurred with those blood samples without their consent and by several researchers. Secondary data analysis using the original blood samples allowed researchers at Arizona State University to conduct additional studies on Native migration, schizophrenia, and inbreeding, all of which occurred to serve academic neoliberalism and imperialistic ideas about Native Peoples and Native Nations instead of the original promised study on diabetes.

Incorporating the 4 Rs and CBPR

A nation-to-nation approach that incorporates the diplomacy of the four Rs – *respect, reciprocity, relevance*, and *responsibility* (Kirkness & Barnhardt, 1991) – might serve as central tenets for cultural expectations and diplomatic requirements for culturally appropriate research collaborations (see also Martinez, 2014). As scholars working in Indigenous research, tribes often ask us if we are willing to use community-based participatory research (CBPR) methods. This type of *action research* uses a methodology in which collaboration is endemic to the research process, benefits and data ownership are made clear, results are expected to be translated for presentation to the community, and tribal people are mentored in the research process all along the way. These efforts reflect Doreen Martinez's (2016) work on holistic social justice. She writes,

> Connell, building off of grounded theory (when we acknowledge theory that comes from the data vs. theory used to analyze the data) offers, "What we might call dirty theory – that is, theorizing that is mixed up with the specific situations. The goal of dirty theory is not to subsume, but to clarify; not to classify from outside but to illuminate a situation in its concreteness," (2007, p. 207). A core premise of dirty theory is to get your 'boots dirty' by being in the community, with people, in their situations, from their perspectives. This is how we engage Indigeneity. Dirty theory then reaffirms, by providing measures of reliability, validity, consistency and compatibility to our holistic social justice research efforts, which provide growth and an expansion of knowledge and culture; a recognition of truths and collective philosophies.

Therefore, we also meet expectations of ethical and just knowledge production that does, can, and needs to take place in the academy.

Furthermore, Native Nations are actively calling for more participatory methods in the research process. Qualitative methods are often preferred, given the narrative nature of centering the voices and experiences of people and honoring stories – our oral lives – and given the reductionist approach often found in quantitative methodology. CBPR methodologies are viewed as a research approach more aligned with tribal sovereignty and Indigenous values where scholars must engage, share power, and listen to Natives as partners and coproducers in the research process (Holkup, Tripp-Reimer, Matt Saiois, & Weinert, 2004; Wallerstein & Duran, 2006, 2010). Tribal participatory methods also serve to place Indigenous communities at the center of every phase of the research process and require researchers to work within a historical framework where the impact of oppression, discrimination, and the disempowerment of Indigenous communities is consciously considered (Fisher & Ball, 2003; Walters et al., 2008) and taken up. Russell Bishop (1999) centers, in a similar yet Maori fashion, the aspirations, understandings, and practices of Maori people in the research process. In acknowledging the politics of the research process, Bishop emphasizes the need to recognize and address the ongoing effects of racism and colonialism in our society and its influences in the academy.

There are serious barriers created with Native Nations, since culturally relevant and informed academics are few and far between in many universities. Native scholars and allies often struggle with the neoliberal demands of the very institutions in which they are employed. Plus, these challenges increase when scholars and the students who work with them are unfamiliar with Native rights regarding participants, data sharing, data ownership, different expectations around research interests and benefits, cultural differences, lack of training around power and privilege, and other ethical challenges that often arise. However, like the trickster, transformative ways of thinking and Indigenous knowledges create new possibilities that can actually contribute to improvements in research design and delivery as well as provide a vehicle for transformation of the researcher and Indigenous Peoples (Grenier, 1998). Scholars involved in responsible Indigenous methodologies and research efforts recount life-changing engagements with Indigenous communities that shaped their lives and career paths (personal communication, Tom Cavanagh, January 22, 2003).

Kovach (2016) adds to this discussion:

> It is within this landscape of efficiencies and silencing, that Indigenous research, methodologies and Indigenous Nations with its relational accountabilities, its trickster energy, and its irreverancy toward established academic orthodoxy makes it appearance. Indigenous researchers academics, and allies – at least those who respect tribal knowledges – are increasingly found within the academy but we are largely an undomesticated bunch. It is our ethic of accountability to Indigenous sovereignty, the community, the teachings, the Indigenous laws, that nurtures this non-conformity, although we often can feel the burn of being told that we are not bringing in enough money, we don't have enough high-impact publications, we are perhaps too collaborative, and that we should do less talking and processing and more writing and producing. Yet, it is it this resistance to the insipid subtleties of neoliberal assimilation that is the source of our resistance and offers the possibility of a trickster transformation within the academy. (n.p.)

It is why Indigenous scholars and allies do service. It is why we search for trickster-like approaches and dream of change.

Our ethic of accountability is why we resist. We know the violence being done, created and permitted by historical academic research with and on Indigenous lives, histories, and futures. We are resisting the violence of academic neoliberalism through our practice of the four Rs in the academy. We must resist because to avoid doing so we participate by omission and render our purpose and reason for doing this work in the academy in the first place hopeless and negligible. With the deployment of trickster activism, we hold steady to the notion that from opposition comes the possibility for transformation and at the very least change in the academy, the world, and in an imagining of Indigeneity by Americans in the United States.

Research has historically been and continues to be used as a tool of colonial control and will continue to provide a vehicle to marginalize and appropriate Indigenous Peoples and their resources if Native Nations are excluded from the processes and policies that guide research with them. Native Nations are actively issuing declarations, policies, ordinances, guidelines, tribal code provisions, and model contracts, and creating IRBs and Native research committees to actively protect their citizens and resources involved in research initiatives. However, Western approaches, philosophies, and the current influences of neoliberalism remain embedded in research methodologies and universities' practices (Smith, 1999). As Indigenous Peoples, scholars, and allies in North America re-center Indigenous methodologies and support Indigenous knowledges as vibrant ways of knowing, we will have to remain vigilant, keeping the trickster at our side to resist not only new and emergent ways of Othering all that is Indigenous in the academy but also the neoliberal audit culture that seeks to commodify knowledge.

Note

1 This quoted material comes from a 1995 essay Louis Owens wrote on Native American literature and literary theory. Although Louis was clearly referring to Native literature, it is insightful how fitting this quotation is when discussing research, ethics, and methodologies.

References

Battiste, M., and Henderson, J.Y. (2000). *Protecting Indigenous knowledge and heritage: A global challenge*. Saskatoon, SK: Purich Publishing.

Belmont Report: Ethnical principles and guidelines for the protection of human subjects and research (1979). National Commission for the Protection of Human Subjects of Biomedical and Behavioral Research, Department of Health, Education and Welfare. Washington, DC: United States Government Printing Office.

Bishop, R. (1999). Kaupapa Maori research: An Indigenous approach to creating knowledge. In N. Robertson (Ed.) *Maori and psychology: research and practice*. The proceedings of a symposium sponsored by the Maori and Psychology Research Unit. Hamilton, NZ: Maori and Psychology Research Unit.

Carjuzaa, J., and Fenimore-Smith, K. (2010). The give away spirit: Reaching a shared vision of ethical Indigenous research relationships. *Journal of Educational Controversy*, *5*(2). *Cherokee Nation v. Georgia*, 30 U.S. 1, 1831.

Cohen, F. (1982). *Handbook on Federal Indian Law*. (1982 ed.). Charlottesville, VA: Michie Bobbs-Merrill Law Publishers.

Crenshaw, K. W. (1997). Intersectionality and identity politics: Learning from violence against women of color. In M. Stanley and V. Naryan (Eds.), *Restructuring feminist political theory: Feminist perspectives*. Cambridge: Polity Press.

Executive Office of the President (2014). *Native Youth Report*. Washington, DC. Executive Order 13175 of November 6, 2000.

Fisher, P.A., and Ball, T. J. (2003). Tribal participatory research: Mechanisms of a collaborative model. *American Journal of Community Psychology*, *32*(3/4), 207–216.

Getches, D. H., Wilkinson, C. F., Williams, R. A., and Fletcher, M. L. M. (2011). *Cases and materials on federal Indian law* (6th ed.). St. Paul, MN: West Publishing Company.

Greiner, L. (1998). *Working with Indigenous knowledge: A guide for researchers*, Ottawa, Canada: International Development Centre.

Harding, A., Harper, B., Stone. D., O'Neill, C., Berger, P., Harris, S., and Donatuto, J. (2011). Conducting research with tribal communities: Sovereignty, ethics and data sharing issues. *Environmental Health Perspectives*, *120*(1), 6–10.

Harmon, A. (2010, April 21). Indian tribe wins fight to limit research of its DNA. *New York Times*. Retrieved from www.nytimes.com/2010/04/22/us/22dna.html

Harry, D. and Kanehe, L. M. (2006). Asserting tribal sovereignty over cultural property: Moving towards protection of genetic material and Indigenous knowledge. *Indigenous Land and Property Rights*, *5*(1), 27–66.

Hill Collins, P. (2000). *Black feminist thought: Knowledge, consciousness, and the politics of empowerment* (2nd ed.). New York: Routledge. (Original work published 1990).

Holkup, P.A., Tripp-Reimer, T., Matt Saiois, E., and Weinert, C. (2004). Community-based participatory research: An approach to intervention research with a Native American community. *ANS ADV Nur Sci*, *27*(3), 162–175.

Kirkness, V. J. and Barnhardt, R. (1991). First Nations and higher education: The four Rs – respect, relevance, reciprocity responsibility. *Journal of American Indian Education* *30*(3), 1–10.

Kovach, M. (2015). Paper presentation on Indigenous Ethics and Neoliberalism Panel at the 12th Congress on Qualitative Inquiry, Urbana, Illinois.

Lalonde, C. (2002). *Grave concerns, trickster turns: The novels of Louis Owens*. Norman, OK: University of Oklahoma Press.

Lomawaima, K. T. (2000). Tribal sovereigns: Reframing research in American Indian education. *Harvard Educational Review*, *70*(1), 1–23.

Martinez, D. E. (2012). Wrong directions, new maps of authenticity and Indigeneity: Cultural tourism, Indigenous commodities and the intelligence of participation. *American Indian Quarterly, 36*(3): 545–573.

Martinez, D. E. (2014). Methodologies of social justice: Indigenous foundations and lessons. In G. Henson, and A. Wilson (Eds.), *Exploring Social Justice: Indigenous Perspectives* (pp. 2–21). Vernon, BC: JCharlton Publishing.

NCAI Policy Research Center and MSU Center for Native Health Partnerships (2012). *Walk softly and listen carefully: Building research relationships with tribal communities*. Washington, DC, and Bozeman, MT.

Owens, L. (1995). The song is very short: Native American literature and literary theory, *Weber Studies*, *12*(3). Retrieved from weberstudies.weber.edu/archive/archive%20 B%20Vol.%2011-16.1/Vol.%2012.3/12.3Owens.htm

Pevar, S. L. (2004). *The rights of Indians and tribes: The authoritative ACLU guide to Indian and tribal rights*. New York: New York University Press.

Presidential memorandum on Tribal Consultation November 5, 2009.

Sahota, P. C. (2008). Research regulation in American Indian/Alaska Native communities: Policy and practice considerations. NCAI Policy Research Center. Washington, DC.

Smith, L. T. (1999). *Decolonizing methodologies: Research and Indigenous peoples*. London: Zed Books.

Spooner, M. (2015, September 1). Higher education's silent killer. *Briar Patch Magazine Fiercely Independent*.

Wallerstein, N. B., and Duran, B. (2010). Community-based participatory research contributions to intervention research: The intersection of science and practice to improve health equity. *American Journal of Public Health, 100*(1), 40–46.

Wallerstein, N. B., and Duran, B. (2006). Using community-based participatory research to address health disparities. *Health Promotion Practice, 7*(3), 312–323.

Walters, K., Stately, A., Evans-Campbell, T., Simoni, J. M., Duran, B., Schultz, K., Stanley, E. C., Charles, C., and Guerrero, D. (2008). "Indigenist" collaborative research efforts in Native American communities. In A. Stiffman Rubin (Ed), *The field research survival guide* (pp. 146–173). New York, NY: Oxford University Press.

Yellow Horse Brave Heart, M., and DeBruyn, L. M. (1998). The American Indian holocaust: Healing historical unresolved grief. *American Indian and Alaska Native Mental Health Research, 8*(2), 56–78.

10

TURNING AGAINST EACH OTHER IN NEOLIBERAL TIMES

The discourses of Otherizing and how they threaten our scholarship

Kristi Jackson

ACT 1: Robert Moses

The Power Broker (Caro, 1974) won a Pulitzer Prize as a biography of one of the most prolific and polarizing urban planners in American history, Robert Moses. Known as the "master builder," his racist and elitist beliefs were evident in much of his work. With the support of the New York City Planning Commission, he publically resisted the move of black veterans into Stuyvesant Town, a Manhattan residential development complex created to house World War II veterans. In addition to these attempts to protect white privilege, he was known for large-scale construction projects that resulted in tremendous business development across the city, while slicing through neighborhoods with a disregard for local community boundaries. Although he was never elected to any public office, he once held twelve titles simultaneously, including New York City Parks Commissioner and Chairman of the Long Island State Park Commission. In his careful review of the history of Robert Moses, Joerges (1999) concludes, "He was an undemocratic scoundrel all right" (p. 418).

In his discussion of "the politics of artifacts," Winner (1980) describes the 204 bridges over the parkways of Long Island that were built under the supervision of Moses. Unusually low for the 1920s, when the bridges were constructed, some had only nine feet of clearance. Based on a claim by a co-worker (Caro, 1974), Moses purposefully constructed the low bridges to prevent busses from traveling through the area's parkways. Winner (1980) argued that Moses intentionally privileged white, upper-class owners of automobiles who could fit their vehicles under the bridges and thereby enjoy the parkways, while simultaneously restricting access to poorer people (often blacks) who tended to ride buses that were typically twelve feet tall. This barrier meant that the widely acclaimed

New York State Park system and in particular, Jones Beach, could not be equitably accessed. This is one of Winner's (1980) examples of the social determination of technology: That there are explicit and implicit political purposes in the histories of architecture and city planning. This view serves as an allegory of the way software architects construct programs such as Qualitative Data Analysis Software (QDAS), although the primary purpose of this chapter is to dismantle the deterministic premises on which this argument depends. Before continuing with the story of Robert Moses, a review of the history of QDAS is warranted, along with a vignette to help explain how such software can be used.

ACT 2: Qualitative Data Analysis Software (QDAS)

QDAS became codified as a software genre in the late 1980s as researchers from Australia, Germany, and the United States began developing them independently (Davidson & di Gregorio, 2011; Jackson, 2014;). The Surrey Research Methods Conference was held at the University of Surrey in the United Kingdom in 1989, and this conference established a dialogue between developers and early users (Fielding & Lee, 2007). Although the early presence of these programs represented great diversity of features, purposes, and software platforms, the software development arc since then has been fairly typical (Gilbert, Jackson, & di Gregorio, 2013; Norman, 1998): The early diversity of programs and their notable limitations in handling only a narrow methodological approach or data type gave way to programs that contained more features. A handful of products with this common set of features were leading the industry by about 2005.

In *The Dictionary of Qualitative Inquiry*, Schwandt (2007) cautioned his readers about the unexamined bias of tools for "computer-assisted data analysis." By echoing "Technopoly" (Postman, 1992) and drawing from a theory of materialism, Schwandt argued that the creation and use of particular tools influenced the ways researchers saw (and created) themselves and their research environment. He said QDAS could foster unreflective processing of qualitative data because of the erroneous assumption that software was "more … systematic, … rigorous" and, therefore, "better" (p. 35) than researcher judgment and intuition. He also stated, "While developers and frequent users of qualitative data analysis tools may customarily reflect on these embedded predispositions," such as the assumption of software systematism, "it is not entirely clear that the casual user does" (2007, p. 35). Schwandt did not thoroughly detail the predispositions of QDAS, but he raised concerns about a common failure to examine the ideological and methodological associations between such software, rigor, and systematicity.

From my insider perspective, those who are experts in QDAS – and who often mentor others in the use of this genre of digital tools for qualitative research – tend to emphasize constructivist perspectives by encouraging researchers to carve out their own paths in the use of the software for a particular study (Silver &

Woolf, 2015). As Miles and Huberman (1994) argued, the flexible, recursive and iterative capabilities of software provide unprecedented opportunities to challenge researcher conceptualizations. In support of this claim, Garcia-Horta and Guerra-Ramos (2009) detailed their use of MAXQDA and NVivo in two different research projects, concluding that, among other things, the programs helped push researchers past the powerful and often unwarranted influence of first impressions of the data.

The Richards (1994) agreed, and said that as they began developing NUD*IST, their analysis "became far surer, with provision for constant inter-rogation of themes. The processes of building and interrogating themes gave an impression of constant working at theory built up and peeled back in onion skin layers" (p. 164). They also reminded us that one of their primary goals during the early development of NUD*IST and NVivo was to allow for a diverse range of methods and methodologies to be applied within the software, and for these to be adjusted over time if the ongoing analysis warranted changes (Richards & Richards, 1994).

Gilbert et al. (2013) argued that as the software became more standardized around 2005, it simultaneously became more versatile. This versatility was often missed by critics (e.g., Coffey, Holbrook, & Atkinson, 1996) who associated the standard tools in QDAS with a trend toward homogeneous research processes. QDAS experts (Gilbert et al., 2013) critiqued this common conflation between standard software tools and homogeneous method, a logical fallacy that was usu-ally lodged by researchers with limited QDAS experience. For readers who are not immersed in the use of this genre of software, I provide a concrete example of handling data with several tools in QSR International's NVivo 11[1] that together allow for (and help to map) adjustments in researcher interpretations. Following this example, I return to the story of Robert Moses and his infamous bridges.

ACT 3: The relationship tool in NVivo

The following vignette of a bully-proofing project in a middle school demonstrates the ways in which NVivo can promote alternative explorations and explanations. In this example, the researcher wants to know more about successful peer media-tion in order to improve a marketing and recruitment program for such mediators in the school district. Rosa is a peer mediator. Hector, one of her classmates, is interviewed to ascertain which peer mediators he turns to, and the characteristics of mediators that either encourage or discourage him from asking for help:

> Interviewer: Tell me about the peer mediators you are most comfortable turning to when there is a problem with another student.
> Hector: Well, I like Rosa because she cares about people, you know? Like, she'll listen and she won't hurt anyone's feelings and she's sometimes like a class clown so she can make people laugh.

This data might be handled in several ways to answer the research questions, and is likely to be tagged (or coded) as "Positive characteristics: Listening" and "Positive characteristics: Humor." In the end (assuming a more comprehensive dataset and more detailed examination), the researcher might present a claim that peer mediators in this school who are known as humorous and outgoing tend to be more actively sought than more introverted ones. The relationship tool, however, provides opportunities to look at alternative explanations. The following series of figures demonstrate how a relationship can be interrogated by the researcher in NVivo 11. First, as in Figure 10.1, Hector seeks assistance from Rosa, and the direction is one-way.

When this relationship is placed in the Project Map in NVivo 11, the researcher obtains a graphic display as in Figure 10.2.

Because NVivo 11 retains and can display all possible relationships (identified by the researcher) in the project, it can generate a social network map based on all pairs[2] as shown in Figure 10.3.

Although the researchers asked students to identify positive mediator characteristics, by viewing the Project Map a new aspect of the context emerges that was not articulated by students as a relevant characteristic: gender. Among the four actors, the boys are never turned to for assistance. Conversely, the two girls receive requests for assistance from at least two other actors in the network.

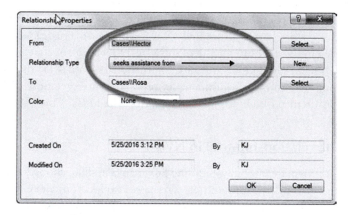

Figure 10.1 Construction of a relationship between two items in NVivo 11

Figure 10.2 Visualization of a relationship in the Project Map within NVivo 11

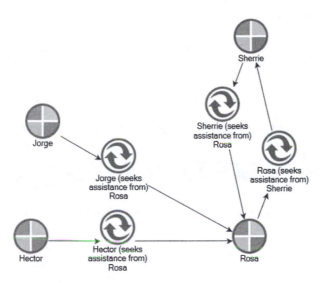

Figure 10.3 Visualization of multiple relationships in the Project Map within NVivo 11

This is an overly simplistic example from which to draw definitive conclusions, although the potential power to reveal an unanticipated pattern is clear. Among other things, this unanticipated pattern might lead to a revision of the research design (including theory), additional data collection, a re-examination of the coding structure, or team meetings to generate new perspectives.

The next unexpected pattern is revealed through an additional, two-step process that was engineered into this relationship tool: First, the relationship between Hector and Rosa is a potential container for evidence (i.e., a code or node), instead of a simple statement that "Hector seeks assistance from Rosa." By using the "drag and drop" coding method (similar to dragging files into folders within the file management system of a computer), a researcher can code text into the relationship, as demonstrated in Figure 10.4.

If the researcher returns to the Project Map and right clicks on the relationship between Hector and Rosa, he or she can "Open Item" as demonstrated in Figure 10.5.

This would take the researcher to the relevant quote, as shown in Figure 10.6.

Thus far we have mapped the network, coded evidence to one of the relationships in the network, and called up this passage to review the text. Instead of stopping here, this tool allows the researcher to select the hyperlink to <Internals\\ Hector> (at the top of Figure 10.6) and then jump immediately to the location of this quote in the context of the full interview, as shown in Figure 10.7.

An examination of the additional context below the highlight reveals an alternative explanation: The presence of other boys in the social context might be a barrier to a boy who would otherwise seek assistance from a girl mediator. Again,

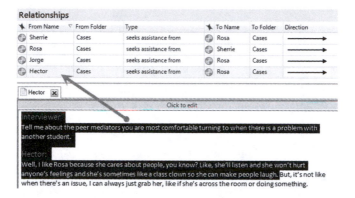

Figure 10.4   Coding a specific passage into a researcher–identified relationship in NVivo 11

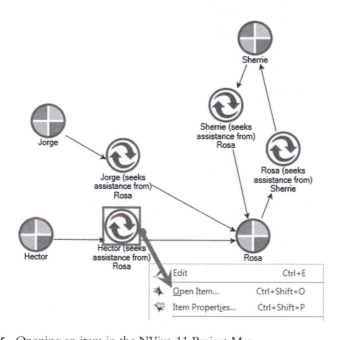

Figure 10.5   Opening an item in the NVivo 11 Project Map

<Internals\\Hector> - § 1 reference coded [12.88% Coverage]

Reference 1 - 12.88% Coverage

Well, I like Rosa because she cares about people, you know? Like, she'll listen and she won't hurt anyone's feelings and she's sometimes like a class clown so she can make people laugh.

Figure 10.6   Examining the content in a Project Map item in NVivo 11

Interviewer
Tell me about the peer mediators you are most comfortable turning to when there is a problem with another student.

Hector:
Well, I like Rosa because she cares about people, you know? Like, she'll listen and she won't hurt anyone's feelings and she's sometimes like a class clown so she can make people laugh. But, it's not like when there's an issue, I can always just grab her, like if she's across the room or doing something. Maybe it's different if it's like an ongoing issue, and I can go to her when I see her in class or in the hall, but not just like when someone like Adam starts saying things just to be an ass while we're working on a project in class. That would just make it worse. So, like if she were right there in the group on the other side of the table, I'd be like, "Well, Rosa, did you catch this?" Which I'd say half-joking to bring it to the surface but also to give me a way to back down, to be honest, in case I get hassled for it. But, I mean, the same thing is true whether I am in class or not, I guess, right? Like, whether she's around and what to say if she is, because you have to think about maybe getting hassled for bringing in a peer mediator. Plus, like if it's guys around, I may not say anything, because they'd tease me for not sticking up for myself, but if it was mostly girls, then they're more likely to stick up for me for some reason, so they won't pick on me if I brought in Rosa.

Figure 10.7 Jumping from a decontextualized quote to the source in NVivo 11

this potential pattern might lead to a revision of the theory or methods, additional data collection, a reexamination of the coding structure, team meetings to gather new researcher perspectives, and so on.

In summary, a relationship in NVivo is created by the researcher to document how two or more entities or concepts relate – they might be people, objects, processes, or abstract concepts. Optionally, it is also a pointer to evidence for that relationship, such as text, audio, video, and reflexive researcher journal entries. In this regard, it is an interesting hybrid between social network mapping (which only provides statistical connections) and qualitative research (wherein the researcher may use codes/nodes, identify connections and interpret meaning through ongoing handling of the data). Researchers can easily obtain a visual of the interconnected relationships via the Project Map (as in Figures 10.2 and 10.3). If a researcher codes evidence of the connection among items, this evidence can be instantly accessed from inside the Project Map (as in Figures 10.5 and 10.6) and also examined in the original context (as in Figure 10.7).

ACT 4: Determinism, constructivism, and QDAS

To help clarify the focus on determinism and constructivism in the remainder of this chapter, it is important to acknowledge that I am not addressing some of the diverse understandings of these approaches to knowledge and am ignoring some of the philosophical controversies around them. My goal is to point to the ways we qualitative researchers often simplistically leverage language related to determinism and constructivism in our narratives to either undermine or support a wide range of claims about the practice of qualitative research.[3]

Determinism presumes that all events, including human actions and choices, are the results of particular causes. Determinism is, by definition, a myopic view because this approach to knowledge isolates elements and tends to treat them as causes or results (or both in sequential linkages). Under this regime, the entire framework of understanding our physical, biological and even spiritual worlds rests on the importance of standardization, principles, universal laws and prediction. It also tends to question the relevance of personal agency.

Constructivism presumes that our views of ourselves and our world are continually evolving according to internal processes of self-organization. These views are not the result of exposure to information, nor do they depend on adherence to principles such as Occam's razor. Rather, our views of each other and our world expand, contract, plateau, and adjust from within ourselves; knowledge and the world are constantly reshaped (and reconstructed) through personal experiences. Moderate constructivists believe that an outside reality exists, but insist that we see it differently. In this regard, individual agency and perception are central and diversity is presumed. This summary points to key characteristics that are at the core of the remaining argument:

1. Determinism's tight limitations on personal agency alongside the implicit acceptance of standardization.
2. Constructivism's presumption of individual agency alongside inevitable variations in perceptions (i.e., diversity).

The above example of the relationship tool in NVivo 11 is intended to demonstrate some of the ways that QDAS can foster opportunities for researchers to generate and pursue alternative explanations and positions; opportunities that are closely aligned with constructivism. The example is not intended to imply that all such pursuits are only possible via software, but rather that these pursuits are often made more practical with software. "Contrary to a common prejudice, a computer can make the analysis process more flexible with the right software. It encourages 'playing around' with the data" (Tesch, 1990, p. 135). For QDAS experts, features such as the relationship tool promote discussions regarding the construction of interpretations and allow qualitative researchers to creatively work with data.

In contrast, many critics who argue that QDAS compromises the qualitative research process are borrowing from some of the tenets of determinism. The most common critiques include the tendency for this genre of software to distance researchers from the data (Agar, 1991), quantify the data (Hinchliffe, Crang, Reimer, & Hudson, 1997; Welsh, 2002), homogenize the research process (Barry, 1998; Coffey et al., 1996), take precedence over researcher choices (Garcia-Horta & Guerra-Ramos, 2009; Schönfelder, 2011) and lull researchers into a false sense confidence about the quality of their work (MacMillan & Koenig, 2004; Schwandt 2007). However, unlike the sociocultural determinism of technology evidenced by Robert Moses's bridges (Winner, 1980), this represents a different type of determinism: Technological determinism. To the QDAS critics, the software limits personal agency by standardizing processes; to the advocates, the software expands options and promotes diversity.

ACT 5: Moses revisited

These explorations now return us to the story of Robert Moses, and in particular the way he was characterized by Caro (1974) and Winner (1980). Both scholars argued that sociocultural privilege allowed Moses to construct over 204 bridges in a manner that was purposefully engineered to limit access for poor, marginalized people. Furthermore, for their scholarship in this matter, Caro received the Pulitzer and Winner has been cited in hundreds of subsequent publications in the fields of sociology, urban planning, education, and environmental design. But, suspicious of some of the characterizations of Moses as "the big bogeyman of urban studies" (p. 412), Joerges (1999) began examining the historical details and presents us with another picture.

First, and perhaps most significantly, at the time that he constructed the bridges, commercial vehicles such as busses and trucks were prohibited from operating on parkways altogether. So, Moses could not have let them on the parkways even if he wanted to. Next, the regional planner who claimed that Moses purposefully built the low bridges to limit access did so almost 50 years after the event, and through his own deduction after measuring the bridge height, not through his retelling of claims made by Moses or anyone else. Third, Kenneth Jackson, a historian and editor of the *Encyclopedia of New York City*, told Joerges that he repeatedly had his students research some of the themes and episodes in Caro's (1974) biography and found that many were "doubtful or tendentious" (Joerges, 1999, p. 417). Fourth, in correspondence with the civil engineers who helped Joerges investigate the bridges, two explanations for the height of the bridges were regularly provided: Commercial traffic was prohibited from such roads, anyway, and because of this restriction, erecting more than 200 unnecessarily high bridges would have been fiscally irresponsible. Finally, adjacent to the parkways, Moses constructed the Long Island Expressway, which did not restrict commercial traffic and provided access to the beaches in any vehicle. What are we to make of these different characterizations of Robert Moses and what do they have to do with determinism, constructivism, neoliberalism, and the scholarship about QDAS?

ACT 6: Boundary-work, Robert Moses, QDAS, and neoliberalism

Thomas Gieryn (1983; 1999) initially introduced the concept of boundary-work to describe the activity among scholars who purposefully attempted to demarcate science from non-science, although it has far-reaching implications beyond the debates about scientific research. Gieryn detailed the ways boundary-work was part of an ideological discourse that functioned to promote a public image by contrasting science with allegedly non-scientific activities. He provided examples that demonstrated how the belief in scientific method was solidified via this ideological discourse early in the evolution of western culture and argued that such discourse continued to shape the way the public perceives scientific activity. However, "The boundaries of science are ambiguous, flexible, historically changing, contextually variable, internally inconsistent, and sometimes disputed" (p. 792), because science is not (and can never be) one, immutable thing.

It is critical to understand that while Gieryn primarily focused on the sociology of science, he also argued that this boundary-work could occur in any discipline. This includes history (such as my description of the bridges of Robert Moses), and research methods (such as my descriptions of QDAS).[4] Critics of neoliberalism would also argue that a systematic construction of discursive boundaries by social elites continues to define what "freedom" means in political and economic arenas (if we take neoliberalism to refer to an alleged *laissez-faire* approach to political and economic processes and structures). Boundary-work is all around us. That qualitative research is often under attack within the neoliberal regime is evident in the other chapters in this book. But, that we qualitative researchers sometimes engage in this boundary-work ourselves is not always as evident. Furthermore, when it is, we sometimes conflate thorough, systematic, well-reasoned boundary-work with overly simplistic sound bites in the form of a handy attack.

What I am pointing to, as part of my conclusion, is that most scholars view the bridges of Robert Moses as the contested entity; the bridges are the artifacts that – depending on one's view – either control human behavior by limiting agency or provide freedom by promoting it. However, as Joerges (1999) noted in his assessment of the many ways the bridges have been described for different purposes, the artifact is the *telling* of the story, not the bridges themselves. Even the way I introduced this story, couched in an already distasteful impression of Moses, made his nefarious intentions and their outcome all the more believable.

Perhaps there is no concrete evidence of his isolationist intentions in building low-lying bridges because Moses was smart enough to know that such a move would not do anything to perpetuate class and race distinctions, given the access to the beaches via the nearby Long Island Expressway. Of perhaps greater interest, from a social justice perspective, is that despite widespread access to the beaches, Jones Beach remained notably white. Surely the tale could be told with greater complexity and nuance if the primary issue was about black access to this white beach. The artifact is not the bridge project, it is the *telling* of it to leverage other understandings and theories, and this is the boundary-work. I use Winner's (1980) rendition of the story because it has been so widely adapted for a range of theories and propositions about the *social determinism of technology*. Indeed, Winner invokes it for this purpose.

The bridge story has been used over and over because it is handy. Because it tells well. Because, in my rendering of it, the telling of the bridge story is an allegory of the endless array of critiques of another artifact: QDAS. Together these critiques amount to a one-sided, inaccurate view of how the software limits agency and limits we who use it, and it is a story told over and over. But, I am afraid the lesson does not end here, and the last portion of this critique carries a sting for my colleagues and me. As a QDAS expert, I am aware of our boundary-work in the way we sometimes talk of the researchers who criticize the use of QDAS. Unflattering comments include words and phrases such as luddites, lazy, afraid, behind the times, and wildly uninformed about the capabilities of the software (e.g., "They don't know what they are talking about"). Few of us experts have a history of talking kindly and in depth with these researchers, nor have we respectfully and thoroughly studied their resistance to the use of QDAS.

I am proposing that qualitative researchers of all kinds often (and perhaps impulsively and without reflection) use the language of determinism to critique the "other" by invoking fairly simplistic, cause-and-effect characterizations. We QDAS experts use it on the critics of such software, and they use it on us. This is a form of boundary-work that both camps leverage to allegedly protect the values of freedom, diversity and individual agency against the oppressive, homogenizing other. After all, that is collectively what we qualitative researchers tend to do when we perform boundary-work with quantitative researchers within a neoliberal regime that privileges the objective, invisible hand of the free market; it is a strategy we have honed over the years to help demarcate and protect our approach to knowledge. As Figure 10.8 illustrates, we talk in constructivist terms about *our* interpretations, reflexivity, flexibility, context, and the importance of diverse methods and researcher choices. We have autonomy, and we do not want *you* to take it away.

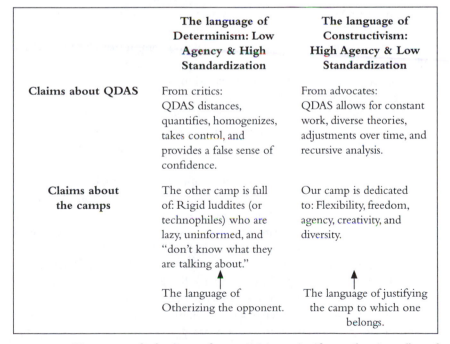

	The language of Determinism: Low Agency & High Standardization	The language of Constructivism: High Agency & Low Standardization
Claims about QDAS	From critics: QDAS distances, quantifies, homogenizes, takes control, and provides a false sense of confidence.	From advocates: QDAS allows for constant work, diverse theories, adjustments over time, and recursive analysis.
Claims about the camps	The other camp is full of: Rigid luddites (or technophiles) who are lazy, uninformed, and "don't know what they are talking about." ↑ The language of Otherizing the opponent.	Our camp is dedicated to: Flexibility, freedom, agency, creativity, and diversity. ↑ The language of justifying the camp to which one belongs.

Figure 10.8 How we use the language of constructivism to justify ourselves (regardless of the camp to which we show allegiance) and determinism to Otherize our opponents

This argument ends with the possibility that the artifact is not QDAS, just as it was not really the bridges of Robert Moses. The relevant artifact for this discussion is the way we tell our stories about the software, primarily through our published scholarship and professional roles. Furthermore, the lesson regarding these determinist versus constructivist discourses may be less about epistemologies and more about the ideological language we use to engage in boundary-work, both the careless and the careful kind. The primary observation on which most critiques of neoliberalism are based is hypocrisy: underneath the discourse of fairness rest mechanisms of power and control, sponsored by political and economic elites. But when this tactic of pointing out hypocrisy is used without full knowledge and understanding of the context, then the neoliberal critic has the potential to become hypocritical. It is the epic failure to do one's homework. As Herman and Chomsky reminded us (1988), the focus need not be on a formal conspiracy that threatens us. Instead, our attention might be best directed toward the subtle workings of cultural norms that often simply go unanalyzed and unpublicized in any systematic way; this is one of the paths to detecting and describing hypocrisy without becoming hypocritical, oneself.

If we intend to develop new opportunities for qualitative research in social contexts (and the leveraging of digital tools in engaging in this research to combat the neoliberal agenda), we must refocus our scholarship about the strengths and limitations of QDAS, because in many ways, the scholarship has not been based in genuine and diligent attempts to understand and learn. Instead, it has been part of a long tradition of the tactics of power and control that effectively enlist 'otherizing' discourses. This has never resulted in positive, innovative changes in any field, because it is the language of exclusion and isolation and is often ultimately revealed as hypocritical.

Our challenge is to find new avenues for innovative scholarship that minimize the careless boundary-work and maximize the collaborative effort to generate thorough, systematic, well-reasoned boundary-work. There is little research from a practice theory perspective (Bourdieu, 1977) that examines the dynamic interplay of qualitative researchers and the technologies they employ, including QDAS (for exceptions see Gilbert, 2002, and Jackson, 2014). We should meet the challenge and push toward understandings that help capture the complex web where researchers and technologies meet. An example of such scholarship that may serve as an example is Henderson's "On Line and on Paper: Visual Representations, Visual Culture, and Computer Graphics in Design Engineering" (1999), which is an ethnography that followed engineers as they transitioned from traditional pencil and paper drafting tools to computer programs. It considered the way they negotiated their status at the same time that they discussed their drafts, and it examined how the use of the technology influenced and was influenced by the relationships within teams of engineers.

From a constructionist and practice theory perspective, the possibility to advance our understandings depends on four things:

1. Resisting the deterministic discourse we use to otherize.
2. Observing specific researcher practices.
3. Examining the construction of technical tools over time (including the role of the industry in creating and marketing them).
4. Conceptualizing how these tools influence and are influenced by researcher use.

We have the skills to meet the challenge and push toward understandings that help capture the complex web where researchers and technologies meet. It remains to be seen whether we have the collective will to do so.

Notes

1 In the remainder of the paper, each reference to NVivo 11 pertains to the Windows Pro and Plus versions. Figures 10.1 through 10.7 in this chapter appear with the kind permission of QSR International.
2 The tool can also be used to map concepts or codes (i.e., nodes) in addition to social networks; the relationship types are user-defined and can be developed from a broad range of theoretical, methodological and conceptual perspectives, such as contradictory, affirming, tangential, hybridized, fragmented, resonant, and so on.
3 For a more nuanced exploration of determinism, see Nagel (1960) and Roberts (2006); for constructivism, see Piaget (1950) and Vygotsky (1978).
4 The three strategies Gieryn (1983, 1989) identifies in the practice of boundary work are (1) acquiring intellectual authority and career opportunities (and thereby staking claims to additional authority and resources), (2) denying these resources to non-scientists or pseudoscientists, and (3) protecting the autonomy of scientific research from political interference.

References

Agar, M. (1991). The right brain strikes back. In N. G. Fielding and R. M. Lee (Eds.), *Using computers in qualitative research* (pp. 181–194). London: Sage Publications.

Barry, C. A. (1998). Choosing qualitative data analysis software: Atlas/ti and Nud*ist compared. *Sociological Research Online*, 3(3). Retrieved from www.socresonline.org.uk/socresonline/3/3/4.html

Bourdieu, P. (1977). *Outline of a theory of practice* (R. Nice, Trans.). New York: Cambridge University Press.

Caro, R. A. (1974). *The power broker*. New York: Knopf.

Coffey, A., Holbrook, B., and Atkinson, P. (1996). Qualitative data analysis: Technologies and representations. *Sociological Research Online*, 1(1). Retrieved from www.socresonline.org.uk/1/1/4.html

Davidson, J. and di Gregorio, S. (2011). Qualitative research and technology: In the midst of a revolution. In N. K. Denzin and Y. S. Lincoln (Eds.), *The Sage handbook of qualitative research* (pp. 627–643). Thousand Oaks, CA: Sage Publications.

Fielding, N., and Lee, R. (2007, April). Honouring the past, scoping the future. Plenary paper presented at CAQDAS 07: Advances in Qualitative Computing Conference, Royal Holloway, University of London.

Garcia-Horta, J. B., and Guerra-Ramos, M. T. (2009). The use of CAQDAS in educational research: Some advantages, limitations and potential risks. *International Journal of Research and Method in Education*, *32*(2), 151–165.

Gieryn, T. F. (1983). Boundary-work and the demarcation of science from non-science: Strains and interests in professional interests of scientists. *American Sociological Review*, 48. 781–795.

Gieryn, T. F. (1999). *Cultural boundaries of science: Credibility on the line*. Chicago: University of Chicago Press.

Gilbert, L. S. (2002). Going the distance: 'closeness' in qualitative data analysis software. *International Journal of Social Research Methodology*, *5*(3), 215–228.

Gilbert, L., Jackson, K., and di Gregorio, S. (2013). Tools for analyzing qualitative data: The history and relevance of qualitative data analysis software. In J. M. Spector, M. D. Merrill, J. Elen, and M. J. Bishop (Eds.), *Handbook for research on educational communications and technology* (4th ed.) (pp. 221–238). London: Routledge.

Henderson, K. (1999). On line and on paper: Visual representations, visual culture, and computer graphics in design engineering. Cambridge, MA: MIT Press.

Herman, E. S, and Chomsky, N. (1988). *Manufacturing consent: The political economy of the mass media*. New York: Pantheon Books.

Hinchliffe, S. J., Crang, M. A., Reimer, S. M., and Hudson, A. C (1997). Software for qualitative research: 2. Some thoughts on 'aiding' analysis. *Environment and Planning A*, *29*(6), 1109–1124.

Jackson, K. (2014). Qualitative methods, transparency, and qualitative data analysis software: Toward an understanding of transparency in motion. Retrieved from ProQuest Digital Dissertations. (AAT 3621346)

Joerges, B. (1999). Do politics have artifacts? *Social Studies of Science*, *29*(3), 411–431.

MacMillan, K. and Koenig, T. (2004). The wow factor: Preconceptions and expectations for data analysis software in qualitative research. *Social Science Computer Review*, *22*(2), 179–186.

Miles, M. B. and Huberman, A. M. (1994). *Qualitative data analysis: An expanded sourcebook* (2nd ed.). Thousand Oaks: Sage Publications.

Nagel, E. (1960). Determinism in history. *Philosophy and Phenomenological Research*, *20*(8): 291–317.

Norman, D. (1998). *The invisible computer*. Cambridge, MA: MIT Press.

NVivo qualitative data analysis Software; QSR International Pty Ltd. Version 11, 2015.

Piaget, J. (1950). *The psychology of intelligence*. New York: Routledge.

Postman, N. (1992). Technopoly: *The surrender of culture to technology*. New York: Vintage Books.

Richards, L. and Richards, T. (1994). From filing cabinet to computer. In A. Bryman and R. G. Burgess (Eds.), *Analyzing qualitative data* (pp. 146–172). London: Routledge.

Roberts, J. T. (2006). Determinism. In S. Sarkar and J. Pfeifer (Eds.), *The philosophy of science*. New York: Routledge.

Schwandt, T. A. (2007). *The Sage dictionary of qualitative inquiry* (3rd ed.). Thousand Oaks, CA: Sage Publications.

Schönfelder, W (2011). CAQDAS and qualitative syllogism logic—NVivo 8 and MAXQDA 10 compared. *Qualitative Social Research*, *12(1),* Article 21. Retrieved from http://nbn-resolving.de/urn:nbn:de:0114-fqs1101218..

Silver, C. and Woolf, N. H. (2015). From guided-instruction to facilitation of learning: The development of Five-level QDA as a CAQDAS pedagogy that explicates the practices of expert users. *Social Research Methodology*: 527–543. doi: 10.1080/13645579.2015.1062626.

Tesch, R. (1990). *Qualitative research: Analysis types and software tools*. London: Routledge: Falmer.

Vygotsky, L. S. (1978). *Mind in society: The development of higher psychological processes*. Cambridge, MA: Harvard University Press.

Welsh, E. (2002). Dealing with data: Using NVivo in the qualitative data analysis process. *Forum: Qualitative Social Research*, *3*(2). Article 26. Retrieved from http://nbn-resolving .de/urn:nbn:de:0114-fqs0202260.

Winner, L. (1980). Do artifacts have politics? *Daedalus*, *109*(1), 121–136.

11

COMMUNICATIVE METHODOLOGY AND SOCIAL IMPACT

Aitor Gómez

Introduction

Today's society is a product of profound changes that have transformed both our point of view and the social perceptions of our surroundings. Dialog constitutes a fundamental concept (Flecha, Gómez, & Puigvert, 2003) used to understand the nature of such changes. Power elements (explaining social class dynamics, gender differences, and ethnic and cultural inequalities) still exist. However, egalitarian dialog is becoming more prevalent, and when authorities deny this dialog, conflict arises (Gómez, Latorre, Sánchez, & Flecha, 2006).

Reflexivity and the central value that the analysis of the subject's actions acquires are consequences of this process. Research methodologies, in this case, also turn to a preference for techniques that allow for an understanding of such intersubjective relations among people when interacting in society, which is more interesting in the study of the life world, the analysis of the daily lives of individuals, and the relationships among us. This understanding necessitates complex analyses based on several intervening variables.

Currently, more researchers are developing new methodologies for analyzing diverse elements that compose social reality. The importance of intersubjective relationships from a communicative perspective serves as an example of this transformation, which is currently affecting the field of scientific research. Present-day society demands complex studies that can explain dynamic situations. Traditional research designs are not useful in understanding what is happening around us because what is happening is changing to the point where if we do not combine techniques and disciplines, studies will become partial accounts of a much broader reality.

At the same time, the social impact of research conducted worldwide is becoming more central. National and international research councils and agencies are now funding research projects with both scientific and social impacts. Researching with communicative methodology has demonstrated ways to achieve high social impact through research efforts. In the following sections, we introduce how we can reach social, political, and scientific impact through communicative methodology.

Conceptual overview of the communicative methodology

The communicative perspective applies elements of several research traditions, including phenomenology, constructivism, symbolic interactionism, ethnomethodology, dramaturgy, transcultural studies, dialogic action, communicative action, and dialogic learning. The most innovative aspect of this methodological approach pertains to the fact that it addresses growing societal demands for dialog, whereby individuals adopt more reflective and critical views on our environment (Gómez, Latorre, Sánchez, & Flecha, 2006). The communicative methodology, with its postulates and research process, is designed to reflect the present moment and to offer innovative and imaginative answers in response to new research requirements appearing in the modern world.

Postulates of the communicative perspective

The communicative methodology is based on one intersubjective/dialogical epistemological concept. This means that a reality-based point of view (phenomena studied) is a product of intersubjective agreements made between individuals who use dialog to define realities around them. In other words, meanings given to objects/phenomena/processes around us are meanings that we share because we have discussed them and reached agreements. This point of view is not a closed point of view. The meanings of objects/phenomena/processes that surround us can change. Whenever we talk about them again or when we reach different agreements based on different arguments, the meanings that we ascribe to them change.

The communicative methodology is a tool that allows us to explain and understand the actions of individuals in reference to phenomena and processes studied. When analyzing reality from this point of view, researchers working with this type of methodology assume (or refer to) contributions made by other individuals (e.g., Chomsky, 1988; Searle, 1999; Mead, 1934; Habermas, 1984; or Beck, 1992). Those contributions lead to several postulates that the communicative perspective assumes (Gómez, Latorre, Sánchez, & Flecha, 2006).

Universality of language and action

Language and action are universal abilities common to all people as a result of their humanness. All people have the capacity to develop language skills and to perform actions (Habermas, 1984; Luria, 1976; Cole & Scribner, 1974). For this reason, from a methodological point of view, we must advocate for methods that compile and make all participants' voices worthy of the reality studied.

Individuals as transformational social agents

Everyone is capable of interpreting the world around us in certain ways and of acting within it. That is, individuals are not "objects" subordinated by the structures that create dynamics that shape us. People are not cultural dopes (Garfinkel, 1967). Rather, they have a critical understanding of reality. They have the option to rebel against power relationships, make their own decisions, and determine their actions as a result. Therefore, from the standpoint of communicative methodologies, the techniques employed allow space for individuals to freely express their agency.

Communicative rationality

Individuals who work under the umbrella of communicative methodology assume that communicative rationality, as Habermas (1984) defines it, is the universal basis for language and action competencies that all people have. Communicative rationality implies that individuals act not only in their own self-interest (instrumental rationality) but also to reach agreements. For this reason, based on this methodological approach, we seek techniques that allow for an analysis of situations based on this postulate.

Common sense

In social sciences and education fields, we study phenomena and processes that involve people. We must bear in mind that everyone interprets reality on the basis of their own common sense or rather based on beliefs and knowledge that they have internalized over their lives, which they use to interpret their surroundings (Schütz, 1967). Individuals who use the communicative approach seek out ways to organize research in a way that allows us to identify the commonsense beliefs of individuals involved in research.

No interpretative hierarchy

Individuals who use the communicative approach assume that the interpretations of research participants have the same value as those of researchers. Given that participants of the phenomena or processes studied offer knowledge and experience on a given reality, that we assume all individuals have capacities for language and action, and that we are able to know our world, researchers who use this approach agree that there should be no interpretative hierarchy. In turn, it is possible to break with the monopolization of expert knowledge. "Experts" are not experts when they do not discuss their ideas with others (Beck, 1994). Through the techniques that we employ, we ensure that all study participant interpretations (all voices) are considered.

Same epistemological level

As a direct consequence of the prior postulate, we assume that there is no epistemological unevenness between the researcher and researched. All individuals involved in research have the same capacity to understand phenomena or researched processes. Thus, there is a need to identify the best way for each individual to contribute his point of view and interpretations. Through the creation of spaces of dialog in which all research participants are offered the same opportunities to contribute knowledge, epistemological unevenness can be reduced considerably. Researchers offer knowledge from the scientific community, while research participants offer knowledge and experiences of reality, which are investigated by all.

Dialogic knowledge

Individuals who apply the communicative approach assume that knowledge is generated through a dialogic process, which is not an objective process that involves searching for knowledge (positivist perspective), nor is it the result of the subjective interpretations of researchers (interpretative perspective). Rather, knowledge is generated through a process in which we all participate. By means of dialog, we share interpretations, points of view, and arguments that facilitate our conception of reality. This sharing thus involves an intersubjective process of knowledge creation focused on possible venues toward overcoming injustices and oppression (Freire, 2003).

The three main methodological facets of the communicative methodology

To apply these postulates, the communicative methodology uses *communicative action:* it facilitates dialog based on understanding between subjects capable of engaging in discussion and action (Habermas, 1984). Contributions are not valued based on the status of the speaker, but rather in terms of his or her arguments. Communicative action cannot be carried out through a research project based on a methodology that allows what is considered good or true to be imposed from the research team's position of power.

In terms of communicative action, the communicative methodology prioritizes the capacities and communicative skills acquired by those who encounter barriers due to a lack of academic skills or due to membership to a socially excluded group. The premise is that facing such barriers generates learning, which is just as or more valuable than learning acquired from academic criteria. Universal structures of rationality must result from interactions between all cultures, and pretensions of truth must seek universal acceptance while they may be rectified upon being exposed to other cultures.

The communicative methodology acts according to its postulates, which are applied through communicative action. To prevent misunderstanding, it must be clarified that concepts such as "ideal speech situation," "egalitarian dialog," "consensus," "creation of meaning," and "solidarity" do not denote that, in reality, everyone and/or all groups function from the same position of power, we participate in fully egalitarian dialog, we always agree (as if disagreement did not exist), or we always enjoy solidarity. There is undoubtedly considerable distance between progressive egalitarian objectives and practical reality. However, such concepts and efforts to develop them and put them into practice help us move closer to them.

Communicative organization of the research

I have described and analyzed postulates and procedures of the communicative methodology. To carry out the postulates more consistently, we require a favorable context that fosters its development. This context is where communicative organization come into play. When defining a project, it is important to reach a consensus throughout the research process with individuals, groups and/or organizations that are part of and/or related to the group studied (Yuste, Serrano, Girbés, & Arandia, 2014; Munté, Serradell, & Sordé, 2011). Communicative organization follows a concrete premise, researching with and for studied communities, in turn highlighting the active role of participation throughout the entire research process (Flecha & Gómez, 2004).

To facilitate this process, communicative organization carry out the following actions, among others.

Advisory committee creation

The creation of an advisory committee entails the creation of a group of people composed of representatives of collectives, groups and/or communities of the population participating in the investigation and including their diverse contributions, modes of understanding and transformative realities into a given study. Representatives of vulnerable groups are those who are considered the most socially vulnerable within certain vulnerable groups. Normally, these committees include at least two representatives of any vulnerable group participating in a given study. Such committees always include researchers and representatives of collectives because egalitarian and intersubjective dialog between them forms an interpreted reality. Those selected from vulnerable groups must determine ways to overcome inequalities.

Such advisory bodies are designed to contribute knowledge, critically revise documents, direct project development and processes, control what is being carried out through the inclusion of all voices, evaluate entire research projects including conclusions, and, most importantly, ensure that the obtained results help transform the conditions of collectives focused upon in studies.

Advisory committee monitoring and participation is best facilitated when daily literature reviews, state-of-the-art information searches, data collection efforts, analysis techniques, and report-writing tasks consider everyone's voices.

Constitution of operative work groups. For an organization to be more efficient, it is helpful to create specific and flexible work groups that are assigned concrete tasks (e.g., elaborating on theoretical bases, defining methodologies, preparing information analyses). These groups, which are formed based on the needs of a given project, are designed to generate knowledge on specific issues.

Plenary meetings. It is important for research teams to meet several times throughout a research project to analyze, discuss and agree on all documents and proposals elaborated through different study groups. Once these tasks are carried out, the team takes the results to the advisory committee.

Communicative data collection techniques

We will analyze the following three strategies of communicative data collection: communicative daily life stories, communicative focus groups, and communicative observations. The position of the researcher is the same for the three techniques. While meeting with participants, researchers always introduce the main theoretical issues on the studied matter. The goal is to interpret reality through egalitarian and intersubjective dialog whereby participants contribute their feelings, suggestions, and opinions and whereby researchers present relevant theories, facilitating a dialogical interpretation of reality. In this sense, through communicative rationality, it is possible to overcome interpretative hierarchies and thus to interpret realities at the same epistemological level.

Communicative daily life story

A life story is a researched subject's biographical narration. In contrast, a communicative life story is created through dialog between two people (a researcher and someone who is recounting information) that involves reflecting upon and jointly interpreting the daily life of the person providing information. The objective of the story created is to record a reflected narration of the participant's daily life and to interpret this story to identify facets of the present and past and expectations for the future. It is important to study thoughts; reflections; and ways of acting, living, and resolving concrete situations in the participants' daily lives. This technique involves using an outline that incorporates key study issues in accordance with the theoretical framework applied and the objectives proposed. It is crucial that representatives of the "studied" collectives participate in elaborating on such questions. In this sense, advisory committees are essential in validating such procedures by bringing research and participants together through egalitarian dialog (Aubert, Melgar, & Valls, 2011; Garcia-Yeste, 2014).

Communicative focus groups

From a communicative orientation, collective interpretations are based on study themes through dialog. Participants must reach an agreement the group's function through prior reflection on themes and on their positions or opinions on a given subject. In such a context, the researcher acts as a group participant while assuming the role of coordinator to ensure that dialog remains focused on the research theme and that everyone participates. Clearly, the researcher should not renounce his or her knowledge to maintain egalitarian dialog; instead, he or she should engage with everyone on egalitarian terms. The group in turn prepares an outline of themes to address. Interpretations and conclusions are then established through group dialog, and these conclusions are then debated and agreed upon definitively in a second meeting (Rosell, Martínez, Flecha, & Álvarez, 2014; Aubert, Melgar, & Valls, 2011).

Communicative observations

In the communicative approach, the observer and subject of observations interact and share interpretations of actions, attitudes, motivations, skills, and non-verbal language on egalitarian terms. As is the case for other communicative techniques, interpretation involves both parties. Dialog occurring before observation facilitates the sharing of objectives, and dialog occurring afterward validates the results obtained. There can be two points of view on the same action, as follows: that of the observer and that of the observed. Both seek points in common through dialog to reach a consensus, which is precisely what makes observations communicative. Communicative observation involves defining possible skills normally employed in daily situations that should be observed, which involves making a list of important facets that a situation or activity in question demands; this list can be prepared jointly with those involved in observation. Observation takes place in the space where a given activity is usually carried out to observe the series of tasks and skills defined in situ while noting everything that is considered relevant and while keeping in mind different ideas and theories constructed throughout the research process. Once observations are made, a consensus with the individual observed must be reached by sharing the text created and by selecting aspects that are relevant to the research project. These aspects must be related to the list previously elaborated and must facilitate interpretation (Gómez, Latorre, Sánchez, & Flecha, 2006; Gómez, Racionero, & Sordé, 2010).

Communicative data analysis

Communicative data analyses are designed to address the need to move beyond exclusionary research in basing all interpretations of reality on scientific evidence with a transformative orientation, thus promoting social inclusion. Information is always analyzed through either exclusionary or transformative dimensions. The exclusionary dimension includes all barriers and obstacles that reproduce social inequalities, and the transformative dimension considers possible solutions to such barriers as a way to overcome social inequalities (Pulido, Elboj, Campdepadrós, & Cabré, 2014).

Communicative methodology is oriented toward social transformation and the best way to analyze and present information involves using both dimensions, as this allows one to identify the main sources of exclusionary information and the main solutions at the same time. Problems and possible solutions are identified through an egalitarian and intersubjective dialog between researchers and participants.

The social impact of research?

The social impact of research in the social sciences and humanities (SSH) has been questioned in recent years, especially due to difficulties associated with evaluating the usefulness of SSH project findings. For instance, the SSH were not presented as a challenge per se in the first H2020 draft.[1] In the end, researchers, international associations and the European Parliament succeeded at including them in the H2020. However, we are "under review."

The H2020 evaluates all research proposals based on the following three main criteria: study excellence, quality, efficiency, and *impact*. Any research project funded by the H2020 must have a potential impact. However, more important than scientific impact, research projects must also concretely benefit citizens through social impact.

Some problems associated with the social impact of research projects are directly related to the objective to measure social impact. Researchers are not used to thinking of their work as a means of generating social impact. As researchers do not think about this issue from the very beginning, it is necessary to clearly show how we can achieve social impact from the start of the research process. There is no tradition of gathering evidence on the social impact of research projects because in the past, this question has not been considered relevant. Finally, there are several problems concerning the measurement of social impact.

For these reasons, the European Commission approved the IMPACT-EV project coordinated by the CREA (Community of Research on Excellence for All). The main objective of the IMPACT-EV is to develop a permanent system of selecting, monitoring and evaluating various impacts of SSH research. The IMPACT-EV evaluates scientific the impact of SSH research with a specific emphasis on policy-relevant and social impact (Flecha, 2014–2017).

Following Burdge and Vanclay, social impact can be conceptualized as "the process of assessing or estimating, in advance, the social consequences that are likely to follow from specific policy actions or project development, particularly in the context of appropriate national, state, or provincial environmental policy legislation, and not of (SSH) research" (Burdge & Vanclay, 1995, p. 31). In this sense, social impact occurs when individuals and societies experienced evidence-based improvements (according to societal objectives) as a result of research results.

Social Impact Open Repository (SIOR)

The SIOR is a non-profit initiative launched by the IMPACT-EV consortium.[2] It is an open source repository that stores evidence of social impact. Any researcher or research group can freely upload evidence of their research study's social impact by registering with the SIOR and creating an ORCID ID. Any institution or citizen around the world can in turn freely review study results, researchers, and research groups based on a social impact factor. The repository only includes research projects that have had a social impact. The evidence is peer reviewed and scored (1 to 10) according to the following criteria.

Connection to EU2020 targets or to similar official international targets. The SIOR uses targets defined by citizens through their democratically elected representatives in defining what is considered social impact. The most important EU2020 targets used in the IMPACT-EV are the following:

- Employment → Increasing the employment prospects of individuals aged 20–64. EU target = 75 percent employed.
- Education → Reducing early school dropout rates. EU target = below 10 percent.
- Increasing the number of 30–34 year olds completing higher education. EU target = at least 40 percent.
- Fighting poverty and social exclusion → Reducing the number of people living in or at risk of living in poverty and being subjected social exclusion. EU target = 20 million less.

Percentage of improvement achieved in relation to initial conditions. The SIOR scores research projects according to such improvements. A maximum of 10 is granted when a project can demonstrate a 30 percent improvement from initial conditions. The score diminishes from 10 to 7 when a project inspires only some improvement.

Impact transferability. Transferability occurs when actions developed based on a project's findings have been transferred to other contexts besides the original one. To achieve a positive score, it is necessary to demonstrate transferability in at least two different contexts.

Publication in scientific journals (with recognized impact) or in publications of official governmental or non-governmental bodies. At least one article citing the main results and social impact a project must be published.

Sustainability. The impacts of actions resulting from a project's findings must be sustained over time. This item is particularly important, as many research projects have social impact during the research process but not after this process ends. It is important to demonstrate how a project can have an impact years after it concludes.

When researchers wish to cite a project in the repository, they must register with an email or ORCID and include all required information regarding their project's impact. They must also explain all project impacts and support them with scientific evidence. Before publishing project information, the SIOR team reviews (peer reviews) all uploaded information. If it is correct, the information is published.

In the repository, only studies with social impact are listed. Even a score of "1" is a good result, as many studies do not have enough social impact to even be included in the repository. The most important facet of the SIOR lies in its role as an open source of information on international research projects that shows data on social impact independent of any score.

The SIOR is already affecting the scientific community. Researchers who are unsure of whether their work has achieved social impact are now considering this resource and seeking evidence (even for completed projects). In addition, researchers whose work has not had social impact are beginning to consider this resource for future research project proposals.

Reaching social impact through communicative methodology

In this last section, I describe two research projects carried out based on the communicative methodology that have achieved the highest social impact scores registered in the SIOR. The projects show how we can achieve social impact in the following two areas: education and employment.

INCLUD-ED: Overcoming absenteeism through successful actions

The INCLUD-ED project (Flecha, 2006–2011) involved analyzing educational strategies that contribute to overcoming inequality and social exclusion while promoting social cohesion (with a particular focus on vulnerable groups). Applying the postulates and organizing, collecting and analyzing information through a communicative orientation, Successful Educational Actions (SEAs) were identified.

Communicative case studies were carried out in two schools as learning communities in Spain from 2006 to 2011. Among other techniques, communicative focus groups were held and daily life stories were recorded during the fifth year of the study. All recorded information was analyzed through communicative data analysis, and the research process was verified and validated by an advisory committee created at the beginning of the research project.

All of the results generated show how SEAs are decreasing early school drop-out rates and risks of exclusion in other areas. Several EU official documents and resolutions demonstrate this fact and prove their political impact. SEAs have had considerable social impact in deprived areas. One school participating in the project reduced absenteeism from 30 percent to 10 percent over one year and over the following two years cited only occasional absenteeism (Aubert, 2011). SEAs have also generated a statistically significant increase in instrumental learning among disadvantaged students (Valls & Kyriakides, 2013).

WORKALO: Employment success

The Fifth Framework Program Project, WORKALO, serves as an example of a research project that has improved employability outcomes. WORKALO (Flecha, 2001–2004) was designed to create new occupational opportunities for cultural minorities, specifically for the Roma. Traditionally, courses oriented toward marginalized groups have not improved employability outcomes for the Roma, because they have been based on deficit thinking theories rather than on the competences and skills that Roma people already offer. While in many cases courses could help students develop specific skills in a specialized profession, course participants often fail secure jobs as a result of ethnic discrimination.

The project analyzed the skills that Roma people already offer, several of which were found to be in demand in the information-based labor market. From the WORKALO project's results and as a result of specific partnerships forged between researchers and Romani associations, specific vocational training courses that connect Roma women and migrants with jobs were designed (Sordé-Martí, Munté, Contreras, & Prieto-Flores, 2012).

This intervention was designed to mitigate the above-mentioned barriers that Roma people face when accessing the labor market. The project involved designing a cafeteria monitor training course. Given Romani women's potential contributions to school cafeterias with Roma children, their labor insertion proved very successful (in comparison to other courses), resulting in an 80 percent success rate. Similar programs typically achieve a less than 20 percent rate of labor market inclusion (Sordé-Martí, Serradell, Puigvert, & Munté, 2014).

Both projects were organized using a communicative orientation through the use of communicative techniques and communicative data analyses and by presenting all results in a communicative way. As a result, vulnerable groups participated from the very start of the research process to the final presentation of results to the European Parliament.

In both cases, the application of communicative techniques allowed for the establishment of egalitarian dialog between researchers and participants based on a common understanding of reality. For the INCLUD-ED, a conceptualization of SEAs was established through discussions on social science theories and on the daily life experiences of the participants involved.

During the presentation of the WORKALO project's results to the European Parliament in 2004, an illiterate Roma woman discussed the results of the project with a Catalan Europarlamentarian. As a result of this dialog, the Europarlamentarian presented a motion to the Spanish Parliament to recognize the Roma population in Spain. The motion was approved unanimously, exhibiting the strong political impact of the research project resulting from egalitarian and intersubjective dialog achieved between all participants.

Notes

1   The H2020 (Horizon 2020) is the new European Framework Program on Research that follows principles and recommendations established through the EU2020 (European Union 2020).
2   The SIOR is accessible at www.ub.edu/sior/index.php

References

Aubert, A, Melgar, P., and Valls, R. (2011). Communicative daily life stories and focus groups: Proposals for overcoming gender violence among teenagers. *Qualitative Inquiry*, *17*(3), 295–303.

Aubert, A. (2011). Moving beyond social exclusion through dialogue. *International Studies in Sociology of Education*, *21*(1), 63–75.

Beck, U. (1992). *Risk society: Towards a new modernity*. New Delhi: Sage

Beck, U., Giddens, A., and Lash, S. (1994). *Reflexive modernization: Politics, tradition and aesthetics in the modern social order*. Cambridge, MA: Polity Press.

Burdge, R., and Vanclay, F. (1995). Social impact assessment. In Vanclay, F., and Bronstein, D. (Eds.), *Environmental and social impact assessment*. Chichester: Wiley.

Chomsky, N. (1988). *Language and politics*. New York: Black Rose Books.

Cole, M., and Scribner, S. (1974). *Culture and thought: A psychological introduction*. New York: John Wiley and Sons.

Flecha, R., Gómez, J., and Puigvert, L. (2003). *Contemporary sociological theory*. New York: Peter Lang.

Flecha, R., and Gómez, J. (2004). Participatory paradigms: Researching 'with' rather than 'on.' In B. Crossan, J. Gallacher and M. Osborne (Eds.), *Researching widening access: Issues and approaches in an international context* (pp. 129–140). London: Routledge.

Flecha, R. (2014–2017). *IMPACT-EV. Evaluating the impact and outcomes of EU SSH research*. Seventh Framework Programme for research, technological development and demonstration. European Union.

Flecha, R. (2006–2011). *INCLUD-ED. Strategies for inclusion and social cohesion in Europe from Education*. Sixth Framework Programme. European Union.

Flecha, R. (2001–2004). *WORKALO. The creation of new occupational patterns for cultural minorities: the gypsy case*. Fifth Framework Programme. European Union.

Freire, P. (2003). *Pedagogy of the oppressed*. New York: Continuum.

Garcia-Yeste, C. (2014). Overcoming stereotypes through the other women's communicative daily life stories. *Qualitative Inquiry*, *20*(7), 923–927.

Garfinkel, H. (1967). *Studies in ethnomethodology*. New York: Prentice-Hall.

Gómez, J., Latorre, A., Sánchez, M., and Flecha, R. (2006). *Metodología comunicativa crítica*. Barcelona: Hipatia.

Gómez, A., Racionero, S., and Sordé, T. (2010). Ten years of critical communicative methodology. *International Review of Qualitative Research*, *3*(1), 17–43.

Habermas, J. (1984). *The theory of communicative action, Vol. 1: Reason and the rationalization of society*. Boston: Beacon Press.

Luria, A. R. (1976). *Cognitive development: Its cultural and social foundations*. Cambridge, MA: Harvard University Press.

Mead, G. (1934). *Mind, self and society*. Chicago: University of Chicago Press.

Munté, A., Serradell, O., and Sordé, T. (2011). From research to policy: Roma participation through communicative organization. *Qualitative Inquiry*, *17*(3), 256–266.

Pulido, C., Elboj, C., Campdepadrós, R., and Cabré, J. (2014). Exclusionary and transformative dimensions communicative analysis enhancing solidarity among women to overcome gender violence. *Qualitative Inquiry*, *20*(7), 889–894.

Rosell, L.R., Martínez, I., Flecha, A., and Álvarez, P. (2014). Successful communicative focus groups with teenagers and young people: How to identify the mirage of upward mobility. *Qualitative Inquiry*, *20*(7), 863–869.

Schütz, A. (1967). *The phenomenology of the social world*. Evanston, IL: Northwestern University Press.

Searle, J. (1999). *Mind, language and society: Philosophy in the real world*. New York: Basic Books.

Sordé-Martí, T., Munté, A., Contreras, A., and Prieto-Flores, O. (2012). Immigrant and native Romani women in Spain: Building alliances and developing shared strategies. *Journal of Ethnic and Migration Studies*, *38*(8), 1233–1249.

Sordé-Martí, T., Serradell, O., Puigvert, L., and Munté, A. (2014). Solidarity networks that challenge racialized discourses: The case of Romani immigrant women in Spain. *European Journal of Women's Studies*, *21*(1), 87–102.

Valls, R., and Kyriakides, L. (2013). The power of interactive groups: How diversity of adults volunteering in classroom groups can promote inclusion and success for children of vulnerable minority ethnic populations. *Cambridge Journal of Education*, *43*(1), 17–33.

Yuste, M., Serrano, M. A., Girbés, S., and Arandia, M. (2014). Romantic love and gender violence: Clarifying misunderstandings through communicative organization of the research. *Qualitative Inquiry*, *20*(7), 850–855.

CODA: ALL I REALLY NEED TO KNOW ABOUT QUALITATIVE RESEARCH I LEARNED IN HIGH SCHOOL

The 2016 Qualitative High graduation commencement address

Johnny Saldaña

Alma mater

(the Valedictorian of Qualitative High School, dressed in a black graduation gown and cap, steps to the podium; he addresses the audience)

VALEDICTORIAN: Could we all please rise, as you're able, for the singing of our school's alma mater. We all know the melody, right? I'll warm up to get us started; join in when you catch on.

(the Valedictorian leads the audience as they hum through the melody of "Daisy")

Everyone, now:

(slides: song lyrics; the audience sings to the tune of "Daisy")

> Qual High, Qual High,
> Oh, what a lovely name!
> Life is our lab,
> Researching is our game.
> Whether narrative, codes, or theory,
> We love to do inquiry.
> And how we write
> Into the night.
> Hail to thee, hallowed school,
> Qual High!
>   *(Valedictorian shouts:* Second verse!)

Qual High, Qual High,
Loyal are we to you.
We're word crazy,
Some of the chosen few.
We don't really crunch statistics,
We're more about heuristics.
And we'll not rest
Until we're the best.
Hail to thee, hallowed school,
Qual High!
   (applause and cheers)
Thank you. Please be seated.

Welcome

(slide: graduation cap and diploma)

Principal Denzin, distinguished faculty and staff, parents, family members, friends, and students of Qualitative High: Welcome, and thank you for the honor of selecting me as valedictorian for Qual High's 2016 graduation commencement address.

Curriculum

We've all worked hard for our high school degrees by studying lots of different subjects in qualitative inquiry. We had a great curriculum and set of classes at Qual High with some really outstanding teachers. Just in my senior year alone, I took:

(slides: class titles)

Period 1, Grounded Theory, with that teacher that everybody loves, Ms. Charmaz.
Period 2, Phenomenology, with the mellow and laid back Mr. Vagle.
Period 3, Ethnography, with Qual High's sweetheart of a teacher, Ms. Tracy.
Period 4, Case Studies, with my soulful mentor, Ms. De la Garza.
Then Lunch, which usually consisted of either barbeque or fried chicken.
Period 5, Autoethnography, with that rockin' dude, Mr. Poulos.
Period 6, CAQDAS Computer Lab, with my gal-pal Ms. Jackson.
Period 7, Ont-Ep, or Ontologies and Epistemologies, with the brilliant Ms. Mirka.
And Period 8, with Mr. Creswell, AP Mixed Methods – or, as we jokingly liked to call it, the "mixed meth lab."

(slide: dancers on stage)

We had great after school extracurricular activities, too, like Poetic Inquiry and Arts-Based Research. These programs were after school for no credit because, you know, they're frills. But our award-winning Qual High drama club did put on some pretty outstanding play productions this year, like:

(*slides: play productions*)

A Datum in the Sun, Category on a Hot Tin Roof, To Code a Mockingbird, the children's theatre touring show of *The Wizard of Observation*, and the club's annual musicals: *The Phenomenology of the Opera* and *Fieldwork on the Roof*.

(*slides: high school proms*)

But at Qual High it wasn't all work. We also had fun, like at the school's annual proms with our wonderful themes: "Enchanted Ethnography," "A Million Case Studies," and "Grounded Theory under the Sea."

Now, you may think that there's more to learn after we receive our diplomas today. But, in a way, all we really need to know about qualitative research we learned in high school.

Cliques

(*slides: high school cliques*)

For example, at Qual High we learned that there are cliques – social groups of like-minded tribes who cluster into categories of affinity such as the arts-based researchers, the autoethnographers, the mixed methods researchers, the grounded theorists, and the poststructuralists.

(*video clip: the cliques and cafeteria scene from* Mean Girls: www.youtube.com/watch?v=IVhfrUkH5JY)
(*slides: high school cliques*)

Cliques usually sat together at their respective lunchroom tables and shop-talked passionately about what they shared in common. We naturally gravitate to those with whom we share a common interest. And, it made us feel as if we belonged to a little community. But remember at lunch how, in our cliques, we sometimes talked smack about others sitting at different tables? Ethnographers would glance toward the phenomenologists and think, "I wonder what it is they do, exactly." Poststructuralists would sneer at the grounded theorists and think, "Losers!" Mixed-methods researchers would glance suspiciously at the arts-based inquiry table and whisper among themselves, "Well, yeah, but it's not *real* research."

What we learned is that Qual High, like life, has cliques. And though some of us crossed borders now and then because of our different interests, there seems to be a tightly controlled mind-set in some of these camps, with their leaders or big dogs who set the tone for the rest of the group. There'll be people in your clique who'll be your best friends forever and ever, and others from different cliques who'll think that they're just too cool for you. We were told by our teachers that we're one big global community and that we should all learn to get along with each other. But at Qual High, we've been taught to compete with our raging hormones of professional disagreement, fighting in the parking lot or locker room over who's got the biggest paradigm.

Rivalry

(slide: high school football players)

Now, sometimes competition can be a good thing. We had great team rivalry with the alternative school, Post-Qual High, with their post-football games at their post-stadium, watching their post-students in the post-stands post-applauding their post-marching band making post-formations on the post-field, with their post-cheerleaders and post-pep squad excitedly waving their post-pom-poms, rallying around the post-football team's post-quarterback making post-touchdowns at the post-goal posts.

(slide: math Olympics winners)

We had great team rivalry with Quant High, too, even though they always kicked our butts at science fairs and math Olympics. After all, their school motto was *(slide)*, "*Gloria in numero*" – "Strength in Numbers." But let's not forget our school motto *(slide)*: "*Ut intellegas omnia*" – "To Understand Is Everything." Yeah, Quant High may calculate the mean, but at Qual High *we* calculate *meaning*.

Literature

(slides: libraries and book covers)

In literature classes, we read the great masterworks of the field, like *The Presentation of Self in Everyday Life, The Discovery of Grounded Theory*, and *Naturalistic Inquiry*. In secret, a few of us even snuck off and delved into the banned books section to get off on such titles as *Sick Societies* and *Tearoom Trade*. We learned a lot from our teachers about the classics. They felt it was important to know our literary history, our scholarly roots.

Admittedly, I originally thought that these moldy-oldies wouldn't have anything to say to me now. But after reading books by Ina Corinne Brown, Clifford

Geertz, and Elliot Liebow – not just reading *about* them in a research handbook but reading what *they themselves* actually wrote – it made me realize how rich our field is, how insightful our ancestors were, and how our own work today is truly built on their foundations. And just because we can Amazon.com or Wikipedia our way through a literature review these days, doesn't mean we should ignore the genius of what's already been discovered and written about social life. I encourage my incoming and current classmates: Don't just stick to what's been published in the last five to ten years. Pick up a 20th-century classic now and then. Read it. Learn for yourself why it's considered a masterpiece.

Composition

Now, reading was hard but writing was harder – even the faculty admitted how tough it was to write qualitatively.

> *(video clip: the writer's struggle scene from* Hamlet 2: www.youtube.com/watch?v=hg10aV0uPQk)
> *(slides: people writing)*

Rivalry wasn't just with other schools, it was even amongst ourselves. Sometimes we felt bullied when a senior mocked us because we couldn't grasp an ontology, or when we hadn't read the latest journal issue, or if we hadn't cited their work in our most recent report. Manuscript submissions were the worst – when our articles that we worked so hard on were ripped apart by badass peer reviewers who tore down our self-esteem. It was qualitative hazing, of sorts – a ritual we had to go through to be accepted into the publications club. But many of us will never forget that day when we finally made it into the journal of life!

> *(slide: the journal cover for* "Qualitative Inquiry")

Teachers kept telling us to "find" our voice. And, that journey took a bit of time. But what I eventually learned at Qual High was that I didn't need to "find" my voice – all I needed to do was to *trust* it.

CAQDAS lab

> *(slides: CAQDAS screenshots)*

I did OK in reading and writing qualitatively, but math and science were not my strong suit. That's probably why I flunked CAQDAS computer lab and had to retake the course – twice. I remember going up to Ms. Jackson one day after my program crashed and whining, "Ms. Jackson – digital tools are, like, *hard*!" She looked me straight in the eye and said, "Johnny, it's not the software that's holding you back; it's your fear." Nevertheless, she placed me in the freshman remedial CAQDAS class. But even there, I had a very hard time trying to figure things out, even after learning that stupid "Qualitative Software Song" – remember it? Sing along with me, if you do:

(slides: song lyrics; sung to the tune of "The ABC Song")

AnSWR, AQUAD, Qualrus, CAT,
ATLAS.ti, Dedoose, INTERACT,
Transana, NVivo,
V-Note, WordStat, Quirkos, oh,
MAXQDA, DiscoverText,
HyperRESEARCH, none of these complex.

(slides: CAQDAS screenshots)

But they *were* complex – to me, at least. Some students aced these courses: tech-head whiz kids who got it and knew all the right functions to click while I was still struggling to learn the difference between a code and a node. But I didn't give up, and I came out with an A-minus – the qual nerd's "F." I'll admit there's still a lot more to learn, and you're never too old to learn, right? Like Ms. Jackson said – it's not the software that's holding us back; it's our fear.

Driving

(slides: high school drivers)

Speaking of fear, high school was also the time we learned how to drive. It was a major achievement to get that license from the PhD-DMV. In dissertation driving class, we were scared, at first, to get behind that wheel, armed only with our master's learning permit and a committee chair yelling at us, "You're going too fast! Slow down, slow down, *slow down!*" But we paid careful attention to the road as we sped down Seminar Street and Doctoral Drive, following the rules and braking quickly when danger lay ahead. We'd steer and swerve and not accidentally step on the fast-track gas pedal and run head on into committee members standing on a sidewalk, even through there were times when some of us really, really wanted to. Oh, but what an achievement, to finally get that license from the PhD-DMV! Yeah, there are student car loan payments to make for what seems like an eternity, but now, we can go anywhere we want.

Detention

Admittedly, a few of us did spend a little time in in-school and after-school detention.

(video clip: the detention monitor's opening instructions scene in The Breakfast Club: www.youtube.com/watch?v=Z2WZrxuwDhs)
   (slides: high school detention)

Detention wasn't all that bad, though. It was a time and place to reflect, to reflex, to refract. A time when the suspension monitor forced us to write analytic memos on our deviant actions and what they all mean. The bad boys and bad girls of Qual High who refused, rejected, avoided, and failed, who wouldn't put up with anyone's othering or interactional BS, critically theorized about the oppressive panopticons of power and the stigma of our presentations of self in this total institutional asylum of a school.

The badasses of Qual High even had a nickname for their gang – the Outliers. The police would sometimes catch them spray painting graffiti on school walls such as *(slides)*: "POWER TO THE PARTICIPANTS," "N = *ME*!", and "FOUCAULT? FOUC YOU!"

Deviance, though, can sometimes be a good thing. It means you're straying away from the norm, challenging the status quo, and presenting an alternative perspective on life. The time it becomes a problem, however, is when resistance transforms into intellectual obstruction. It becomes a problem when ontological defiance transforms into epistemological bullying and axiological manipulation. Walk your own path, but don't peer-pressure or kidnap others along the way. Butting heads with someone may get yours bitten off. As we were taught in our Ethics class *(slide)*: "Do no harm, but take no shit."

(aside)

Sorry, Principal Denzin.

Teachers

Us students had a tough time at Qual High, but we also know our teachers did, too.

(video clip: the literature class scene from 10 Things I Hate About You: www.youtube.com/watch?v=H_3eOtD_0GA)
   (slides: high school teachers interacting with students)

Sometimes when I passed by the faculty lounge, I heard teachers saying things behind the door such as, "I can't teach my students how to think," or "He wouldn't know a paradigm if it fell on his head," and "What do those kids expect me to do, pull a grounded theory out of my butt?" Some teachers made darn sure that when it came to research methods, it was either their way or the highway, while others nurtured and encouraged us to find our own ways of working.

Perhaps you're hoping some of us will become the next Arlie Russell Hochschild or the next Erving Goffman. But maybe, just maybe, I want to be the next Barbara Ehrenreich or the next Dwight Conquergood. Or maybe I just want to be the *first* Johnny Saldaña. After we leave Qual High, the methodological decisions are up to us.

Teachers: We appreciate what you did for us, shaping, sharpening, and challenging our minds. We know that qualitative teachers work hard, put in long hours, and you're grossly underpaid. But we'll never forget what you did for us. You taught us how to look at life in new and different ways. You taught us how to think for ourselves, to not be swept away by what's trendy in the field. And you taught us to strive for rigor, credibility, and trustworthiness in everything we do. You have influenced and affected our lives for the better, and we are eternally grateful to you.

Sex

All we really need to know about qualitative research we learned in high school. For example, we learned about sex.

> (*video clip: the fake bedroom sex scene from* Easy A: www.youtube.com/watch?v=QGIQQBEj9uU)

Oh yeah, our classes in qualitative health care taught us about the biological and reproductive aspects of being human, but the teenagers in us fooled around. We even had labels for it, too *(slides)*:

1st base: Codes
2nd base: Categories
3rd base: Theories

It was a time to naturally experiment, to discover what turned us on. I'm not ashamed to admit it, we all did it. When we should have been constructing matrices, flow charts, and diagrams for mixed-methods class, sometimes I was locked away in my bedroom under the covers − writing autoethnography.

> (*slides: terms*)

But, I mean, let's face it − in high school, sex was all around us: gender studies, women's studies, masculinity studies, feminist theory, queer theory, trans studies − it seemed as if every course in junior year was about sex, sex, sex. I mean, come on, the terms our teachers used: *raw data, horizontalization, probing, oral history, thick description.* Some days I didn't know the difference between an IRB and an STD.

Qual High was a magical period, though, for first-time experiences: Losing our virginity on the first day of fieldwork; that awkward moment of silence during our first formal interview; and the heartbreaking crush of our first journal article rejection letter.

Yet through it all, we were taught to analyze responsibly in ethics class, to practice safe research. And we learned that no matter what our methodological preference or orientation – qualitative, quantitative, or mixed – we are all loved. We are OK, just as we are.

The real world

(slides: people in despair)

People say that high school prepares you for the real world. And, unfortunately, the real world waiting for us consists of bad things like government accountability, massive cuts to higher education, restricted or conditional funds for our research, unsolved social problems all around us, and some really, really stupid people with way too much money and power.

(slide: "Hope")

But we're a resourceful graduating class – we have to be. We have skills that can change the world. We have knowledge about the way things work that can make a significant impact on others.

Life learnings

All we really need to know about qualitative research we learned in high school. But like they taught me in Constructivism class, I acknowledge that my perspective is not the only one that exists. So, I asked my Facebook friends from our graduating class what *they* learned at Qual High, and this is what they told me:

(slides: high school yearbook photos from the 1950s to today)

Being a researcher means to find your passion and follow it. Getting involved in projects you love makes life worth living. If you have an interest in a research topic, it's up to you, and only you, to pursue it. You can let research happen to you, or you can make research happen. Other scholars may come and go and be supportive or not, but it's your responsibility to be in the world, so it's your responsibility to know the world.

Research isn't always as hard as we make it out to be. Maybe you don't want people to know how dumb you *think* you are, or how smart you *really* are. Nobody, not even you, will remember in a few short years the stupid things you said in a seminar that you made you feel like hiding away forever. And even if you're a senior researcher with a kick-ass publications record, you're not entitled to anything; if it's worth having, then it's worth working for. Teachers aren't always right; sometimes students are.

Yeah, there were some mean bullies at Qual High who shoved us into methodological lockers. It made us want to build walls to protect ourselves. But we survived. Life goes on after we graduate from Qual High. There are many more great inquiries ahead. Life isn't always fair, but *you* can be. Put good into the world every day. Despite what our teachers told us, these weren't "the best years of our lives," because it gets *better*.

If you're new to Qual High, not fitting in is OK; everyone's insecure. Find a paradigmatic place where you can be who *you* need to be. If you get tired of grounded theory, then write an autoethnography. If you're bored with generating codes and categories, then write a data poem. Reinvent yourself.

Good research colleagues, good friends, are the most important thing. Don't put your heroes on pedestals, though, because it'll hurt really bad when they come crashing down. It's better to be you than someone else. Like our teachers taught us in Autoethnography class: "You can't learn how to tell someone else's story until you first learn how to tell your own."

The future

High school is the time for the search for our identities. And some of us have already found a focus as grounded theorists, arts-based researchers, mixed methodologists, and so on. But you know what? That may change in the future. We are adolescents – or dare I say, young adults – with a lot more growing up to do. There are many opportunities ahead of us, and we need to be ready for them in any way we can.

(slide: forks in the road)

Like baseball great Yogi Berra said, "When you come to a fork in the road, take it!" We need to keep ourselves open to *all* quests for knowledge. We'll interview when we need to, we'll observe when we need to. We'll crunch numbers when we need to, we'll think with theory when we need to. We'll write a poem when we need to, we'll compose an autoethnography when we need to. We'll code when we need to, we'll categorize when we need to, we'll use a CAQDAS software program when we need to. We need to know how to do it *all* – because we never know what our futures hold.

Farewell

(slide: Qual High motto)

"*Ut intellegas omnia*" – "To Understand Is Everything."

(slide: graduation cap and diploma)

Qual High class of 2016, we did it! We've gotten through, and we've received our diplomas. We're research geeks, and damn proud of it. So let's go out there, raise some qualitative hell, and change the world! Thank you, and *congratulations*!

(recessional music: Elgar's "Pomp and Circumstance": www.youtube.com/watch?v=Q0PHWKRFgZ0)

LIST OF CONTRIBUTORS

Editors

Norman K. Denzin (PhD, University of Iowa) is Distinguished Emeritus Professor of Communications, College of Communications Scholar, and Research Professor of Communications, Sociology, and the Humanities at the University of Illinois, Urbana-Champaign. One of the world's foremost authorities on qualitative research and cultural criticism, Denzin is the author or editor of more than 30 books, including *Performance Ethnography; Interpretive Ethnography; The Qualitative Manifesto; Qualitative Inquiry Under Fire; Reading Race; The Cinematic Society; Images of Postmodern Times*; and a trilogy of books on the American West. He is past editor of *The Sociological Quarterly*, coeditor (with Yvonna S. Lincoln) of five editions of the landmark *SAGE Handbook of Qualitative Research*, co-editor (with Michael D. Giardina) of thirteen volumes on qualitative research and interpretive methods, coeditor (with Lincoln) of the methods journal *Qualitative Inquiry*, founding editor of Cultural Studies–Critical Methodologies and International Review of Qualitative Research, editor of three book series, and founding director of the International Congress of Qualitative Inquiry.

Michael D. Giardina (PhD, University of Illinois) is an Associate Professor of Media, Politics, and Culture at Florida State University. He is the author or editor of 18 books, including *Sport, Spectacle, and NASCAR Nation: Consumption and the Cultural Politics of Neoliberalism* (Palgrave, 2011, with Joshua Newman), which was named to the 2012 CHOICE "Outstanding Academic Titles" list; *Sporting Pedagogies: Performing Culture & Identity in the Global Arena* (Peter Lang, 2005), which received the 2006 Outstanding Book Award from NASSS; and *Qualitative*

Inquiry – Past, Present, & Future (with Norman K. Denzin; Left Coast Press, 2015). He is editor of the *Sociology of Sport Journal*, Special Issues Editor of Cultural Studies–Critical Methodologies, co-editor (with Brett Smith) of the Qualitative Research in Sport & Physical Activity book series for Routledge, co-editor (with Norman Denzin) of the ICQI book series for Routledge, and Associate Director of the International Congress of Qualitative Inquiry.

Contributors

Roe Bubar is a Native Studies Scholar and Associate Professor jointly appointed in the Department of Ethnic Studies and School of Social Work at Colorado State University. Her current research considers intersectionality and sexual violence, health disparities, child maltreatment in tribal communities, and Native youth and STD/STI messaging. She has over 20 years of experience in the field and continues to work with tribes, states, federal agencies, and NGOs in tribal communities on a variety of issues.

Julianne Cheek is a Professor of Nursing at Ostfold University College, Norway, and the University of South Australia. One of the leading qualitative health researchers in the world, she is the author of *Postmodern and Poststructural Approaches to Nursing Research* (Sage, 2000). She also holds numerous honorary professorships in South Africa and the United Kingdom, and serves on the editorial board of academic journals, including *Global Qualitative Nursing Research, Qualitative Health Research*, and *International Review for Qualitative Research*.

Anna Montana Cirell is a PhD candidate in Learning, Literacies and Technologies at Arizona State University. Her interests focus broadly on the complex dynamics of literacies and learning, with specific attention to how these are mediated through technology across the socio-spatial design of everyday life. In her current research, she is interested in combining geographic information systems (GIS) with spatial theories, particularly Soja's concept of "Thirdspace," to challenge deficit-based notions of the digital divide in the lives of low-income families.

Lise Claiborne is Associate Professor in the Te Oranga School of Human Development and Movement Studies at the University of Waikato, New Zealand. She is the coeditor of *Human Development: Family, Place, Culture* (McGraw-Hill, 2014), and has published in a wide range of journals, including *Knowledge Cultures, Journal of Moral Education, International Journal of Inclusive Education, Feminism and Psychology*, and *Gender and Education*.

Bronwyn Davies is an Independent Scholar and Professorial Fellow at the University of Melbourne, Australia. She is the author of more than 130 book chapters and articles, as well as 17 books, including *Listening to Children: Being and*

Becoming (Routledge, 2014), *Deleuze and Collaborative Writing* (with Jonathan Wyatt, Ken Gale, and Susanne Gannon; Peter Lang, 2011), and *Frogs and Snails and Feminist Tales* (Hampton, 2003), which has been translated in Swedish, German, and Spanish.

Michelle Fine is Distinguished Professor of Psychology and Urban Education at the City University of New York Graduate Center, and a Founding Member of the Public Science Project. She is the author of numerous books, including the classic *Framing Dropouts: Notes on the Politics of an Urban High School* (SUNY, 1991); *Working Method: Research and Social Justice* (with Lois Weis; Routledge, 2004); and *The Changing Politics of Education* (with Michael Fabricant; Routledge, 2015). Among other major awards, she has received the 2013 American Psychological Association Award for Distinguished Contributions to Research in Public Policy and the 2012 Henry Murray Award from the Society for Personality and Social Psychology of the APA.

Aitor Gómez is Associate Professor of Research Methods at the University Rovira I virgili (Tarragona) and a Visiting Scholar at the International Institute of Qualitative Inquiry. He is currently the principal investigator (PI) of "SALEACOM: Overcoming Inequalities in Schools and Learning Communities: Innovative Education for a New Century" a Marie Skłodowska-Curie Research and Innovation Staff Exchange (RISE) with Stanford University aimed at extending successful educational actions across educational systems.

Byoung-gyu Gong is a doctoral student of educational policy and evaluation program at Arizona State University. He earned his MA in Global Education Cooperation Program at Seoul National University in South Korea. He has also worked in Korean government research institutes such as Korea Educational Development Institute and Korea Research Institute for Vocational Education and Training as a researcher for several years. During his training and working period, he concentrated on studying international and cross-national policy trend of education, experiencing different national education contexts of Botswana (2013–2015) and Uzbekistan (2015–2016).

Stacy Holman Jones is Professor in the Centre for Theatre and Performance at Monash University, Australia. She is the author or editor of eight books, including *The Handbook of Autoethnography* (Left Coast Press, 2013 coedited with Tony E. Adams and Carolyn Ellis); *Autoethnography* (Oxford University Press, 2015, coauthored with Tony E. Adams and Carolyn Ellis); *Stories of Home: Identity, Place, Exile* (Lexington, 2015, co-edited with Devika Chawla); *Writing for Performance* (Sense, 2016, coauthored with Anne M. Harris); and *The Handbook of Performance Studies* (Wiley Blackwell, forthcoming). Dr. Holman Jones is the founding editor of *Departures in Critical Qualitative Research*, a journal dedicated to publishing innovative, experimental, aesthetic, and provocative works on the theories, practices, and possibilities of critical qualitative research. Her teaching focuses on performance studies theory and practice, critical qualitative methods, and gender and critical theory.

Kristi Jackson is President of Queri, a qualitative research and training company. She is the coauthor of *Qualitative Data Analysis with NVivo* (Sage, 2013; with Patricia Bazeley) and Chair of the SiG on Digital Tools for Qualitative Research at the International Congress of Qualitative Inquiry. She has consulted with a number of agencies, including U.S. Centers for Disease Control, U.S. Government Accountability Office, NIH National Human Genome Institute, and the World Bank.

Mirka Koro-Ljungberg is a Professor of qualitative research at the Arizona State University. Her scholarship operates in the intersection of methodology, philosophy, and socio-cultural critique and her work aims to contribute to methodological knowledge, experimentation, and theoretical development across various traditions associated with qualitative research. She has published in various qualitative and educational journals. She is the author of *Reconceptualizing Qualitative Research: Methodologies without Methodology* (Sage, 2016).

Maggie MacLure is Professor of Education at Manchester Metropolitan University, and the Founder and Director of the international Summer Institute in Qualitative Research. Her book *Discourse in Educational and Social Research* won the 2004 Critics' Choice Award from the American Educational Studies Association. She is a former member of the Executive Council of the British Educational Research Association.

Doreen E. Martinez is an instructor in the Department of Ethnic Studies at Colorado State University and Director of Grants/Program Manager for 2040 Partners in Health, an organization which aims to advance the health and healthcare of people living and working in Colorado by informing and facilitating health programs and policies using Community-Based Participatory Action Principles (CBPR) through collaboration with community members, researchers, local organizations, and students/academics from the University of Colorado.

Johnny Saldaña is Professor Emeritus from Arizona State University's School of Film, Dance, and Theatre in the Herberger Institute for Design and the Arts. He is the author of a dozen books, including *Qualitative Data Analysis: A Methods Sourcebook* (Sage; 2014); *Ethnotheatre: Research from Page to Stage* (Left Coast Press, 2013), which received the American Educational Research Association's Qualitative Research SIG 2012 Outstanding Book Award; and *Longitudinal Qualitative Research: Analyzing Change Through Time* (AltiMira, 2003), which received the 2004 Outstanding Book Award from the National Communication Association's Ethnography Division.

Margaret Somerville is Professor of Education and Director of the Centre for Educational Research at the University of Western Sydney, Australia. She is also the Chair of the Greater Western Sydney chapter of the United Nations Regional Centre of Expertise on Education for Sustainable Development (one of only four in Australia). She is the author of six books, including, most recently, *Children, Place, and Sustainability* (Palgrave, 2015) and *Water in a Dry Land: Place-Learning through Art and Society* (Routledge, 2013).

Elizabeth Adams St. Pierre is Professor and Graduate Coordinator of Language and Literacy Education at the University of Georgia. Her work has appeared in a range of scholarly journals, including *International Review of Qualitative Research, Educational Researcher, Qualitative Inquiry, Journal of Contemporary Ethnography,* and *International Journal of Qualitative Studies in Education.* She is also the editor of *Working the Ruins: Feminist Poststructural Theory and Methods in Education* (Routledge, 2000; with Wanda Pillow).

Marek Tesar is a Senior Lecturer in childhood studies and early childhood education at the University of Auckland, New Zealand. His research focuses on decentering the human subject, subject-object relations in childhood places and spaces, and thinking and working with philosophy as a method.

Harry Torrance is Professor of Education and Director of the Education and Social Research Institute, Manchester Metropolitan University, United Kingdom. His substantive research interests are in the interrelation of assessment with learning, program evaluation, and the role of assessment in education reform. He has undertaken many applied, qualitative, and mixed-method investigations of these topics funded by a wide range of sponsors. He is an elected member of the UK Academy of Learned Societies for the Social Sciences.

INDEX